THE PALE-FACED LIE

A TRUE STORY

DAVID CROW

SANDRA JONAS
LARGE PRINT

Sandra Jonas Publishing House
PO Box 20892
Boulder, CO 80308
sandrajonaspublishing.com

Copyright © 2020 by David Crow

All rights reserved. No part of this book may be used in any form whatsoever without the written permission of the publisher, except for brief quotations included in critical articles and reviews.

LARGE PRINT EDITION

Printed in the United States of America
25 24 23 22 21 20   2 3 4 5 6 7 8

Book and cover design by Sandra Jonas

LCCN: 2018960909

ISBN: 978-1-7333386-0-8

All photos are from the author's private collection.

This large print edition published in accord with NAVH standards.

To my wife, Patty

AUTHOR'S NOTE

This is a true story. Some of the recollections come from my parents since I was too young to fully understand what was happening. I have followed up relentlessly with family members, neighbors, classmates, and others to make sure the events depicted are as accurate as possible. In some cases, I relied on family photographs and public records to verify my memories. The names and identifying details of some individuals and places have been changed.

PART 1

Navajo Station
1956

My dad and me (age three) in front of our house at Navajo Station on the Navajo Indian Reservation. 1955.

CHAPTER 1

I was three and a half the first time my dad told me we had to get rid of my mother. On that bitter cold morning in February, he jumped up from the table after eating his usual eggs, grits, and bacon and threw on his coat. Lonnie, Sam, and I had finished our cornflakes long before he sat down.

"Thelma Lou, get David ready," he told my mother. His deep voice filled our tiny house. "He and I are going for a ride."

Mom lurched into the living room with that twitchy look she got whenever Dad asked her to do something. I sat cross-legged on the floor watching **The Little Rascals** as she jerked back and forth in front of me like a broken wind-up toy. "Get ready, David!" she shrieked.

My younger brother, Sam, still in diapers, pushed his Tonka truck across the worn carpet and giggled when Mom stumbled over his toys. Our cat, Midnight, leapt out of her way and glided to safety under a chair. As usual, Lonnie, then seven, was camped out in her room with the door closed, listening to her radio and ignoring the rest of us.

Mom always acted nervous, like something bad was going to happen. It got worse when Dad was around. Before she could touch me with her clammy hands, I ran to the closet, put on my jacket and boots, and bolted out the door.

On the front porch, I hung close to the house and shivered while Dad scraped snow and ice off our Nash Rambler, or what I called the Green Bomber. I had a nickname for everything. White smoke poured from the exhaust and filled the air. I wished Dad would hurry up, but I would never tell him that. Behind him, the giant Navajo Compressor Station where he worked rose into the sky. Dad told me millions of pounds of natural gas flowed through the huge pipelines. They were connected to turbine engines that rumbled so loud I thought they would shake apart.

A fence surrounded the station and the twenty houses belonging to El Paso Natural Gas workers and their families. Everybody called the company EPNG for short. Our only other neighbors were rattlesnakes, stray cattle, sheep, coyotes, jackrabbits, and roadrunners. They all disappeared when it got cold. Dad said we lived on the Navajo Indian Reservation, but because we were Cherokees, we didn't have to follow any of the damn Anglo rules.

The snow blew hard, stinging my face, and I hopped around to stay warm. Dad carved out two openings on the frozen windshield, then snapped ice off the handle on the passenger door and signaled me to get in. "It's colder than a well-digger's ass, so move it," he shouted, hustling to the driver's side of the car. "We're gonna have some fun."

Dad knocked the snow from his boots and slid onto the seat. His burly arms and barrel chest seemed even more massive in his heavy work coat, the one with the familiar red-and-yellow EPNG logo. His head almost touched the ceiling.

"Let's go!" He stomped on the gas pedal and the Green Bomber sped out into the snowy Arizona desert. Just as I got up on my knees to see where we were going, he hit the brakes and yanked the steering wheel to the side, throwing me against the door, like the whirlybird ride at the Navajo fair.

"See—isn't this fun, boy?"

He stepped on the gas and we jolted forward. Seconds later, he slammed on the brakes again. I bounced up to the dashboard and underneath it, banging my head on the hard metal. Dad laughed. "Hey, don't break the glove compartment," he said. "We can't afford a new one."

The next time he stopped, I flipped upside down, and he laughed some more.

"You sure as hell better be tough." He wagged

his finger at me as I crawled back onto the seat. "I hate sissies. You're scrawny and you can't hear worth a damn, but you're a determined little son of a bitch. Remember, you're a Crow, by God, a Cherokee Indian of superior intelligence and courage."

Dad straightened the wheel but didn't slow down. The wipers screeched against the icy windshield as snow whipped around us. "Now it's time for a real talk," he said. "I have something important to say, and you need to promise not to tell anyone." He reached over and squeezed my arm with his gigantic hand. "Got it?"

"I promise," I blurted through nervous laughter. I grabbed the door handle to keep from falling, afraid it would turn and I'd fly out into the cold.

"We need to get rid of your mother," he said, his voice low and sharp. "She's no goddamn good, and if you grow up with her, you'll become just as loony as she is. She's worthless and destructive. She'll ruin you—ruin us all. You know we can't keep her around, don't you, boy?"

No, but I nodded anyway. He said bad things about Mom all the time, that she was a crazy, stupid, whiny bitch just like her mother and the other freeloading assholes in the Dalton family.

But he wouldn't really get rid of her, would he? He yelled at her to go away and not come back, and sometimes he slapped her hard. Even then, she never left the EPNG compound unless Dad drove her to town. And usually things returned to normal after dinner. I could hear them laughing in their bedroom at night.

I wrapped both hands around the door handle and studied Dad's face. Below his thick, wavy black hair, a Y-shaped vein popped out on his forehead, and his large blue eyes bulged like they might explode. His mouth stretched tight. He always looked scary like that when he was angry.

Would he leave Mom at the trading post? Or on the side of the road next to the Navajo drunks? Maybe he'd put her on a bus and send her back to her mother like he threatened so many times. But Dad said her whore of a mother didn't want her. Neither did her two shiftless, alcoholic, mooching brothers. And Granddaddy Dalton could barely take care of himself.

The only time Mom went anywhere alone was when she borrowed a cup of sugar from one of the ladies in the compound—though she always dumped it down the sink when she got home. Once in a while, she dragged me with her, and I listened to her tell them that her mother was cruel and her brothers beat her up. Even her daddy couldn't save her. Clutching the ladies' hands, she would put her face close to theirs and say her life was no better now, because Dad hit her and her kids didn't behave. The women pulled away, handed Mom the sugar, and closed the door as fast as they could.

Poor Mom. She'd lie on the couch most of the day and call to Lonnie and me to do things for her. "I need help," she'd say. "I can't do this by myself." My sister would roll her eyes. Mom never had energy for anything. Sometimes she stayed in her nightgown and didn't get dressed until just before Dad got home—or not at all.

The other moms in the neighborhood weren't like that. They smiled and laughed. They packed lunches for their kids and talked to them while they waited at the bus stop. When the bus came, the moms hugged them and told them to have a good day, and then they walked back to their houses, full of energy, their arms swinging.

Not my mom.

Lonnie packed her own lunch, got her homework ready, and fixed her own breakfast. Our mom went from the bed to the couch. I felt sorry for her, but her whiny, squeaky voice made my head hurt.

If she disappeared, who would be our mom? That nasty, old Mrs. Bell from next door?

Dad slammed on the brakes and returned to spinning the car in circles. The tires crunched across the icy ground. His face was loose and relaxed again, like it was when he joked with the guys from work. My hands were tired and sweaty.

"Having fun, boy?" He laughed.

Maybe he didn't mean what he said. Maybe he wouldn't leave Mom so she couldn't find her way back home.

But he sure seemed serious about it.

Dad probably told Lonnie the secret too. My sister knew everything about our family, though she never talked about Mom other than to say she was nuts.

Lonnie was thin like Mom and had her reddish-blond hair and green eyes, but they acted nothing alike. My sister had a happy, bright face and a spring in her step. She played the piano, read constantly, and got straight As. Everyone liked her. Lonnie was full of life—and Mom flopped around like a deflated balloon.

Most mornings after Dad left for work, I ran through the house and Mom would tell me to stop yelling like a banshee. I'd kick my rubber ball, swing my bat, and throw baseballs into lamps, pictures, and the lazy Susan on the living room coffee table. Mom chased after me, trying to grab a piece of my shirt or pants, but I was too fast for her. Once I made a big enough mess, she would let me go outside.

One morning she made me stay in because it was raining. To change her mind, I climbed on top of the washer and tossed in a baseball bat during the spin cycle. Mom came running right away, but the cylinder was already dented so bad it had to be repaired. Dad spanked me really hard for that dumbass stunt, as he called it. The marks stayed on my legs a long time.

On another rainy day, I put Midnight in the dryer after he came in soaked. He screeched like mad. When Lonnie got him out, he tore through the living room and flew onto the venetian blinds, clawing them off the windows. As soon as someone opened the door, he took off.

Lonnie slapped my face and called me a wild animal. She said all the neighbors called me that too. But I just wanted to dry him off. I didn't mean to scare him.

Dad told Mom he hoped I'd run away and join the circus.

On the mornings Mom would let me out of the house, I'd race over to the compressor station looking to break a few rules. Dad told me to get away with whatever I could. "But don't make anyone important mad at you," he said. "If you do, I'll have to punish you hard."

I would carry a small wrench from his toolbox, making believe he had forgotten it and needed me to bring it to him. When I crawled up the metal steps and banged the wrench on the compressor building's giant steel door, one of the workers would open it and smile down at me. Then he would turn and cup his hands around his mouth. "Go get Thurston," he'd yell above the noise.

All the guys laughed. Kids weren't allowed to go inside where the big engines lived, so Dad pretended to swat my butt. Sometimes while I was there, he gathered his men around to tell them stories about me. "No other boy would have the gumption to come here and knock on the door." He'd rub my head and smile. "David is the only one who would pull that kind of stunt."

Before sending me home, Dad would take the wrench, and I'd find it in the same spot the next morning. As I left the station, the men would say, "See you tomorrow, sport."

When I turned four that summer, Dad started putting me through drills before he went to work. I needed to be strong and brave like our Cherokee ancestors, he said. He would toss me into the air and hold out his hands to catch me, but then he'd often pull them away, letting me drop to the ground. My body was covered with scrapes and bruises.

Dad would laugh. "I'm teaching you to be on guard, boy. I won't always be there to protect you."

He yelled at me when I got scared, telling me not to watch his hands. "Put your arms out to brace the fall," he said. "Protect yourself. Do I have to tell you everything? Besides, a little bump on your head won't hurt you."

Other days, Dad tied me to the pine tree in our front yard. He'd wrap a thick, scratchy rope around my chest and ankles and tug on it hard to make a tight knot.

"Try to get out of that, you clever little bastard." He would turn and walk away.

"Dad, please untie me . . . please . . . please."

"Not a chance. I don't want you to be afraid of anything—except me," he'd say over his shoulder.

I would squirm and squirm, but that never worked. The rope burned my skin and pulled snug like a Chinese finger trap. Soon my body started shaking, and I struggled to breathe. The tears came next, dropping on the rope. I didn't feel like a brave Cherokee.

If someone walked by, I'd yell out, "Hey! I tied myself to a tree by accident. Can you help me?" I forced out a laugh, but it sounded strange, kind of ragged and uneven.

Often Mr. Bell came over and untied the rope. "I know your dad did this," he said softly. "And what he's doing is wrong."

If Mr. Bell didn't set me free, Mom would scurry from the house and do it as soon as the Rambler was out of sight.

CHAPTER 2

Dad worked directly under Champ, the guy who ran the whole plant. Champ was my best buddy. He told me that many times.

When no one was looking, I would carry a wooden milk crate over to his big red EPNG truck parked next to the compressor station, climb into the bed, and lie on my stomach, waiting for him to drive off to survey the miles of pipelines. Then I'd jump up and bang on the back window. Champ would laugh and let me sit beside him in the cab.

We ate sunflower seeds and drank the Cokes he kept in a cooler on the floorboard. I rested my feet on it and talked nonstop, asking about turbine engines, roadrunners, rattlesnakes, or anything else that popped into my head. Champ said there was a motor attached to my mouth.

I giggled when he called Dad on his walkie-talkie to let him know we were patrolling the pipelines.

"That mischievous son of a bitch," Dad would say, but he never minded if I was with Champ.

Though he only finished high school, Dad could outtalk anybody on any subject. Our house was full of engineering and math books, and he had read each one from start to finish. Dad knew more than all the other guys in the compound about the turbine engines and how to keep them running.

No one interrupted him, and no one ever disagreed with him. If his voice got extra loud, his men would back away and leave as soon as they could. Sometimes they laughed too hard or quick at his jokes. Still, when I brought Dad his wrench, they would tell me he was the smartest man they'd ever met.

The men talked about gas all the time, and the smell of it was everywhere. After a while, we didn't notice unless someone visiting mentioned it. An older boy told me that EPNG used buffalo farts to make the gas smell funny. Dad called it sulfur.

"Without the odor, we can't detect a leak," he said, standing and puffing out his chest to make sure everyone paid attention to him.

We had just finished one of Mom's dinners of fried okra, roast beef, and iced tea, the same meal she served every night. Lonnie and I loved sitting at the table listening to Dad tell us how the powerful engines pushed the gas all the way to Los Angeles. Sometimes he drew pictures of them to show us how they worked. The turbines were enormous, and the inside parts moved faster than my eye could see.

"And if we can't detect a leak, an explosion will blast our dead asses clear to Mexico."

I always got a sick feeling in my stomach when Dad talked about explosions. The year before, the compressor station had blown up during a test run of some new turbines. Everyone still talked about it as though it had happened yesterday.

The morning had begun as usual, with Mom asleep on the couch, me in front of the TV watching cartoons, and Sam in the playpen. First came a rumbling noise, and then a loud boom rocked the house, making the pictures tumble off the walls. I ran to the window as the emergency siren pierced the still air and people scattered in all directions. Midnight went berserk, tearing through the room before climbing the curtains and hanging there, his hair standing on end.

The second explosion shook the ground much harder than the first, knocking me down. Giant balls of fire erupted from the station, and smoke billowed high into the bright blue sky. The building disappeared behind a black cloud. As the siren blared, another blast shook the house. The buffalo farts smelled extra nasty, like they'd caught on fire.

Mom sprang from the couch and ran around in circles, crying and shaking. I huddled in the corner, hands over my ears, afraid the ceiling would fall on us. Sam's eyes darted back and forth between Mom and me before he scrunched up his face and started crying too. Lonnie was in school, so it was up to me to comfort Mom, but I didn't know what to do when she dropped to the floor screaming. And the rumbling kept going on and on. Soon black smoke filled the house, and the air hung thick and heavy.

I shook Mom a few times, but that didn't help. It never did. She curled up into a ball, closed her eyes, and moaned. Then Mrs. Bell burst into the living room. Her husband had worked the midnight shift and was home asleep when the station blew up.

"Thelma Lou," she said, "we don't know what happened yet. Every spare man is there to help. Thurston is probably fine. Stay calm."

No one locked their doors in the compound—we were one big family. During an emergency, all the moms and dads helped out like they were relatives. Even people who avoided Mom came over to see what they could do.

Mrs. Bell got down on the floor. "Thelma Lou, come on now, you have to get a hold of yourself." She patted her back. "We'll figure this out together."

Other neighbors streamed into the house and said nice things to Mom. Mrs. Bell helped her up to the couch, and when she got her a glass of water, Mom shook so hard it spilled all over the floor. Dad said Mrs. Bell despised Mom, but she was kind that day, gently rubbing Mom's shoulders and trying to get her to relax. She talked to Mom like she was a little kid, asking her if Lonnie was at school. Mom nodded, her sobs coming in such big spurts it was impossible to understand her.

The loud noises finally stopped, but the smoke and fiery clouds kept coming. Sam cried harder in the playpen, and one of the neighbors picked him up and rocked him, settling him down. A few minutes later, he started up again when we heard the loud siren from a fire truck. I ran outside to see, and Midnight followed, diving under the neighbor's bushes. Mrs. Bell yelled at me to get inside, but I ignored her, and she flew out the door, her face all red, and grabbed my shirt with one hand and my cheek with the other to drag me into the house.

Mrs. Bell was one of the ladies who called me a wild animal. She smelled kind of funny, like medicine, and was always bossing people around. Her first name was Beatrice, and Dad called her Blubber Bee because she was so fat. Mr. Bell complained about me too, even though he had untied me from the tree more than once. I never saw him smile. Dad said he was a miserable henpecked son of a bitch.

By the time Champ showed up and asked for Mom, her cries had become sniffles. She was still in her robe, and her hair was messy as if she had just woken up. Her eyes twitched wildly. Dad had been badly burned, Champ said, and he was in the emergency room. Though Champ rubbed my head and smiled at me, his gray eyes were sad. He said that some of the injured men might die, but he wasn't sure about Dad.

Soon more teary-eyed neighbor ladies stopped by to check on Mom. Champ's wife drove her to the hospital, and the other ladies sat in our living room with Sam and me, whispering to one another and shaking their heads like Dad was never coming back—but I knew he would.

When Lonnie got home from school, she had tears running down her cheeks. One of the men told her what had happened. "Dad tried to close the shut-off valve for the gas, but the turbine exploded," she said, wiping her face on her sleeve. "He barely got out, and then he rushed a bunch of guys to the hospital in one of the trucks. He's alive but burned all over."

It was dark when Mom came back from the hospital. She shook so much she couldn't walk, and Champ's wife had to help her inside. "Your daddy was wrapped up like a mummy," Mom told us as she fell back onto the couch. "His chest didn't move. They said he was still alive, but he looked dead to me."

Lonnie and I cried—after all, Mom had to know if Dad was really dead.

"Thurston," Mom yelled, "it's not fair for you to

die and leave me alone with the kids. You're supposed to take care of me!"

She got up and went to bed. Lonnie told me to pick up the toys on the floor and then opened cans of pork and beans for dinner. I minded my seven-year-old sister better than I did my mother. After Lonnie changed Sam's diaper, fed him, and put him in his crib for the night, she tried to get Mom to eat.

For many days after that, the neighbor ladies brought food and sat with Mom. They took turns driving her to the hospital, and when she walked through the door every night, we asked if Dad was alive. She'd shake her head. "I don't think so, but they say he is."

One evening when she came into the house with her usual scared, frantic look, she said, "Your daddy is alive. I didn't believe it—his face was so swollen and puffy after they took the bandages off. But he called out my name, so it must have been him."

Even then, Dad couldn't leave the hospital for a long time, and the doctors wouldn't let us visit. Our germs might kill him, they told Mom.

When she finally brought him home in the Green Bomber, Lonnie and I ran to the car to meet him. Mom was right—he didn't look like our big, strong dad. His head had swelled to the size of a pumpkin, and his eyes were like tiny BBs. His forehead and nose shined bright red, and flaky skin fell off his face. He moaned in pain. Mom changed Dad's bandages, and he didn't yell at her or hit her once.

The people in the compound stayed sad for months, but Dad told us that EPNG employees understood the risks. Seven of his guys were badly burned in the explosion, and two never returned. New men replaced the injured ones, the turbine engines were repaired, and everyone went in and out of the compressor station just like before.

Dad's skin eventually healed, and he went back to work. Soon after, he started yelling at Mom again, telling her to go away.

Most of the time Mom didn't know where I was. The neighbor ladies complained to Dad that I ran outside the entrance gate where kids weren't supposed to go. Mom needed to watch me better, they said.

"He can't wreck anything outside," he told them. "And nothing seems to hurt the little bastard." The women didn't think he was funny, but Dad didn't care. He said breaking the compound rules was good training because Cherokees always had to make their own rules to survive.

While driving their red trucks, the EPNG men would find me far from home, and they always stopped to pick me up. When they told Dad it wasn't safe for me to be out in the desert, he laughed. "Don't worry about David. He always finds his way back."

One morning after Dad sent me home from the compressor station, I got in line for the school bus. Neither Lonnie nor the driver saw me sneak on board. When we pulled up to the elementary school in Ganado, I hid in the middle of the students as they got off the bus and walked into the building.

But I didn't get far. Lonnie ratted on me. The driver had to make the trip back to the compound with only one passenger. She yelled at me for being a bad boy. I laughed, running up and down the aisle of the empty bus.

My sister told everybody I was a snot-nosed little brat. When I slipped onto the bus again, Lonnie didn't spot me until I rolled out from under one of the seats. She wanted the driver to make me walk the twelve miles back home. And I would have done it, but I didn't have to. The driver told me that if I'd wait until first grade to get on the bus, she'd give me a Davy Crockett canteen with a compass on it. That sounded like a good deal, so I took it.

On Saturday mornings, Mom and Dad always knew where I was—with them getting groceries at the Hubbell Trading Post, just down the street from the school. Nothing excited me more than to see Navajo Indians up close. All our neighbors were either

Mexican or Anglo, and they never dressed the way the Navajos did when they came to town. The men braided their long, dark hair into a ponytail and wore turquoise bolo ties and black hats with bands of silver. The women wore beaded necklaces and bracelets and red velvet skirts. And the children looked like miniature versions of their parents.

When we pulled into Hubbell's, I'd dash over to the Navajo pickup trucks and horse-drawn wagons. Sometimes I chased their herds of sheep, making loud bleating noises. They would run in all directions, and the trading post manager would throw his hands in the air and yell at me. He would have to start counting them all over again.

I thought it was funny, but Dad would whop me on the butt real hard. "Stop being a pain in the ass," he'd say. "The Navajos want to sell their sheep, buy some stuff, and get the hell out of here. They don't want to be bothered by your nonsense."

But I wanted to talk to them. I'd yell "**Yá'át'ééh**," or "Hello" in Navajo, and make whooping noises like the Indians in the movies when they raided wagon trains. The men turned their backs, and the children dropped their eyes to the ground and stuck their hands in their pockets. The mean, older women tried swatting me, but I was too fast for them. I wanted to have fun—no one else at Hubbell's did.

CHAPTER 3

During the school day, I had the compound to myself. None of the other young kids were allowed to roam free looking for trouble. One morning before Dad went to work, he saw me watching Shorty John through the living room window. "Look at that dumb Mexican shuffling. He barely lifts his feet off the ground."

Shorty worked at EPNG as a maintenance man. Every day he carried a long hose from house to house to water the tiny patches of grass in the yards.

"He has no energy, David. No brains. I bet you could trick him easy, couldn't you? Wouldn't it be fun to sneak up on him and get him with the hose?" He laughed.

Dad and I started playing what-if games. What if I stopped Shorty from watering the grass? What if the son of a bitch chased me—could I outrun him to the house or get beyond the cattle guard and make him give up? What if I made his job so unbearable he quit? Dad kept shaking his head. "A snail could move faster and with more purpose."

I sat on our front porch and studied Shorty and the hose. Then I'd creep up behind him and squeeze the hose into a V shape until the water stopped flowing. When he pointed the hose at his face to see what was wrong, I let go and watched the water shoot up his nose. I giggled and ran away, always knowing the number of steps to my house so he couldn't catch me.

Sometimes I'd run up to him, pull on his pants, and laugh when he stumbled after me. After that got boring, I would wait until he went down the street, and then I'd run over to his truck and fill his lunch pail with fire ants and lizards, an idea I came up with on my own, without Dad's help. I hid more ants inside his sandwich. When Shorty discovered what I had done, he chased me, but he was too slow to make the game much fun. He was easier to fool than Mom.

Each time I told Dad how I outran Shorty or what his face looked like when water squirted out of his nose, Dad laughed and asked me to tell him more. He'd slap me on the back and say, "You are the cleverest little shit I've ever known."

And when the poor man requested a transfer because I wouldn't stop, Dad treated me like a heavyweight boxing champion. He asked me to flex my muscles or run fast in front of his men, telling them that I could fool anybody and I would become a great fighter someday.

Whether he and I were at Hubbell's or in stores and gas stations outside Ganado, Dad told anyone who would listen how his four-year-old son defeated a full-grown man. He'd pull strangers aside. "Look at my boy," he would say. "Listen to what he did."

But the men in the compound weren't happy about what happened to Shorty. They said that the little guy had only been trying to do his job, that Dad had gone too far, egging me on the way he had. Dad just laughed.

What were they talking about? Messing with Shorty was hilarious.

At the dinner table, Dad told us stories about the Crow family. His big blue eyes teared up when he described how his Cherokee parents had struggled to survive the vicious white sons of bitches who abused them and how hard it had been to eke out a living in the Texas and Oklahoma dust bowls.

"My parents worked me like a rented mule, forcing me to pick cotton for twelve hours a day by the age of six," he said, shaking his head. "And white people hated our red asses."

His voice got quiet when he told us about his superior Cherokee intelligence and courage and how he could read at age four even though his dad never learned to read or write a single word of English. Dad went on to teach himself math, science, and physics and study the English classics by reading every book he could get his hands on, often by stealing them.

Taylor, his father, drew his name on the army application when he signed up to serve in World War I—being able to read and write wasn't necessary to handle a machine gun or march all day and night. His ship narrowly missed being sunk by a German U-boat on the way to Europe. He survived the war, but his lungs were damaged by mustard gas during a ferocious battle in France.

It wasn't Taylor's fault he was so mean, Dad said. The war had destroyed his mind and health, and he was never the same. Indians were treated horribly even when they defended their country against the German bastards.

After the war, thirty-three-year-old Taylor married fourteen-year-old Ella Mae, a cousin of his first wife, who had been killed in an automobile accident. Dad was the only one of Taylor and Ella Mae's children to survive. Taylor spent the rest of his life in and out of Veterans Administration hospitals and roughnecking in the oil fields, which amounted to hauling heavy pieces of drilling equipment. When that work dried up, he picked cotton, bootlegged, and fought any dumbass who crossed his path—a trait he passed on to his son.

"My father sure as hell didn't treat me right," Dad said, stabbing the air with his fork. "He'd guzzle down moonshine and then storm home in a drunken rage and beat me with a wet rope."

But it was his mother, Ella Mae, who made Dad the angriest. She constantly smacked him around and yelled at him for not picking cotton fast enough, despite his ability to outdo most grown men.

"She couldn't wait to humiliate me, that miserable bitch." He spat out the words, his nostrils flaring like he smelled something bad. "She worked me into the ground—no matter what I did, no matter how hard I worked, it was never good enough."

The three of them lived in rusted-out cars, under bridges, and anywhere else they could hide from the elements—or the police. Taylor had been caught selling moonshine, and he was always in debt. Dad scavenged trash cans for food. Mostly the Crows drifted from town to town looking for work and trying to stay alive.

When he got to the part about his mother killing his father, Dad's voice would break. Ella Mae, beaten one too many times, bumped off her husband by putting rat poison in his food. Twelve-year-old Thurston soon gained a stepfather and two stepbrothers—"three of the most ignorant dipshit Okie inbreds ever conceived." The happiest day of his life came when he turned eighteen and signed up for the navy. He ate regularly for the first time, gaining thirty pounds.

Then came the stories we loved best. Dad told us how he shot down countless Japanese Zeros in the Pacific as they swooped down to attack his aircraft carrier. All those suicide-bomber sons of bitches sank to their deaths in the cold ocean.

Dad could have been killed. He was so brave.

When he talked about Mom's side of the family, Dad said that she was an Indian too because she was born in Quanah, Texas, named for the great chief Quanah Parker. Dad had to be right about that, Mom said. She remembered when the chief's son wore an Indian headdress and paraded by her house on a tall, spotted horse.

The Daltons had blue eyes, reddish-blond hair, and the whitest skin I'd ever seen. Like Lonnie, both Sam and I took after that side of the family. We didn't look like the other Indians on the reservation or the ones on TV. We were the pale kind. Lots of Cherokees were as pale as ghosts, Dad said, so they could outrace the wind and the cavalry.

Mom hated her mother too. Mary Etta left her husband, John Ben, several times, dragging her daughter across Texas from one crummy hotel room to another, making her scrub bathrooms and wait for her while she spent time with some of the men who stayed there. Mary Etta despised her husband. He lost their ranch during the depths of the Great Depression, forcing them into poverty. Mom said she was sad from her first memory, and so was everyone in her family.

Even at four, I knew something wasn't right about my parents' stories. When Dad got excited, the details changed enough to make me think that some parts were missing and others weren't true. One night after I used the bathroom, I heard them talking and crept to their bedroom door. They didn't whisper, probably never suspecting anyone would listen.

That was a good thing because my ears weren't perfect, especially the left one. Dad didn't believe in "con artist doctors," and the previous summer, when I got an ear infection and a fever that lasted for days, he said my body would heal fine. But it didn't, and now I had to press my better right ear to the bedroom door.

Mom said something about a guy named George who wanted to kill Dad. She didn't make any sense. Dad was a war hero who helped beat the Japs—why would anyone want to kill him? But after listening in over time, I managed to figure out what she was talking about.

Mom was fifteen and Dad was nineteen when

they met in Los Angeles following the war. Mom's brother Bill worked with Dad and introduced him to his sister in the Daltons' home in Cleo Cole's Trailer Court. Dad would say that Mom was the most gorgeous girl he'd ever seen, and he knew he'd have to marry her to get a piece of that.

When he got mad, Dad claimed that Mom trapped him into marriage by pretending to be pregnant. But she insisted she was a virgin the day they ran off to Arizona to get married, five months after she turned sixteen. Within weeks, she was pregnant with Lonnie. Since Dad didn't have enough money to support his bride, they moved into the Daltons' new house, thirty miles from the trailer court.

According to Dad, Cleo had been tapping Mary Etta's fat ass in exchange for lower rent and help with car repairs and jobs around the house. Mom didn't deny it. Her daddy, John Ben, might have thought something was going on when Cleo continued making regular stops at the Dalton house after they moved. But John Ben worked the night shift and slept during the day, so it's possible he didn't know what his wife was up to. More likely, he didn't care, considering how long he and Mary Etta had hated each other.

When Mom found out she was pregnant, she dropped out of ninth grade and rested on her parents' couch every day. One October afternoon, Cleo came out of Mary Etta's bedroom and stopped in front of Mom on his way out. He was a fat, dirty old man, Mom said, with brown teeth and a disgusting grin.

"My, Thelma Lou," Cleo said that day, "aren't you a fine young thing. Maybe I should be spending time with you instead of with your mom."

That night, Mom told Dad about Cleo's comment in front of Mary Etta. Dad erupted in a volcanic rage, screaming that he was going to smash that son of a bitch into pieces.

"Thurston," Mary Etta said, "a real man wouldn't put up with that kind of shit. You need to defend your wife's honor—get yourself over there and give Cleo an ass whipping he'll never forget."

She might as well have kicked a sleeping bull in the balls.

Dad raced out of the house and grabbed his boss and best friend, George, to help him avenge this wrong. Dad plotted their strategy on the half-hour ride to the trailer court. The plan was simple. Since Cleo fixed cars and rented out trailers, George would knock on Cleo's door saying that his car had broken down and that he'd like to rent one of the advertised trailers. Dad was certain the promise of cash for repairs and a rental would be enough to lure the old lecher outside so late at night.

Dad parked the car a block away from Cleo's trailer and sent George to knock on the door. When he walked back to the car with Cleo, the hood was open as if George had already tried to fix the engine. Dad crouched behind the rear fender, a monkey wrench in his hand and a handgun in his back pocket. Cleo placed his toolbox on the ground, hooked a flashlight inside the hood, and leaned over the engine to take a good look.

While Cleo checked the distributor, George slipped on a pair of gloves so he wouldn't get blood on his hands. When Cleo straightened up, George swung his fist into the old guy's face as Dad shot out from the rear and slammed the wrench into the back of his head.

Dad couldn't take the chance Cleo would recognize him. "Gouge his eyes out!"

Still standing, Cleo turned toward Dad and tried to run. Dad smashed one of his eye sockets with the wrench and the other with his fist.

Cleo fell to the pavement unconscious, bleeding profusely from his head. Dad and George left him, sure he would bleed out shortly, and hurried into the car.

But it didn't start.

Unbeknownst to them, while Cleo was under the hood, he sensed something wasn't right, so he removed the rotor from the distributor, slipped it into his jacket pocket, and put the distributor cap back in place.

Alarmed, Dad jumped out of the car, rolled Cleo over, and stole his wallet and keys from his pants, missing the rotor. He and George hopped into Cleo's car and drove it a few miles before pulling into a vacant lot to toss out the registration and other papers identifying Cleo. Panicking beyond reason, they didn't stop to think that the car alone would be a dead giveaway.

Meanwhile, Smiley, Cleo's wife, thinking her husband had been gone too long, went looking for him and found him down the street in a pool of blood, his breathing shallow and irregular. The ambulance attendants told her he would have died had they picked him up fifteen minutes later.

The LA police began their search in Cleo's neighborhood, shining a spotlight as they drove through the streets. It didn't take them long to come upon two men throwing papers out of a car. Dad and George confessed immediately. "Cleo was still breathing when we left," Dad told them.

That had to be the easiest arrest the cops had ever made.

On Dad's twenty-first birthday, a guard at San Quentin State Prison, or "the Q," informed him that his wife had given birth to a beautiful baby girl named

Lonnie. Dad wasn't sure he'd ever meet her. He had only a seven-year sentence, but that could change—depending on Cleo.

The old guy was still in serious condition. Following the assault, he had fallen in and out of consciousness for days, close to death. He needed several blood transfusions and remained on a respirator for weeks.

Miraculously, Cleo pulled through, but it would be a year before the doctors felt confident he'd survive. He remained blind in one eye and severely impaired in the other and never recovered his ability to speak and walk. If he had died, the charge would have changed to premeditated murder, and the judge had vowed to give Dad the death penalty or at least life in prison without parole.

If that had been the case, I would never have been born.

At San Quentin, the chief psychiatrist claimed Dad's IQ was the highest they had ever tested. During one of their many conversations, he told Dad his smarts would help him adjust to the outside world when he got out. But Dad didn't wait—he used his smarts on the inside, finagling a job in the psychiatrist's office helping with autopsies and medical records, a highly coveted position.

In no time, Dad convinced the psychiatrist that Mom had been raped and he'd gotten a bad deal. The psychiatrist then convinced the warden that Dad deserved an early parole, so he was released after serving only three years. He laughed all the way home.

The night of the crime, the police chief had interviewed Dad and George separately. George held to the story that he was simply helping a friend and that Cleo deserved what he got. But Dad gave a different account, claiming George used the monkey wrench without his knowledge and got out of control. Dad just meant to rough up Cleo.

The only time George and Dad saw each other in the prison yard, his former friend told him, "I'll kill you, you hear me? You double-crossing son of a bitch."

Whenever Mom talked to Dad about George, she would cry, yet she'd bring up his name all the time. She was like that—saying the same things over and over again. It was tiring and made Dad mad.

On many nights when I listened at their door, Mom would say, "We're stuck on this ugly reservation where everyone hates me because of what you did. No one checks—how many other violent criminals are here?"

"People will hate you wherever we live. And for the millionth time, it's a good thing they don't check or I'd be out of a job, and we'd be living on the street."

"You think George won't find us? Someday he'll come and kill us all!"

"Goddamn it, Thelma Lou, shut up for once. No

one will look for us here. This mess is all your mother's fault. If that fat-ass whore had stuck around for my trial, she would have convinced the judge that Cleo deserved what he got. I'm sorry we didn't kill the bastard."

The bed would creak then, signaling my dad had turned over on his side, the conversation now over. That was my cue to leave. I'd tiptoe back into the room I shared with Sam, no one the wiser.

CHAPTER 4

In June of 1957, EPNG transferred Dad to a station ten miles outside the town of Belen, New Mexico, about two hundred miles southeast of Navajo Station and thirty miles south of Albuquerque. Dad said it was a little fart of a railroad town on the edge of the Rio Grande River, which on most days was no wider than the piss stream of a drunk. When we drove up to our new house, nothing looked different except for the kids playing in the street.

A month later, Dad brought Mom home from the hospital with a new baby girl they named Sally. Dad yelled at Mom and said she couldn't be his because he hadn't had sex with her in years. Lonnie blushed and said Sally was the only one of us who had Dad's darker coloring and broad cheeks. We loved her from the first moment we saw her big brown eyes.

As the days passed, Mom became sadder and more tired, which I didn't think was possible. She crept around the house in her nightgown, moving from the bedroom to the couch, holding Sally and crying most of the time. Every morning, Lonnie fixed us breakfast. She was nine years old.

I began running farther and farther from home into the desert. Mom didn't notice. Neither did Dad. Although he worked the four-to-midnight shift, he wasn't around much during the day, even on weekends. After sleeping in, he'd go to the plant to work extra hours or to study for the engineering correspondence classes he was taking from the University of New Mexico night school. Sometimes he would go to the plant when he wasn't working or studying so he could be alone, he told us.

One day after lunch, I took off without telling Mom and kept going until I couldn't see the houses anymore. Lizards scooted out of my way as I ran faster and faster through the tall weeds, trying to kick pebbles. A husky that belonged to one of the neighbors caught up with me, barking like crazy. When I glanced over at him to see what was wrong, he stopped in his tracks—and I tumbled headfirst into a deep hole.

I didn't panic at first. After all, I was a tough Cherokee. Pretending I was in a Western, I let out a war cry and scrambled up the sides but made it only halfway before sliding back to the bottom. After several more tries, I gave up and yelled as loud as I could.

The husky ran around the edge and barked, sometimes pawing at the dirt like he wanted to get down into the hole with me. I yelled until I was hoarse, and he continued barking. No one came. This was a whole lot scarier than being tied to the tree.

It was getting dark when I heard a truck door slam and looked up to see a tall, skinny EPNG guy with a crew cut. The cigarette in his fingers glowed red. "Don't worry, son, I'll drop a rope and pull you out."

I hung on tight as he lifted me up and then grabbed my arm. The husky ran around me and licked my arms and legs, nearly knocking me down. He raced after the truck until we reached the main road, barking the whole time.

At home, the man followed me inside, and we found Mom dozing on the couch, unaware that I'd been gone. The man said he would let Thurston know I was okay. The next day, Dad told me, "If you'd stayed in the hole overnight, maybe you would have finally learned your lesson."

Mom and Lonnie said they were glad I had started kindergarten—but now three-year-old Sam was running around the house and yelling like a banshee while I was at school. Mom moaned that making meals, doing the ironing, and keeping the house clean with two wild sons and a baby in diapers was too much for her.

"What's your problem?" Dad asked her. "Do you expect to live the life of Riley? Or maybe you want to be a contestant on **Queen for a Day**?"

She hurried into the bedroom, slammed the door, and cried some more.

One Saturday morning not long after, Dad told Mom to stop bellyaching and took off in the car. At lunchtime, he pulled into the driveway with a huge box in the back. "I got this industrial iron for you," he told Mom. "It'll make life easier if you get off your dead ass and use it."

We gathered outside to watch him unload it. A neighbor lady came by and said the only time she'd ever seen such a large contraption was in a dry cleaner that pressed clothes for the whole town. She couldn't imagine needing it for one family's ironing.

After hauling the box into the living room, Dad took out the instructions and packets of screws and bolts and began assembling it. Sam and I handed him screwdrivers and wrenches, but he pushed us away. "Hey, get the hell out of my hair." When he finished, the ironing machine had two giant hinged plates and two pedals on the floor like the ones on Lonnie's piano.

Mom jerked around the room watching. "I can't work that big thing," she yelled, her arms waving wildly in every direction.

Dad poured water into a large cylinder and flipped

on a brass-colored switch. In no time, the water turned to steam and made a sizzling noise.

"Thelma Lou," he said. "Watch my feet." One pedal made the plates clamp together, and the other one released them. "You have to press hard on the release pedal or the plates won't open up until the two-minute cycle is finished."

He demonstrated with a pair of jeans. Sam squealed when they came out looking like they'd been run over by a steamroller. Reaching down to the overflowing laundry basket, Dad pulled out a shirt and handed it to Mom. "Okay, now you do it."

She placed it on the bottom plate, pushed down on the start pedal, and stood back as the top plate lowered into place. When the plates released, Mom peeled off the shirt, now as flat and thin as a piece of paper and smelling like the air after it rained.

"Thelma Lou, I expect all the clothes to be ironed when I get back from my shift."

Her lower lip trembled. "I'll try."

Once he left, Lonnie took Sally into our parents' bedroom, and Mom sat down to iron. "I can't use this," she kept muttering. "I don't understand it." And then she complained that the vapor from the steam burned her eyes.

Everything would have been okay if she had sent us outside to play that day. Stuck in the house, Sam and I raced around, and every time I hit him with my rubber-tipped arrows, he fell down and kicked his feet in the air, pretending to die. When he got tired of that game, he bolted into the living room and knocked Mom's knickknacks off the lazy Susan.

Yelling, she moved to catch him just as the ball I kicked against the wall ricocheted into the back of her head. She turned to chase after me, and Sam darted toward the iron.

It took us a moment to realize what had happened. The air filled with smoke, howling, and a terrible smell. Lonnie ran into the living room with Sally to see what was wrong. Sam stood by the iron, screaming, trying to pull himself free—the top metal plate had somehow clamped down on his left hand. Mom raced to the iron and pulled on his hand, but it wouldn't budge. Lonnie stomped on the release pedal with all her might, but the plates wouldn't open.

Mom let out a loud scream and fell in a heap on the floor. Lonnie pulled on Sam's hand, but she couldn't get it out either. I wrapped my arms around Lonnie's waist and pulled her to help free Sam's hand. But it didn't work. Sam jumped and shook, wailing so loud I thought he was dying.

It seemed like hours before the plates released. When they did, Sam's hand was a mass of blood and flesh, as if it had melted. Grabbing Sam, Lonnie ran into the bathroom and came out with a towel wrapped around his hand, a trail of blood following them. Tears flowed down her cheeks, but she acted calm. She gave Sam to me and rushed to the phone to call Dad.

Sam fell limp in my arms. I couldn't stop crying. My baby brother was hurt worse than anything I could have imagined, and it was all my fault.

"He's on his way," Lonnie said.

Mom stopped crying but kept whimpering and slowly got up off the floor.

A few minutes later, Dad screeched the Green Bomber into the driveway so fast I thought it would smash into the house. Bounding inside, he yelled for us to get some clothes and hustle to the car because we'd be gone for a long time. He told Mom to wrap Sam's hand in gauze filled with petroleum jelly and to get clean bandages.

Hoot, Dad's boss, had called a hospital in Phoenix after Dad relayed what Lonnie had told him, and they promised to have a surgeon waiting for us when we got there. Albuquerque didn't have a doctor who could fix Sam's hand, Hoot said.

The family piled into the car and tore out of the compound. Lonnie cradled Sally in the back seat next to me, and Mom sat in front holding Sam and crying in sniffling spurts. Dad stared straight ahead. His fingers gripped the wheel with such force the bones almost popped through his skin.

Sam's face turned a scary red color, but he didn't

move or cry. His eyes were closed like he was sleeping. Dad said he was in shock. I was afraid he'd never wake up.

Lonnie leaned forward. "Dad, what about Midnight?" she asked softly.

"He'll be okay."

We would never see him again.

The dust kicked up around the Green Bomber as if we were trying to outrun a tornado. For the first time in my noisy life, I didn't utter a sound. Sally squirmed and cried in Lonnie's arms. When it got dark, I stared at the star-studded desert sky, listening to the hum of the tires, and pretended that nothing was wrong with Sam's hand.

We arrived at the hospital in the middle of the night. Dad parked at the entrance and ran inside with Sam in his arms. Nurses in white uniforms put him on a gurney and hurried him down the hall, and Mom and Dad followed behind. Lonnie, Sally, and I weren't allowed to go with them, so we sat in the waiting room.

Lonnie changed Sally's diaper and gave her a bottle and then sent me to the vending machine for crackers and soda pop. She squeezed my hand and said the accident wasn't my fault, but I shook my head and cried. Most of the night, I walked around the waiting room counting the square tiles and imagining that Sam would come out running and giggling.

It was daylight when Mom and Dad came back to the waiting room. Through Mom's muffled tears, we found out that the doctors were still operating. Her eyes were red and her skin was puffed up, as if someone had stuffed cotton balls in her cheeks.

"Dad," I said, "is Sam gonna be all right?"

He raised his hand, signaling me to stop as tears filled his eyes. It must have been really bad if he couldn't answer me. I went back to counting tiles, but I kept thinking about Sam and I'd lose track and have to start over.

Staring at the wall, Mom shook and muttered that it wasn't her fault. She knew the ironing machine would break and hurt one of us kids. It was too fancy for her, she said to no one in particular. Lonnie rocked Sally in her arms singing softly. "Don't cry, baby." No one paid any attention to us—we blended into a room full of sad, tired people who looked like they didn't want to be there either.

After what felt like forever, a doctor came out and pulled up a chair in front of Mom and Dad. "Sam will regain most of the use of his left hand," he said. "But it will take a couple of months before he can leave the hospital. We've grafted skin from his stomach to grow over his hand. It's a new technique that has shown promising results."

• • •

We moved into a roach-infested motel room with two beds and a small TV. I slept on the floor with a pillow and my Roy Rogers blanket, and Lonnie and Sally slept in the bed next to Mom and Dad's. Mom didn't say much other than occasionally mumbling that everyone blamed her for Sam's accident. Her eyes seemed to be in a continual trance. Sometimes I'd walk right in front of her and she didn't see me.

Dad acted like she wasn't there.

For many long weeks, Sam lived behind a glass wall in a tiny bed under a clear plastic tent. We weren't allowed to go inside. Every day Dad picked me up, held me against the glass wall, and told me to wave to him. Sam's left hand was taped to his stomach and his other hand was under a bright blue blanket. Straps held his chest and feet tight so he couldn't move except for his head. He turned to look at me, and I cried, but he gave me the biggest smile I'd ever seen.

"When will he be able to play again?" I asked a stern-faced nurse in a white uniform and funny hat.

"Not for a long time," she said. "He has to live in a germ-free oxygen tent until he's healed enough not to get an infection."

Dad called his boss to update him on Sam's progress, and Hoot told him he could take as much time as he needed. His job would be waiting when he got back. But Dad wasn't getting paid and soon our money would run out, so he needed Lonnie and me to help him pick fruit and cotton—the same thing he did when he was my age.

In the hot Arizona desert, we worked alongside Mexican field hands, and my peashooter came in handy for blowing tiny pebbles at them. Sometimes I hit them in the butt with apples or pears when they bent down. They would yell something in Spanish and shake their hands at me.

Other times, I lobbed tomatoes at the sides of the trucks to see them go splat. I didn't think Dad was watching me, but after one of my best throws, he grabbed me by the arm and said the next time he saw anything flying, he'd whack my little ass hard. So I did it only when he wasn't around.

When I got bored with that, I'd throw apples high in the air and catch them, pretending I had gotten the third out in a big inning. Or I would aim for the baskets we used to collect the fruit. Messing around was the only way I could take my mind off Sam.

We ate fresh fruit from the farm and groceries that didn't need cooking, like salami and cheese sandwiches. Dad ate sardines from a tin can that smelled as bad as the buffalo farts. Mom mixed powdered milk with the rusty water from the bathroom sink, making it taste even worse than it normally did. I poured it down the drain when no one was looking.

The day finally came for Sam to leave the hospital. A nurse carried him out of the tent room and handed him to Mom. I ran to hug him, and Lonnie gave him a kiss on top of his head. He giggled. His hand and stomach were covered with giant bandages. The nurse said we needed to be careful around him because his skin was still very tender.

A doctor told Dad that Sam had to have the skin on his hand and stomach sanded to make it look natural when he got older.

"I'm not paying for any sanding," Dad said. "Sam isn't going to be a movie star. Hell, his skin looks rugged, and nothing's wrong with that."

On the drive back, I promised to be a better boy so Sam wouldn't get hurt again. Dad said it wasn't my fault and not to worry about it.

But I did.

We stopped at a small diner to get Cokes and hamburgers, and Dad launched into more stories about his World War II adventures. I made my best machine gun impression and twirled my arms to look like a Japanese Zero falling from the sky. Even Mom laughed at that. Dad didn't yell at her once.

• • •

We made it home for the Halloween party at the EPNG rec center. I dressed up as Roy Rogers and ate as much candy as I wanted. Dad didn't seem to mind, and Mom smiled when she saw me dance with Ginger, Hoot's daughter. She was three years older than I was, but she let me play with her.

Not long after the party, everything returned to normal. Dad yelled at Mom, Lonnie took care of Sally, and I shot rubber arrows at the pictures on the wall, begging Mom to let me out. It worked every time. Sam still had a soft wrap on his hand, and his stomach was covered with rectangular red scars, but we got used to seeing him like that.

One warm afternoon the following March, Mom called out from the kitchen, "David, wouldn't it be nice to take Sam on a bike ride?" She came into the living room where I was stretched out on the floor with my cowboy and Indian plastic toys.

I looked up and blinked—her hair was combed and she was dressed, ready to go. Lonnie would stay in the house playing the piano and watching eight-month-old Sally while we used her bike.

In front of the house, Mom sat Sam in the basket hooked to the handlebar. He was wearing only a diaper, without shoes or a shirt. Since the ironing accident, Sam had gone back to diapers, and he didn't talk as much as he used to.

Mom turned to me. "Sit on the rack in back to

keep the bike balanced." It took her three tries to get on the seat while holding wiggly Sam with one hand and the handlebar with the other.

I steadied myself on the rack. "Are you sure we won't tip over?"

"We'll be fine. I've been riding bikes all my life, and there's no traffic to worry about. It'll be fun."

Mom began pedaling, and the bike wobbled as my brother kept trying to get out of the basket. "Sam, stay put," she said, pushing him back down.

The bike jerked, moving too slowly to stay upright, so she pedaled faster. By that time, Sam had managed to stand in the basket, and he fell forward out of Mom's grasp. His left foot got lodged between the wheel and the fork, causing the bike to tip over.

Sam's head slammed against the sidewalk with a loud crack and Mom dropped on top of him. I fell off the back and hit my head on the sidewalk too, but I managed to roll to my feet. Blood gushed from Sam's skull and foot, and the raw skin on his stomach was also bleeding. His big left toe hung on the spikes, nearly cut off from the rest of his foot.

He screamed almost as loud as he had when his hand got caught in the iron. How could Sam be hurt again? How could Mom be so stupid?

"What happened, Sam?" Mom yelled. She acted like it was his fault and he knew what had gone wrong. When she realized how seriously he was hurt, she picked him up and ran into the house with me right behind. Lonnie jumped up from the piano and helped Mom wrap his foot in a towel.

"Be careful, Mom! Don't tear off his toe."

Lonnie called Dad, and he rushed the three of us to the hospital in Albuquerque. I had forgotten about the blood oozing from the back of my head, but compared to my poor brother, I was fine. I cried hard, not just for Sam, but for how unfair it was for him to be hurt again.

Since Mom and Dad always did better in a crisis, there was no yelling or hitting. Dad took me into the hospital bathroom to wash the blood off my scalp, joking that he hoped I hadn't broken the sidewalk. Back in the waiting room, Mom cried and shook, as usual, but we didn't pay any attention to her.

It was getting dark outside when a grim-faced doctor came to talk to us. "Your son has a fractured skull and a concussion. We've sedated him until the swelling in his brain goes down. As for his big toe, a surgeon is working to reattach the tendon. It's a tricky procedure, but I'm optimistic he will keep the toe. Your son won't be out of surgery for at least another hour, and he'll need to stay here for a few days because of his brain injury."

We sat some more and then another doctor appeared. "Sam's toe will eventually heal," he said. "But he won't walk normally again for a long time."

Days later, I went with Mom and Dad to get Sam out of the hospital. Mom held him in a blanket, but Dad ripped him out of her arms, yelling that she was too goddamn incompetent to hold him without dropping him. As we walked toward the exit, an older doctor came up behind us. "Mr. and Mrs. Crow, may I speak with you in my office?"

I tagged along since no one told me not to. "Please, have a seat," the doctor said, closing the door. He picked up a clipboard from his desk and looked at Mom. "I'm trying to understand what happened. Why would you place a small child in a bicycle basket?"

Waiting for Mom to answer, Dad mumbled to himself, his voice low like a record player spinning too slowly. The usual signs of anger were there: the bugged-out eyes and pulsing Y vein on his forehead, along with dancing crisscrossed lines. It sounded like he was arguing with himself.

"I couldn't leave David alone," Mom said through sobs. "He causes trouble all the time. Lonnie watched Sally in the house . . . so they were okay. I put Sam in the basket and held him with one hand. It seemed safe . . . There weren't any cars . . . Sam was having fun . . . David balanced the back end, but he's so heavy I could barely get going . . . Sam wriggled out of my hand. The accident could have happened to anybody. It wasn't my fault."

The doctor stared at her, frowning, and then bent over the clipboard and wrote quickly.

"Thelma Lou couldn't take care of plastic fruit," Dad said.

The doctor raised his head. "You shouldn't talk about your wife like that, mister."

"Really?" he yelled. "If you want the dumb bitch, I'll leave her with you."

The doctor got up and walked out.

As we passed through the waiting room, everyone stared at us. I focused on the floor, my face growing hot. I wanted to disappear.

On the ride home, Mom held Sam in a blanket and retold her side of the story. Dad gripped the steering wheel, working his jaw back and forth.

"I can't understand why you're so mad," Mom said, her voice shaky with tears. "Sam giggled up a storm and kicked his little legs when I told him we were going for a bike ride." She turned to the back seat and nodded for me to agree with her.

But I couldn't. I looked down at my lap, realizing for the first time that Dad might be right—maybe Mom **was** crazy.

CHAPTER 5

My parents stopped talking to each other. In their bedroom at night, they didn't laugh anymore either. All they did was yell and scream, and the hitting got worse. Mom shuffled around the house with the dull, vacant look I saw in the eyes of the stray compound dogs.

The neighbors avoided her the way they had at Navajo Station—they wouldn't answer the door the few times she went outside. "I know they're home," she'd tell me. "Maybe they didn't hear me knock." She and I walked from house to house, but no one came to the door.

That's when Mom started bothering us at night. At bedtime, she came to life and hurried from one bedroom to the next, pretending she was helping us get ready for bed when we were already **in** bed. "Did you wash your face, David?" she would ask, and even when I told her I had, she'd bring in a washcloth. The same thing happened with the toothbrush. Then she would straighten my sheets and open my drawers, asking me repeatedly if I was ready to go to sleep.

Finally, she'd leave, and as I drifted off, I would jolt awake, feeling like I had ants crawling in my hair. But it was Mom, tapping my head with her fingertips. She'd put her face close to mine as if she wanted to swallow me whole and then ask pointless questions.

"David, do you know who left a cup in the sink?"

"No, Mom," I muttered.

Minutes later, she would swoop back and touch me again. "David, I found your shoes on the porch. Did you leave them out there?"

"They got wet, and I wanted to let them dry."

Later, after I'd been asleep awhile, Mom would wake me again with more random questions. Sometimes she shook me so hard I thought Sam had had another accident or Belen Station had blown up and I hadn't heard the siren or smelled the smoke. She would grab me with clammy hands, holding on as if she were slipping, tears streaming down her face.

After she repeated this a few times, I couldn't get back to sleep, anxiously awaiting her quick steps into my bedroom. None of our rooms had locks, so I'd move a chair against the door, only to have her push it away, telling me not to do it again. When Lonnie shoved her bed against the door, Mom would stand in the hallway and pound. "Lonnie, let me in. We need to talk."

She did the same thing to Dad. He typically came home from the evening shift, ate, and went straight to bed. Mom would wake him up minutes after he'd fallen asleep. He would yell at her to stop being a stark raving lunatic, and just as I was falling asleep again, he'd stomp through the house, a blanket and pillow in hand, and head for the Green Bomber.

Soon I would hear Mom's birdlike feet pitter-patter down the hall and the screen door bang. "Thurston," she'd yell, pounding on the car window, "we have to talk!"

"Go to bed, you dumb bitch," Dad would yell back at her. "I need to sleep so I can work to pay for all your accidents."

Mom would stand on the porch until Dad got quiet and stopped moving. Then she'd run to the car and pound on the window again, screeching that they needed to talk. When he ignored her, she pounded harder and screamed until he got out of the car and hit her. Then she would run into the bedroom crying as Dad went back to sleep in the Rambler.

Neither of them paid any attention to Lonnie and me as we watched from the porch.

One morning in the middle of the summer, I spotted a group of older boys down the street with their bikes. I raced home and got my bike, my first without training wheels. I would turn six in August and was ready to ride with the big boys. But they didn't see it that way.

"Get out of here, you little pest," they said.

I followed anyway and convinced one of them to tie a rope from the seat pole of his bike to my handlebar. As he pulled my tiny bike, I pedaled hard so we wouldn't fall behind the others. But my little legs couldn't keep up, and the boy jumped off his bike, untied the rope, and took off, yelling over his shoulder, "Go home, kid."

I didn't care what he thought and slowly, steadily rode toward Belen. The compound was ten miles from town, and I'd been on the road for what seemed like hours. It couldn't be much farther.

My legs felt wobbly when I finally reached the bridge crossing the Rio Grande River. By then, the boys were nowhere to be found. That was okay—I didn't need their help. The sun wasn't high in the sky anymore, but I still had lots of time for fun.

I didn't cross the bridge and go into town. There was no sidewalk, and I was scared to ride where the cars drove. Putting down my kickstand, I got off the bike and spotted a small corner store that sold candy and soda pop, the "capitalist crap" Dad never let us have. It had been a long time since breakfast, and I was hungry.

"Can I get some things while I wait for my mom

and dad?" I asked the pretty lady behind the counter. "They'll pay for them when they come get me, after they run some errands."

"You're cute," she said. "Sure, get what you want."

I roamed the aisles, picking up candy, cookies, bubble gum, and a comic book. The lady winked at me when I thanked her. This was the best day of summer ever. I went back so many times for Sugar Babies that my pockets bulged, and it didn't take long before my stomach hurt.

I gathered a bunch of rocks to throw into the river. The muddy water was moving slowly, and I wanted to make some big splashes.

As I sat on the riverbank, the sun began to sink. It would be dark soon. The lady closed the store and came over to ask if I was okay. I told her Mom and Dad would be along anytime, but after she left, I started crying. I should have told her the truth.

Cars and trucks passed me by as I watched the headlights shine on the water. I wished someone nice would pick me up and take me home, but no one noticed me. It was like when I'd fallen into the hole, except the husky wasn't there to help.

The sun faded, and the red streaks across the sky dimmed. I could see a few stars now. Alone and afraid, I knew it would be hard to find me, even if someone were looking. I stuck my hands in my pockets and shivered as the temperature dropped, the way it always did at night in the desert.

A short time later, bright truck lights blinded me, and I heard a man shout, "There he is. Go get Thurston!"

I recognized the man as one of the new EPNG workers. He smelled like grease and cigarettes. "You created quite a scare, little fella," he said. "Every spare man in the compound has been looking for you for hours." He wrapped me in a blanket and carried me to his truck. Another man picked up my bike and followed.

Two more trucks pulled onto the side of the bridge. Dad jumped out of the last one. I couldn't see his face as he yanked me high in the air and said, "Are you all right?" As soon as I said yes, he threw me over his knee and hit my butt so hard it knocked the breath out of me. The men watched, but no one said a word.

Why was he so mad? He never cared when I ran off before. I sniveled the entire ride back.

Mom's usual okra, roast beef, and iced tea dinner was waiting for us. Lonnie and Sam had already eaten, but they stayed at the table and watched Mom, Dad, and me, their eyes wide. "Thelma Lou!" Dad yelled. "What the hell is the matter with you, not paying attention to the kids—especially David? I swear, if breathing wasn't automatic, you'd be dead."

"He's impossible to watch!" She ran into their bedroom and slammed the door.

I found out later that the older kids had fessed up—they knew I had followed them into town, but they didn't try to look for me. One boy's father called Dad to let him know. A neighbor lady came by to tell Mom what happened, waking her from a nap.

After everyone went to bed, I crawled down the hall in the dark and curled up on the floor outside my parents' room.

"I wasn't worried the little bastard had been kidnapped," Dad said. "Even if he had been, they would have given him back when they realized he was such a pain in the ass." He chuckled. "But if he froze to death and you didn't even know he left the compound, they would have locked you up in the funny farm, which is what I should have done a long time ago."

Mom laughed, even though what he said was mean.

I liked my first-grade teacher, Miss Gardner. She was young and pretty and never made fun of me when I wrote my letters backward or couldn't remember words. One day she pulled me aside and asked if I had trouble seeing the blackboard. How did she figure that out? I nodded, and the next morning, she moved my seat to the front of the class.

As nice as she was, though, it wasn't long before the kids started calling me **estúpido**. Whenever Miss Gardner returned a paper with a lot of red marks, they'd laugh and try to rip it out of my hands. Every afternoon, I hopped off the bus and ran as fast as I could away from the house to forget all about it.

On the weekends, Dad would tell me to get into the car, and we'd drive to Belen to check on the cigarette machines he leased. As we refilled them and collected the money, he would say, "Ignorant Indians and Mexicans are paying me to wreck their health. You'd never catch a Cherokee smoking this shit. When I was in the Q, I did autopsies on smokers who had black lungs. I always knew cigarettes were bad."

Dad would blurt out things like this when we were alone. By that point, I'd put together pieces of his story from listening in. He never mentioned the Q in front of my siblings, but he talked to me about it as though I knew everything.

"Pay attention, David—I'll teach you how to make money off other people's idiocy. It's the easiest money you'll ever make."

When we got back in the Rambler and headed home, he would go on about taking advantage of morons or rail against the person who had broken into one of his machines and stolen his money. As the miles passed, I'd think that maybe he wouldn't bring up Mom. Not this time. But no matter what he was saying, he'd interrupt himself, and his voice would turn ugly. "You understand that we need to get rid of your mother, right?"

He had been saying the same thing for years now, but Mom was still at home.

I said yes and nodded, knowing I couldn't answer any other way.

CHAPTER 6

Not a week went by without a screaming match that led to Dad sleeping in the Rambler and Mom running into the house after he hit her. The next day they'd both act as if nothing had happened. Then it would be quiet for a few nights before the yelling and hitting started up again.

The neighbors weren't happy. After more than two years of yard fights and Mom's whiny complaints, they wanted nothing to do with her or Dad. When either one went out during the day, the neighbors quickly turned in the other direction. They didn't allow their kids to come over to our house, and Sam and I weren't invited over to theirs, so we all played together at the compound playground.

After second grade ended, I spent every day there with Sam. He liked to dig in the sandbox so much I started calling him "Diggie." Once in a while, we wandered off the compound, but we never went far. When it was time for him to go in, I took off on my own, running into the desert. No one stopped me, and it meant not having to be around Mom and Dad.

One night, the fighting went on longer than usual. I found Lonnie on the porch sitting on the top step wrapped in a blanket.

"Mom has woken him up three times in the car. She's nuts. It's like she wants him to hit her." Lonnie stood and opened the door. "Be back in a second." She returned with two glasses of Kool-Aid and handed one to me. "It looks like we might be here a while for this one."

Dad opened the side window a crack. "Thelma Lou, get in the house before I whip your ass," he said through gritted teeth.

Mom didn't budge. Dad drew up his knees and kicked open the door against her legs, knocking her onto the dirt. She struggled to get up and then ran around the car, crying for help. The lights came on at the Sanders' house next door, and the husband and wife watched from the front porch in their robes. The wife shook her head, and they disappeared back inside. The house went dark.

Dad closed the car door and pulled the pillow over his head. Mom stormed into the house past Lonnie and me and came flying out with a frying pan. Raising it into the air, she walloped the roof next to the window closest to Dad's head. He leapt out of the car and shoved Mom's shoulder, knocking her down again.

"You don't love me," she cried, curled up on the ground. "I hate it here. I hate these compounds. I hate the mean neighbors. I'm taking the kids and leaving!"

Lonnie and I laughed. Mom needed help with everything. She couldn't take care of herself, much less us.

Dad stepped over her and walked into the house. Mom hurried to her feet and followed him inside, both of them still acting like we weren't there. By then, Sam had joined us. Sally cried from her crib, but we knew she'd go back to sleep once the yelling stopped, so we ignored her.

We went back to our rooms, thinking that Mom and Dad had settled down for the night, but minutes later, their bedroom door flung open and whacked the wall. Mom ran for the front door, Dad close behind. Standing in the middle of the yard in her nightgown and slippers, she screamed at the top of her lungs. I made it to the porch in time to see Dad slap the top of her head with his powerful left hand, knocking her to the ground a third time.

But Mom wouldn't stop. She got up, ran next door, and disappeared inside the Sanders' dark house. Dad tore in after her. Seconds later, she ran out the back door and reappeared in front, Dad close behind her. The lights in the house went on again, and the husband and wife came outside. Other neighbors came outside too. Dad grabbed Mom by the arm and dragged her into our house.

Her muffled crying continued, but there was no more yelling or hitting. At last, I could fall asleep.

The next morning, Dad sat Lonnie and me down at the kitchen table while Mom was still in their bedroom. "Your mother isn't fit to live around normal people," he said in a tired voice. "Everyone blames me for hitting her, but she brings it on herself. Nothing else works."

When I listened at their bedroom door that night, I heard Dad say, "My boss told me to clean up my family mess or I'd be transferred to another station. If the problems continue, I'll be asked to leave EPNG."

How much longer would he let Mom stay?

Soon after I started third grade, I was convinced my classmates were right—I was **estúpido**. Second grade had been hard enough as I stumbled through the Dick and Jane books and the blackboard got fuzzier, even though I sat at the front of the class.

But third grade was impossible. I had to read out loud, and sometimes I skipped words or lines, so none of it made sense. When I stopped and started over, the kids would laugh. No matter what I did, I couldn't get the words to hold still—they shook across the page the way a pond ripples after you toss in a pebble. And I couldn't print any of my letters correctly. My cursive was even worse—one large, smudged mess.

My new teacher, Mrs. Jimenez, said I was a smart boy but just needed some help. I didn't believe her. At home, Dad would test me, asking me to read from the newspaper. He'd call me stupid and shake me as I struggled to keep my place. When I tripped over the words, he would wave his hand back and forth in my face, saying, "Why bother?"

At the end of September, he and Mom woke us up in the middle of the night with yet another fight in their bedroom. More yelling and wailing, along with an occasional grunt and shout from Dad. Gradually their voices faded into silence. I didn't hear Mom at all. It had become so quiet—too quiet. Had Dad finally suffocated her with a pillow?

The next morning, I was relieved to see Mom in the kitchen making coffee. When Dad appeared and poured himself a glass of orange juice, they didn't talk to each other or to us. Dad ate his breakfast, drank his juice and coffee, and hurried to the plant, covering a shift for someone on vacation.

For the next several days, they were unusually quiet and calm. Dad didn't pay attention to anything I said or did. Being the oldest, Lonnie knew the most about our parents' problems, but she couldn't figure out their silence. "Something's up," was all she said.

That weekend, Lonnie, Sam, and I were sitting around the table in our pajamas eating cereal, the television blaring cartoons in the living room, when Dad came in. "Time for a family meeting."

He told us to move to the couch, and he and Mom sat in front of us. "We're leaving EPNG for good," he said. "Your mother needs to live in a real town, with different neighbors, and I want to make more money and go to college at night."

Dad set down his coffee cup and smiled at Mom, and she smiled back. It was the first time in years that we'd seen them be nice to each other. I figured we weren't getting rid of Mom yet.

"We're moving to Albuquerque," Dad said. "I'll be selling life insurance for a big company based in Nebraska called Woodmen Accident and Life. I'm giving EPNG my notice today."

But he'd always said you didn't leave EPNG unless you died or retired. And I didn't want to move. I liked Mrs. Jimenez and the older boys in the compound. I didn't want to be the new kid somewhere else.

When Dad came home that night, nothing seemed different—we had the usual fried okra, roast beef, and iced tea for dinner—so maybe he hadn't told EPNG we were leaving.

Later, I listened for a long time outside their bedroom door.

"What about the guy who threw a brick at you from the top of the turbines?" Mom asked. "Did you ever catch him?"

"No. Probably one of the dumb bastards I had to discipline. Hell, someone has to roll a few heads once in a while."

"It's a good thing we're leaving."

Another person wanted Dad dead? I worried about George finding us and kept a lookout for anyone who seemed to be sneaking up on Dad, like I was a detective. I daydreamed about San Quentin, even calling it the Q the way he did. I'd save him by jumping on George just before he shot Dad in the head.

And I pretended to talk Dad out of trying to kill Cleo. "You'll get caught. Don't do it. Tell George to forget it. The bastard isn't worth it."

On the day we left Belen Station, Mom gathered our dishes and helped Dad load the lamps, tables, couch, piano, and chairs into the green wooden trailer hitched to the back of the Green Bomber. Lonnie, Sam, and I each filled a box with our belongings and put them in the trunk.

The next-door neighbor worked in his front yard

without looking at us. No one helped us load the trailer or said goodbye.

When everything was almost packed, I walked slowly through the empty rooms.

"Anything's better than living here," Lonnie said behind me. "I'm tired of everyone hating Mom. Dad isn't happy either. There will be way more to do in a big city."

Maybe she was right. Maybe the fighting would stop after we moved.

Two Mexican men who lived in Belen and worked for Dad drove up before we left. I remembered them from Dad's deer hunting trips. They got out of their truck and waited for him. The older man, his face creased with deep lines, started talking to Lonnie and me.

"Last fall, a huge momma bear charged our camp when her cubs wandered by. We couldn't get to our guns." He removed his straw hat and wiped his brow. "I thought we were going to die, but your dad calmly picked up his rifle and fired two rounds into the bear's chest, dropping it less than ten feet from us. We'd be dead without him."

The younger man nodded. "We panicked, but not your father."

When Dad came back from that trip, the dead bear took up the back of a flatbed truck. He held me up to see it. The massive head and claws scared me so bad I wet my pants. I wondered why Dad had killed the bear. Now I knew. He'd done it to save them.

"And your dad taught me math and engineering in his off-hours," added the younger man. "I named my son Thurston after him. I'm really going to miss him."

Dad put the last of the boxes in the trailer and came over to greet the men. They shook hands warmly and said their goodbyes. Dad handed the younger man an engineering book and a slide rule. The man's eyes filled with tears. The older man gave Dad a broad smile and said, "Adios, amigo."

They got back into the EPNG truck and drove slowly toward the compressor station. When I grew up, I wanted to be just like Dad—smart and strong and brave.

CHAPTER 7

I looked out the back window at the dust whirling around behind us. The compound got smaller and smaller until the desert swallowed it up. The car was silent, except for Mom's crying. She cried the way she breathed, which is to say all the time. We were doing what she wanted us to do, so why wasn't she happy?

It took only an hour to get to our new house, but it felt like we'd entered another world. There were miles and miles of stores and neighborhoods—an entire EPNG housing compound could fit in one city block. Lots of kids jumped rope and played catch or stickball in the streets. And none of their parents knew Mom or Dad. Maybe no one would avoid Mom or ever see her fighting with Dad.

We settled into 720 Vassar Drive, NE, a gray, one-story stucco house with a small front porch, a one-car garage, and a concrete back patio shaded by a canvas awning. The rest of the backyard was gravel. It was the fanciest house I'd ever been in. Mom said we could have picnics at the wooden table on the patio. We were one block from Lomas Boulevard, a four-lane highway where more cars sped by in an hour than I'd seen in my whole life.

Dad traded in the Green Bomber for a shiny, hot-off-the-lot green Rambler Ambassador station wagon. He used it for work, driving to his office and to his customers' houses to sign them up. He called them prospects. During his first weeks, he sold a policy to a University of New Mexico football star named Don Perkins, who'd signed to play with the brand-new Dallas Cowboys. Soon afterward, Dad sold a policy to Bobby Unser, the famous race car driver. I was positive Dad would become famous too.

Dad bought me a bigger bike and let me share a paper route with a teenage boy in the neighborhood, a kid almost twice my age who supervised my deliveries. The canvas **Albuquerque Journal** bag hung like a poncho, nearly reaching my knees. When the adults on my route saw me, they smiled and waved—before long, they called out my name.

I wanted to know everything about my new city, so I read some of the articles in the paper, though I didn't understand many of the words. The local section had lots of stories about the Southwest in the days of the Spanish conquistadors. On my paper route, I pretended to be one of Coronado's men storming the countryside, slaughtering my enemies.

When I made my weekly rounds collecting payment, my customers tipped me nickels, dimes, and quarters, filling my pockets with change. I jabbered on, the way I had with Champ, and they would tell me about their day or their job or what they were cooking for dinner. I hung around at each house until the man or woman would have to go do something. "Have a good week, David," they'd say.

Lonnie went to the fancy school down the street called Jefferson Junior High, home of the Jets. It looked like a huge hotel. School was easy for her, and she was always the smartest student in the class. Lonnie could do everything, just like Dad.

A few blocks away, I resumed the third grade and Sam the first grade at Monte Vista Elementary, a two-story building with a red tile roof that looked like a Spanish fortress. Our new school had a big playground with swing sets, a dirt running track, a high-jump pit, and a baseball field. I loved everything about it.

But I didn't do any better in class than I had in Belen. Many times, I couldn't make out what Mrs. Salazar said. Her voice was so soft, though everyone else seemed to hear her just fine. And the blackboard was still as difficult to read.

One day, Mrs. Salazar called on each of us to write

our name and address on the board, along with a sentence about something we'd read or done that week. In Belen, Mrs. Jimenez didn't make me write on the board if I didn't want to—and I never wanted to. At Monte Vista, I didn't have a choice.

"David," Mrs. Salazar said from her desk, "you're next." I crept to the board, thinking frantically for an excuse that would spare me, but nothing came to mind, other than running out of the room.

After I wrote my name, the entire class laughed. My cheeks burned. When I looked at what I'd written, I could see that both Ds in my first name were backward. Before I could finish my address, Mrs. Salazar said, "You've done enough for now. Go back to your desk." As I walked down the aisle, she asked me to stay after school, and the class snickered again.

I wasn't just the new kid, but the new **dumb** kid.

"David," Mrs. Salazar said later after everyone had gone, "we can run some tests to find out how to help you with reading and writing. Your eyes aren't working the way they're supposed to—but there are ways to fix that. I need to talk to your parents. What's your number? I couldn't find it in your file."

"I can't give it to you—my father won't let me." We weren't listed in the phone book, and Dad made us promise never to give out our number.

Her eyebrows shot up. "Oh?"

"If you write a note, I'll give it to him."

Walking home, I kept thinking about what Mrs. Salazar had told me—that something might be wrong with my eyes. How could that be?

But everyone in my class could see and read better than me. No one wrote their letters backward. It took me a long time to read the assigned books, and my head hurt from squinting to bring the letters into focus and stop them from moving.

The school nurse gave me a hearing test, but I already knew my ears were bad, so it wasn't a surprise that I couldn't hear many of the beeps, especially out of my left ear. When she gave me an eye test, the letters were too blurry to read, which wasn't a surprise either. It seemed that the only things working in my head were my mouth and imagination.

The nurse sent home the test results with a note saying Mom and Dad had to take me for further testing. Dad said forget it. Cherokees had perfect hearing and vision and didn't need any of that goddamn nonsense. It took several more notes from school before he agreed to make an appointment with an eye doctor.

When I climbed up into the doctor's large chair and looked through his strange machine as it twisted and turned, every letter sharpened—I couldn't believe the difference. But Dad refused to buy me glasses, saying he was ashamed of me. More notes came home from school, and he finally bought me a pair. Sam would go through the same thing when he needed glasses a couple of years later.

As for my ears, Dad would never have taken me to a specialist. I could hear enough with my right ear to get by, and that was the end of the discussion. The school didn't push it.

But they did follow up on my eyes. The letters still jumped around on the page despite my new glasses, so they sent me to a special clinic where doctors ran more tests. Afterward, they told Dad I had dyslexia, a form of brain confusion that made it hard to read and write, and recommended classes to help me re-train my brain. Dad left without saying a word. On the drive home, he was quiet, his face twisting into different shapes, always a sign he was mad. After Mom's okra, roast beef, and iced tea dinner, he told me to go into the living room and sit on the couch with him.

"**Dyslexia** is a fancy word for stupid," he said, his cold eyes boring into me. "I'm not paying good money to help you read. I can read upside down and backward, so don't give me any crap about not being able to read left to right. Hell, I didn't go to school and could read at age four."

He jumped up from the couch and turned on the TV. "We're done. I'm sick of talking to you. You're stupid, and it has nothing to do with your eyes and ears."

That night, I listened to what Dad said to Mom about me. "Maybe David is just plain stupid like everyone in your dumbass family," he said in his usual loud voice. "I'm going to find out."

A week later, he dropped a booklet on the kitchen table in front of me, an IQ test he'd bought from a correspondence course company. "Fill this out as fast as possible," he said. "Piece a cake. Every blank should have a word or number." He pushed a pencil into my hand. "I need to know how stupid you are." He turned the knob on the kitchen timer. "Go."

After guessing most of the answers, I handed him the booklet, my heart racing. Dad flipped from page to page shaking his head. "Your results are far below average." He looked at Mom at the sink washing dishes. "David won't amount to much." He slammed the booklet down and left the kitchen.

The room started spinning, and I couldn't breathe—he might as well have punched me in the stomach. As I heard the TV come on, I vowed to learn more than anyone in our family and at school—in my own way. I promised myself that someday, when I became rich and famous, everyone would be sorry for making fun of me.

Every night, I read until bedtime. Then I read with a flashlight under the covers until I fell asleep. In the morning, I often woke up on top of a book or magazine, and some of the pages would be crinkled or torn. The reading specialist at the clinic had taught me to read with a ruler, to keep my eyes following the print. I still read slowly, but the ruler helped relax my mind. In time, I learned to memorize everything, even the smallest details.

In addition to the **Albuquerque Journal**, I read history and adventure books from the school library. I loved reading about people who overcame great odds and handicaps. The Helen Keller book was my favorite. She had more troubles with her head than I did, and she found a way to overcome them. My classmates never made fun of me when I remembered things they had forgotten or never knew. During tests, though, I continued to do poorly, seldom having enough time to finish.

I was happiest alone, either running or reading a book, creating an imaginary world starring me as the hero, a place where none of the kids laughed at me. The people in my dreams became my best friends.

CHAPTER 8

Mom returned to her old routine of calling on the neighbors. After dinner, she would drag me along to knock on someone's door to say hello. At first everyone was nice and talked with her, asking her questions about where we were from and what Dad did for a living.

The next time we dropped by, she fell back on her excuse of needing a cup of sugar, like she did at the EPNG compounds. After the neighbors let her in, Mom told them how hard her life had been and that she was always sad. The ladies got her out of the house as fast as possible.

When we visited again, they didn't answer the door, but Mom was convinced they couldn't hear her knock. She went back to lying on the couch all day watching TV. Nothing for her had changed.

Not long after we moved to Albuquerque, Sam, now six, started climbing one of the poles holding up the awning above the back patio. Dad called him a little monkey. Mom called him a little daredevil. Sam did it over and over until he could pull himself onto the flat roof. Then he'd jump onto the awning, lean over to grab a pole, and slide down like a fireman.

As soon as we got home from school every afternoon and changed into play clothes, Sam would run to the backyard and jump onto the awning yelling like a wild man. With each jump, the small tears in the canvas got bigger and bigger.

I screamed at him to stop and so did Mom and Lonnie, but he ignored us. Then it happened. I was in the front yard when I heard the loud cry and dull thud. I raced around to the back and found Sam sprawled on the concrete, blood pouring out of the side of his head. His face was full of gravel. Looking up, I saw the large hole in the awning.

"Lonnie! Mom! Come quick."

Lonnie and I carried Sam inside, and Mom tried to clean his head wound and pull out the gravel. Lonnie called Dad. Luckily, he was in his office.

"Dad, hurry!"

Within minutes, he pulled up to the house—like old times. We all rode with him and Mom to the emergency room. In the front seat, wrapped in a blanket, Sam stretched across Mom's lap and didn't make a sound. She sobbed, muttering something about not knowing how a six-year-old could get on the roof. Dad remained silent, but the Y vein pulsed on his forehead and his eyes bulged, ready to shoot out of his head.

At the hospital, Dad carried Sam in his arms, and Mom followed. Again, we weren't allowed to join them. Lonnie held three-year-old Sally on her lap while I walked around looking for tiles to count, but this waiting room had stained, worn carpeting. How many more emergency rooms would we have to visit before Sam grew up—if he made it that far?

Mom and Dad finally came out and told us that the doctors were operating on Sam's head. They sat apart from each other, Mom shaking and Dad muttering to himself, his face tight and dark.

A few hours later, a doctor came out to speak with us. "Your son has two skull fractures and a concussion," he said. "He'll need to remain sedated until the swelling in his brain goes down."

We'd heard that before.

"Several pebbles are embedded in his skull. The tissue will remain tender for some time, and there's a risk of infection."

We visited the hospital every day. Sam lay silently in a bed. His head was red and swollen, his eyes just slits in his puffy skin.

On the day Sam could leave the hospital, all of us piled into the Rambler to bring him home. Dad said he'd be okay, but he had to be really quiet for a while and couldn't go outside to play.

I followed Dad into a big office where he signed the medical release forms. The doctor behind the desk asked him, "Mr. Crow, how did your son get on top of the house and fall onto the concrete? He's only six years old."

Dad blasted out of the chair, waving the forms in one hand and the pen in the other. "The little son of a bitch thinks he can fly," he said. "And his mother sits on her ass all day watching TV."

The doctor frowned. "Sir, that's—"

Dad leaned over and jabbed the pen into his white smock. "All of you goddamn doctors are capitalist frauds making money off people's misery and suffering. You bastards don't care if you cure anybody as long as they keep coming back to spend every last dollar you blood suckers can extract."

What was Dad talking about? Every time Sam got hurt, the doctors patched him up. It was Mom's fault he kept getting hurt.

That night, after everyone had gone to sleep, Mom's screeching voice filled the house, waking me up. "Thurston, we need to talk!" she yelled. When the front door banged, I knew Dad had gone out to the car. Seconds later, Mom followed him. I met Lonnie in the hallway, and we watched from the front porch—as we had in Belen.

Mom stood in the yard looking at the car, her body twitching. Several minutes went by, and then she strode over and banged on the windows. Dad got out and smacked her in the face. She ran into the house howling, "You don't love me." And again, the neighbors' lights came on.

It was like watching a rerun.

After that, none of the kids were allowed to play at our house, or at least that's what they told us. And when the neighbors saw Mom outside, they turned the other way.

It didn't take long for Mom and Dad to have another yelling-and-hitting fight in their bedroom. Once things quieted down, I listened outside their door.

Sniffling, Mom said, "The judge warned me about your violent temper. He called you a coldhearted killer. They should throw you back in prison where you belong."

"No one can touch me now. I'm clean as a whistle. It's like the whole thing never happened." He used his braggy voice, which probably meant only part of it was true.

"How can that be? What you did to Cleo was wrong—the judge said so."

"The son of a bitch needed killing, and if your whore of a mother had testified, I would have been given a medal instead of a prison sentence."

"Who says they can't put you back in prison?"

"The governor of California, that's who. I applied for a pardon, and he gave me one. I have the letter to prove it."

"But you were guilty!"

"Doesn't matter. I had to put a notice in a couple of LA newspapers for a month to see if anyone objected to the pardon. Nobody did—hell, old Cleo is blind, and his wife must not read the back of the paper. So now the violent felony is gone from my record, which means I'm free to do whatever I want and go wherever I want. I never should have been in prison in the first place."

"But what about George?" Mom shrieked. "He'll find us here and kill us for sure!"

"Our number and address aren't in the phone book. He'd have to get awfully lucky to find me. He isn't that smart, and I'd probably get him before he got me. Anyway, my bosses at Woodmen think I'm a fine, upstanding citizen, and that's all that counts."

One evening after work, Dad burst through the front door, and I ran out of my room to see him. He stood in the living room holding his black-and-silver briefcase, staring at Mom on the couch in her nightgown.

Dad had changed a lot in our short time in Albuquerque. He smoked a pipe now like the smart guys on TV and wore suits instead of the usual EPNG uniform. That day, he had on a white shirt, a red tie, and polished black shoes. Even his voice seemed different, smoother somehow.

"Dad, did you sell policies to anybody famous today?" I asked.

He rubbed my head. "Not today, but I'm working on it."

I glanced at him and then at Mom and couldn't believe how different they were.

"Is dinner ready, Thelma Lou?" Dad asked. "It doesn't look like you've even started." He rolled his eyes in disgust.

"I'm too tired to fix dinner." Mom pushed her straggly hair away from her face, groaning as she sat up on the edge of the couch, leaving behind a large crater from lying there for hours.

"Tired from doing what?" Dad laid his briefcase on the newspapers scattered across the coffee table. "Sitting on your ass all day watching TV?"

She jerked to her feet, waving her arms. "You work with gals who talk pretty and finished high school. You'll go for a young one who looks like I did when we first met. Let's move back to Belen. We knew who we were there. People here are too fancy and stuck up. None of the neighbors like me."

Dad shook his head and walked out of the room.

"I wanna go back," she yelled after him.

Mom didn't belong anywhere.

• • •

Every weekend, while Lonnie watched Sally and Sam, Mom and I went to the laundromat. The parking lot was filled with men who didn't work and sad-looking women dragging dirty laundry and kids behind them. Getting out of the car, Mom would say, "Your daddy needs to make enough money to buy a washer and dryer so I don't have to drive to the crummy part of town to clean our clothes."

One Saturday, I followed her into the place, lugging a big duffel bag of laundry. After sorting the colored and white clothes into separate piles, I put everything into the machines and Mom poured in the soap powder. When she reached into her purse for quarters, she mumbled something about not having any change and told me she'd look in the car.

But she never got out the door. Halfway there, she stopped abruptly and scanned the room, trying to make eye contact with the other customers. No one paid attention to her. Then she fell to the floor in a heap, closed her eyes, and began crying.

I ran over to her. "Mom, please get up. Let's go home and get some quarters from Dad."

She acted as if she couldn't hear me, but I knew she was okay. "I hate it here," she muttered between sobs. "We don't have enough money for anything."

"Get up, Mom. The manager is staring at you.

He'll want us to take our dirty clothes out of the machines."

She tucked into a tight ball and closed her eyes. I shook her hard. "Mom, everyone is looking at us, and we have to go."

The manager came over to me and nodded toward Mom. "What's wrong with her?"

"I don't know," I said. "We don't have quarters for the machines, and I guess she's upset. Don't worry. I'll get her up." I tugged her arm, but she wouldn't budge. Several minutes went by, and Mom wouldn't get up or open her eyes.

"I'm calling an ambulance," the manager said, walking over to the pay phone on the wall.

I dropped down next to her. "Mom, get up now!" I yelled into her ear.

"I'm not sure what's wrong with her," the manager said into the phone. "Her eyes are closed, and she's been on the floor for nearly ten minutes."

"Mom, an ambulance is coming for you!"

She didn't move.

I raced over to the machines, yanked out our dirty clothes, soap flying everywhere, and stuffed them into the duffel bag. After hauling it to the car, I ran back across the parking lot. By then, Mom was walking out. As we drove into the street, an ambulance sped past us.

"Mom, why did you do that?" I yelled. "We could

have gotten into trouble with Dad if he had to get you out of the hospital."

"Do what? I was just resting for a minute."

I stared at her in disbelief. "The manager called an ambulance, and it was almost at the laundromat when you got up."

She shrugged. "Why would he do that? There was no reason for that. I was going to get up."

I thought about all the times she woke Dad up in the middle of the night and pretended the next morning that she hadn't done anything. And how she always asked Sam what happened when he had a terrible accident, as if she weren't the parent. Something was seriously wrong with her. She didn't know it, but the rest of us did.

CHAPTER 9

At Belen Station, the older boys threw firecrackers at lizards and ants in the desert, but they wouldn't share them with me. When I discovered you could buy them year-round in Albuquerque, I stopped thinking about how crazy Mom was and started making plans.

As soon as Sam recovered, he and I headed down Lomas Boulevard with my paper route money. About a mile from home, we found a fireworks stand in the parking lot of a small shopping strip. A skinny Mexican kid with horn-rimmed glasses and a pimply face smirked at me when I pulled change from my pocket.

"How can I help you boys today?" he asked.

I pointed at a package of Black Cat firecrackers.

"Nope." He shook his head. "You have to be eighteen to buy firecrackers. Or bring your mom or dad."

The only thing he'd sell us were Black Snakes, harmless little tabs that expanded into "snakes" of ash when lit. They barely made smoke much less blew up anthills, our number one goal, but we bought a pack anyway and walked back home.

I sneaked into the kitchen and grabbed the matches Dad used to light his pipe. On our front porch, we lit three tabs and watched them rise in a tiny anticlimactic arc of ash. We didn't get to blow up anything or even make some noise. It was the biggest waste of a nickel ever.

Sam and I were in the backyard throwing a baseball on the gravel when Mom yelled, "I smell smoke!"

We found her standing on the front step. "Oh no!" She pointed down. "Wires are coming out of the porch. They'll burn the house down!" She ran around in circles and then dashed inside, the screen door banging behind her.

My little brother and I laughed. When she came back out and looked at the ashes again, she'd have to realize her silly mistake. Wouldn't she? Surely, Mom couldn't be that dumb.

Sam and I went back to playing catch, and several minutes later, we heard sirens blaring louder and louder. We ran out front as two fire trucks roared to the curb, lights flashing. Sam and I grinned at each other. Had Mom actually called the fire department? We hid behind the bushes in front of the living room, laughing, as she ran to the trucks with her arms flailing like a windmill.

A fireman wearing a black helmet, black pants,

and a yellow coat pulled a hose out of the truck while another fireman quickly connected it to a hydrant. A third fireman raced to the side of the house with a long ladder and scrambled to the roof. The driver of the hook-and-ladder truck hopped out, an ax in hand, and hurried over to Mom, his coat stretched tight around his enormous belly.

Sam and I should have told the firemen what we had done, but it was so much fun to watch them and Mom. They would laugh too when they saw the snakes, I was certain. Everyone would get a kick out of it.

"Is anyone inside the house?" the fat guy asked Mom.

Her hands flew to her mouth. "My daughters are in there!"

"You stay here. I'll get them out." He put on a mask and rushed through the front door.

Seconds later, little Sally sprinted into the front yard, followed by Lonnie, her lips curled in that weird way when she got annoyed. Soon after, the fireman came out carrying his mask.

"I can't find any problem with the wires inside," he told Mom. "Can you show us?"

Sam and I burst out laughing again. We couldn't help it. Mom and the firemen glanced our way, but they didn't think we had anything to do with the fire, so they ignored us.

Between sobs and gasps, Mom pointed at the ash snakes on the porch and said, "Those wires . . . the house . . . burn my house . . . down."

The three firemen on the ground tilted their heads in confusion, knowing that what they saw wasn't a problem.

The fireman on the roof called down, "There's no fire up here."

"None down here either," the fat fireman said.

Just then Dad got home. Bad luck for Sam and me. He screeched the station wagon into the driveway, jumped out, and ran into the yard, where Sam and I had now joined our sisters. Dad looked at us kids and then at Mom.

"What the hell is the problem?" he asked.

Mom pointed again at the snakes. Shaking and sobbing, she grabbed Dad's arm and pulled him toward the porch. He yanked his arm away, bent over, and squeezed the snake tubes into dust with his fingers. Muttering, he stood and ground the residue into the concrete with the heel of his shoe.

Dad turned to the firemen and thrust out his chest. "Get your dumbasses off my lawn!" he yelled. "Go put out some real fires. You've been tricked by two little bastards who are about to get first-class ass whippings."

The fat fireman nodded at the other men, and they all walked toward the trucks. He said over his shoulder, "Your wife said the house was going to burn down."

"And you believed the idiot?"

Mom ran toward the firemen, yelling, "Thurston's going to hurt me. Please help me."

Avoiding eye contact with her, they got busy wrapping up the hose and putting back the ladder.

"Thelma Lou, if brains were dynamite, you couldn't blow a pimple off your ass. David has been tricking you since he was three, and you fall for it every time."

Across the street, a neighbor lady watched from her porch, frowning, her arms crossed.

I went over to one of the firemen standing by the first truck. "Can I try on your helmet?"

He shook his head and laughed. "You've caused enough trouble for one day, little man."

The radio on the dashboard started squawking. "Truck number five, are you all clear? Over."

The fireman climbed into the cab and reached for the microphone. "All clear," he said. "False alarm. Two kids burning fireworks. Over."

He scribbled something on a clipboard. I wanted to see what he had written. It had to be funny. I was about to step up into the cab when Dad seized my arm. "David, I'm going to beat your ass for this stunt," he said, taking off his belt with the other hand.

"But, Dad, we didn't know the Black Snakes would scare Mom. How could they?"

"You're a disaster." Dad raised his arm, twirling the belt in the air like a lasso, the buckle dangling.

We were used to being spanked, but this was the first time he came after us with a belt. I danced around, trying to be a tough target, but it didn't work. He hit me again and again and again. Pain blasted my legs and rear. The skin tore under my jeans. When he let go, I fell to the ground.

Then it was Sam's turn. I winced at the sound of the belt slicing through the air and the whacks against his butt. I was the one who bought the snake tabs. Sam just went along with me. Dad had to know we didn't mean to upset Mom, but that didn't keep him from beating Sam even harder than he did me.

The snakes wouldn't have fooled Sally at age three. No other mom in the world would have been tricked. And only our dad would have hit us so hard. Mom couldn't be as dumb as she made out. This had to be another way for her to get attention.

Even though Dad had beaten us, fooling Mom made me remember the fun I'd had with Shorty John, and I came up with all kinds of pranks to play on people.

When Sam and I told Dad about them, he laughed and rubbed my head. "Just don't pull any of them on your crazy mother. We don't need fire trucks at our house again, do we?"

We promised to stay away from the house and not get caught. I told him how we hid in the stairwells of office buildings and dropped water balloons on people's heads at the bottom of the stairs. He laughed hard and looked at us with a big, proud smile. "You two are slicker than snot on a doorknob."

I spent a lot of my time dreaming up even funnier things to do and asked Dad what he did as a kid. He used to tie a fishing line to the handle of his mother's purse and toss it into the street. When a car stopped and someone got out to pick up the purse, his friend would pull the line so the purse moved out of reach, and Dad would try to rob them.

We did the same thing with one of Mom's purses, putting it on the street corner a couple of blocks from our house. Sam pulled the line when a car stopped and a passenger tried to pick up the purse. But we didn't want to rob anyone. Instead, I fired eggs and water balloons at them. A perfect throw hit the victim in the face. We'd run off before they realized what had happened.

We also threw eggs and water balloons at cars driving down Lomas Boulevard. It took some practice to throw far enough in front of them to hit the windshields, but we mastered it in no time.

Mom said she couldn't figure out how our family ate so many eggs. She didn't remember cooking that many.

CHAPTER 10

I entered the house after finishing my paper route, and it felt oddly calm inside, even peaceful. The late-afternoon sun lit up the living room and all the nice things Dad had gotten after we first moved in—a red couch, two plush brown chairs, a wooden coffee table, and a new bench for our piano. We kept the new black-and-white Zenith TV in our playroom at the back of the house.

Dad hadn't bought anything in months. No washer and dryer for Mom. He wasn't selling as many policies, he said, but it was bound to turn around.

As I stood in the entryway, I heard a crinkling sound from across the room. Mom knelt on the floor, still in her nightgown, her side facing me. She had pulled up the corner of the carpet, including the padding, and was shoving papers underneath. I spotted the familiar blue Woodmen Accident and Life symbol.

I watched in silence. That was why the carpet had lumps in each corner and under the couch. But why would she hide Dad's papers? He didn't make any money unless they were properly delivered. She had to know he'd eventually find out.

Suddenly the hair rose on the back of my neck.

Dad was right behind me.

Over my shoulder, he watched Mom as she spread out the papers and patted down the carpet to make it flat. My heart beat in my ears. Dad would hit her hard this time. I wanted to yell for her to run, but nothing came out of my mouth.

Dad carefully put his briefcase on the floor and then took off his sports coat and loosened his tie. He stared at Mom for the longest time, his eyes bulging like squeezed balloons. At last, she sensed our presence and stood up, her hair matted from sleeping all day. Her lips quivered.

"Goddamn it, Thelma Lou, you worthless bitch." Dad's voice thundered through the house. "What the hell have you done?" The house shook as he marched across the room and yanked up the carpet corners, exposing dozens of Woodmen insurance papers.

Dad couldn't afford a bookkeeper or secretary, so he had asked Mom to sort bills and mail policies when they arrived at our house. But why would he have trusted her? And why would she have betrayed him? Weren't customers complaining that they hadn't gotten their policies?

Hearing Dad yell, Lonnie, Sam, and Sally appeared in the hallway off the living room. I shook my head and waved them away. Lonnie stopped midstride, picked up Sally, and took her back to their room. Sam retreated to the playroom. I should have joined him, but my feet were rooted to the floor. Dad ripped open letters, memos, and policies, each with more force. He read some out loud, including the dates they were written.

"I have to make you lose your job or you'll leave me," Mom said, tears streaming down her face. "When Bob was here, he saw you go into a hotel room with a woman in a short skirt. You kissed her, and he heard you say, 'I love you.'"

Dad stopped to look at her. "Your brother is dumber than you are, if that's possible. He's a moocher, lazy-ass, shiftless, alcoholic son of a bitch who stole money from me and some of my clothes. I'll kill him if he comes back."

I waited for Dad's fist to fly into Mom's face, but she didn't give him the chance. Crying out, she hurried off to their bedroom and slammed the door. Dad continued reading the hidden mail as he paced and Mom sobbed loud enough for all of us to hear. I ran to my room and tried to read, but my hands shook too much. Finally, I heard Dad drive away.

Several hours later, after we had gone to bed, he stormed back into the house, ranting to himself. The four of us came out into the living room, but Dad stared into space, yelling as though we weren't there. "The bitch is ruining my life. She's completely nuts. I can't live with her. I've got to get rid of her."

"Come on," Lonnie whispered, motioning with her hand to follow her. She took Sally's hand, and we went to their room. Lonnie sat on the bed next to Sally. Sam and I sprawled out on the floor.

"Mom isn't going to be around much longer," Lonnie said. She sounded more like a grown-up than a twelve-year-old kid. "Dad says that I'll be the new mom for a while. If all four of us agree to go with him, he'll take us away and leave Mom behind. She'll lose custody of us because she's crazy. They'll put her in the nuthouse." She paused to look at me. "Dad thinks you won't go along."

But Mom couldn't survive without our help. "Dad might really hurt her this time," I said.

"No, he won't." She scrunched up her face as if it were the most ridiculous thing she'd ever heard. "And if the nuthouse doesn't take her, Dad said she could go live with her mother. You need to cooperate, David."

Lonnie didn't know what Dad was capable of. Without responding, I went back to my room and climbed to the top bunk. Soon after, Sam wandered in, and I pretended to be asleep. I waited and then peeked over the edge of my mattress to see him hidden under the covers below me.

Would we really leave Mom?

Sometime during the night, I heard two sets of footsteps leave the house, followed by car doors closing. The Rambler's engine turned over, then came the snap and ping of the tires on the gravel as they backed out of the driveway. What would Dad do to her?

When the front door creaked open later and Mom pitter-pattered down the hallway whining, I let out a deep breath. She was still alive. I crept to their bedroom door to listen.

"You tried to push me out of the car tonight," Mom said. "If I hadn't locked the door, you would have killed me. I've stood by you through prison and everything."

"Shut up and go to sleep, Thelma Lou," Dad said in a tired voice.

I went back to bed, and the house was quiet for the rest of the night. Mom and Dad didn't say much to each other over the next several days. They never yelled once.

But the constant ache in my gut told me that it wouldn't last.

Dad left Woodmen Accident and Life. He wasn't selling enough policies, and thanks to Mom, the policies he did sell never made it to his customers.

"We're flat-ass broke," Dad said.

Within days, he had found a job as a welder and started wearing workman's clothes again. I knew from listening to him and Mom in their bedroom that he had learned how to weld in the prison workshop so he could earn a living right away on the outside. Though he was a good welder, he hated it. He was smart enough to do so much more, he told me.

Every night after cleaning up, Dad read the want ads. One night, he jumped up and yelled, "Hell, I found the perfect job!" He wrote a letter, put it in an envelope, and drove to the nearest post office.

We didn't hear anything more until after school started almost a month later. I walked into the kitchen at breakfast time, and Mom and Dad were talking softly. She refilled his coffee cup and added two cubes of sugar, just the way he liked it. Sam and Sally sat next to each other, eating their Frosted Flakes and staring at the cereal box. Lonnie was in the living room playing the piano. I poured myself a bowl of cereal, watching everyone, the air heavy with something about to happen.

After Dad finished his coffee, he told us to sit on the couch. Mom sat with us. "We're heading back to the reservation," he said, his face relaxed. "But not to EPNG. I'll be working as a safety officer for the BIA—the Bureau of Indian Affairs—in Fort Defiance, Arizona. They don't have a vacancy yet in the government compound where non-Navajos live, so we'll rent a house just off the reservation in Gallup and I'll commute to Fort Defiance."

The next day, Dad took me on a drive in the Rambler. Once we left the city limits, he pulled onto the shoulder and stopped. "Lonnie says you feel sorry for your mother and you want to stay with her." He reached over and clamped his hand around the back of my neck. "But that isn't going to happen. When the time is right, we are leaving her behind, and you're going with the rest of us. Do you understand—or do I have to knock some sense into that thick head of yours?" He tightened his grip and shook me once before letting go.

I stared out the window as Dad threw the car into gear and squealed back onto the pavement. Neither of us spoke on the ride back.

Mom had run out of chances.

PART 2

GALLUP
1961

Pino's Curios and Indian Trading Shop on Route 66 in Gallup, New Mexico. 1965.

CHAPTER 11

The day we moved, we loaded the station wagon in silence, except for Mom's moaning and nonstop twitching. We didn't have much to take with us. Dad had sold most of the furniture to pay bills—all we had left was the red couch. The piano was gone now too.

Sally held on to Lonnie's leg with one hand and clutched a doll tight to her chest with the other. "Everything will be all right," Lonnie kept whispering to her. "I'll take care of you." Sam waited in the driveway with his bat, ball, and mitt.

I took a long, last look at our street and Lomas Boulevard, watching the cars speeding past us. I'd miss Albuquerque and the people on my paper route. At school, my teachers had helped me get glasses and read and write better. They told me that even smart kids had dyslexia. Now I would have to start all over somewhere else—again.

Dad signaled for us to get into the car. The four

of us jumped in before he could grab us and throw us in. Mom was already in the passenger seat holding onto a Kleenex, dabbing her eyes. None of the neighbors came out to say goodbye as we pulled away, the green rickety trailer shaking behind us.

We had lasted only a year there. By then, Lonnie was thirteen, I was nine, Sam was seven, and Sally was four.

We drove down Nine Mile Hill on Route 66, the two-lane highway that connected hundreds of no-name towns, each with a gas station and an Indian trading post. Gusts of wind pounded the car, whipping the trailer back and forth. I turned away from the Sandia Mountains behind us and focused on the roadside places selling Indian curios, or, as Dad joked, "fake tourist shit." All the stores had funny signs, like "Savage Indians Inside: See Them While You Can."

Mom sniffled the entire 140-mile trip. Just when she seemed to be quieting down, Dad yelled, "Thelma Lou, shut up, goddamn it." That got her crying again.

Outside Gallup, we passed a gigantic yellow metal Indian kachina doll standing on a huge sign: "Gallup, New Mexico, the Indian Capital." Minutes later, we turned off Route 66 onto South Second Street, and the station wagon slowed next to a gully full of weeds, rocks, and broken glass. On the other side of the road, men poured in and out of a liquor store, all of them carrying a bottle in a brown paper bag. Others were scattered around the dirt parking lot facedown as if they had fallen asleep in the middle of a stride.

Dad shook his head in disgust. "Money flows through Gallup like shit through a goose." He stopped in front of a dilapidated gray duplex and turned off the engine. "Get out and unload."

No one moved. Mom sobbed harder. Lonnie and I looked at each other.

The duplex foundation sat on the edge of the gully with little visible support. How had it not caved in? The front was covered with black tar paper, rusted chicken wire, a thin piece of buckled plywood, and moldy gray drywall. A shredded screen door hung by a corner. Our side of the duplex had a spray-painted number: 709½.

In front of the other half, the more prestigious 709, sat a fat, greasy-faced Mexican smoking a cigarette and chugging a bottle of wine. His blubbery body spilled over the broken wooden step outside his door. He grinned at us with tobacco-stained teeth that made him look like a jack-o'-lantern.

As I opened the car door, the Mexican leaned over and let loose a series of loud farts. From his side of the house, three barefoot children burst into the yard, jumping over broken glass, wine jugs, beer cans, and rocks. A short, barrel-shaped woman lumbered out of the front door wearing a threadbare dress. She grunted when I said hello.

How could we have ended up in this pigsty with them as our neighbors? After all, Dad was the smartest man in the world.

"Is this a mistake?" Lonnie asked Dad.

"No, unfortunately, it's not," he said in a low voice without looking up.

Mom grabbed a box of dishes from the back of the station wagon. "I've lived in some pretty sorry places," she said, "but this is the sorriest."

"You're the reason we're here!" Dad yelled.

Mom scurried to the front door, tripping on the lopsided wooden steps. Plastic bowls, cups, and plates tumbled onto the dirt. Sam and I rushed to pick them up and went inside to the kitchen. When we set the dusty dishes on the chipped tile counter, Sam cried out and jumped back as cockroaches bolted out of the rust-stained sink.

Whiskey bottles and beer cans littered the living room floor. On Lonnie's way to the kitchen through all the trash, she let out a shriek. "I just stepped on a mouse!" Sally ran out the front door screaming.

The front window had a diagonal crack from corner to corner and was held together with peeling masking tape. Big dark blotches covered the walls, and a nasty urine smell filled the air. I held my nose, but that didn't help much.

Sam and I went back outside to get boxes from the car, stepping around a drunk passed out in our half of the front yard. Another guy opened his pants and whizzed on the side of the house by the gully.

"Dad, make him stop peeing," Sam said, throwing a rock at the man. It ricocheted off the wall next to him, but he didn't seem to notice.

"At least the poor son of a bitch knows what he's doing," Dad said with a forced laugh. "Leave him alone."

When we finished unloading, I stood by the car and looked down the street. I could see a pawnshop, a trading post, a bail bond business, another liquor store, and a junkyard full of wrecked trucks, broken concrete, wine jugs, whiskey bottles, and beer cans. Our block was one giant garbage dump.

Dad came up behind me and said, "This is an idiot's paradise."

Lonnie got out all the cleaning supplies and began working on the bathroom while Mom sat on the couch, her head in her hands. Sam and I promised we'd help later, but first we had some exploring to do. Out on Route 66, we walked past trading posts, restaurants, gas stations, and bars, happy to get away from our house.

"Every Navajo within two hundred miles comes to

Gallup to sell stuff, buy stuff, and bomb their asses on firewater," Dad told us. "This isn't how Cherokees live. They have more respect for themselves than that." He shook his head. "Indians aren't allowed to drink on the reservation. This town has enough whiskey to drown every single one of them. Half of America drives on Route 66 from Illinois to California hoping to touch a real Indian."

The streets were filled with Navajos. The men staggered around, often stopping to pee right in the middle of traffic. Occasionally they looked around and asked sober passersby for money. Little kids and their mothers wandered aimlessly, oblivious to the trucks wobbling back and forth across the white lines. And on the sidewalks, Sam and I had to navigate around the sleeping drunks, like the one in our front yard.

Within a couple of days, I had a paper route with the **Gallup Independent**. Most of my new customers were poor and rarely smiled or said more than a couple of words when I collected. After my first week, I had some money, so Sam and I prowled the stores looking for friendly merchants willing to supply us with fireworks.

Less than a mile from the duplex, we stumbled upon Pino's Curios and Indian Trading Shop. Looking through the window under the giant yellow and red neon sign, I spotted plastic cowboys and Indians, rubber tomahawks, and cap guns lining the shelves and the shiniest fake turquoise display I'd ever seen.

Inside, a skinny Mexican man with large brown eyes and aviator glasses greeted us with a wide smile from behind the counter. "I'm Ray Pino," he said with a huge laugh, a cigarette dangling from his thin mustached lips. "I haven't seen you boys before. Did you just move here?" He sounded like a big kid, excited to meet us.

"Yeah, about a week ago," I said. "We're looking for firecrackers and big action."

Sam giggled, and I shot him a dirty look. He always did that when I tried sounding older, not helping either one of us.

Mr. Pino waved his hand, motioning for us to follow him. "I've got something you might like." He laughed so hard his head shook and ashes from his cigarette sprinkled onto the concrete floor. His Wrangler jeans bagged around his skinny legs as he ambled to the back of the store, sidestepping boxes of curios. He stopped in front of cartons of Roman candles, sparklers, Whistling Jupiter rockets, and Black Cat firecrackers. I'd never seen anything so wonderful.

"I like fireworks and always keep a good supply." Mr. Pino chuckled and slapped his knee. "These red donut-hole-sized balls are called cherry bombs." He held one up and made an explosion sound with his mouth. "You'll like these babies but be careful. If one blows up in your hand, it'll take off a few fingers."

It was our lucky day! I pulled my pocket inside out to get all my tip money. "How much will this buy?"

"Let's see . . ." He handed us mounds of cherry bombs and packs of Black Cats—we needed a bag to carry everything. "Come back when you run out, and don't get into any trouble."

Did Mr. Pino know what we were going to do with them? He had to know. For a moment I got nervous because he didn't give us any matches. When we returned to the store a few minutes later, he tossed several packs into our bag. "There are plenty more where those came from."

On our way home, we blew up several anthills. Red body parts shot high into the air along with dirt and pebbles. When we threw a cherry bomb into an empty bucket, it popped off the ground and landed all dented up, as if it had been run over.

As soon as we entered the house, we went to our bedroom, closed the door, and threw our stash into the bottom dresser drawer. We counted the cherry bombs and Black Cat firecrackers over and over, not believing how many he'd given us.

That afternoon, Mom stood at the front door in her nightgown and stared out at four drunks lying facedown. Sam and I walked up behind her, eager to go out and use our new ammo. She turned to me, frowning. "David, honey, those poor men haven't moved for hours. It's just awful to have them there. Will you see if they're dead? If they are, I'll call the police so they can be properly buried."

"We'll find out," I said, as Sam and I went into the yard.

One of the drunks was sprawled out on our side of the duplex next to the gully. "Sam, see that guy over there? Let's see if this wakes him up."

I held a cherry bomb up in the air. It took Sam three tries to light the match, and he flashed a huge smile when the fuse ignited and hissed. I bounced a perfect shot between the guy's legs, inches from his crotch. BOOM! His body quivered, and he staggered to his feet, getting out of our yard before falling down.

I laughed. "No need to call the morgue yet."

On to the second drunk. Sam took off the man's hat and placed it over a cherry bomb on the ground about a foot away from his head. With the blast, his hat blew high into the air, splitting into pieces before falling back to the ground. The man winced and rolled to his feet only to drop a few seconds later.

Sam got creative with our third victim. He poured honey on his head, and soon a mass of stinging red ants appeared. The guy didn't move for a long time, but when he did, he jumped into the air with a screech that reminded me of Midnight when he came flying out of the dryer. For the last guy, we dropped a Black Cat into his boot, and he got up and danced around, shaking his foot like it was on fire.

"David," Mom called through the screen door, "do you boys need to use firecrackers? You might hurt them."

"It's the only way to make sure they're alive. They leave the yard, don't they?"

"I guess you're right." She shrugged and moved away from the door, leaving us to patrol our territory.

Whenever Sam and I came outside armed with firecrackers and cherry bombs, the drunks would stagger off, but once we left, a whole new group showed up. It was a constant fight to keep our yard clean at 709½ South Second Street.

CHAPTER 12

School was a lot easier in Gallup. None of the teachers knew I was dyslexic, and I didn't tell them. They could barely keep up with the constant flow of students coming and going and never pushed us to do much. No one called me stupid.

Sam and I lived for the weekends. Because Gallup was the only major town for over a hundred miles in each direction, it began filling with Navajos at about three o'clock on Friday afternoon and didn't empty out until nearly noon on Sunday. The tourists stayed on the strip on Route 66, where there were clean gas stations, nice restaurants, and good hotels. The locals and Navajos who came into Gallup for shopping rarely frequented those establishments. They drove to the side streets for groceries, dry goods, trucks, and alcohol.

Right after breakfast, we would race to Pino's Curios, usually finding Mr. Pino talking to a customer while he leaned over the glass case full of merchandise. As soon as he finished, I'd pour my tip money onto the counter. "Today is going to be a big one, Mr. Pino."

He would flash a huge smile and invite us to his back room, grabbing the change without counting it. "That's enough to buy the good stuff," he'd say, his cigarette bobbing on his thin lips. He would fill our paper bag with all kinds of explosives. "Don't get into any trouble." Then he'd laugh hard.

He knew we were going to raise as much hell as possible. But the cops wouldn't bother us—they were too busy with all the Navajo customers ready to hit the bars around the clock. The paddy wagons picked up drunks from sunup until long past sundown, carted them to the jail, which Mr. Pino said was one of the largest in the country, and let them sleep off their celebration.

By first light on Saturday, Navajo families in horse-drawn wagons and pickup trucks were already backed up for miles trying to cross Route 66. They poured in by the thousands. Long freight trains interrupted their flow at fifteen-minute intervals around the clock. When the railroad gate lifted, a stampede of traffic rushed across the tracks in a mad dash.

Sam and I set up our headquarters next to the Bubany Lumber Company, hiding behind a stack of boards piled close to the tracks. We would lay out explosives at our feet for quick access, along with eggs and water balloons. The biggest challenge of the day was how to get the most out of our arsenal.

I imagined us as underground soldiers, fighting the Germans or Japanese, reclaiming lost territory. We stashed enough weaponry to dramatically change the course of a battle. For a while, I wasn't part of the Crow family—I was a courageous captain in the US Army.

And Sam, my trusty and fearless lieutenant, would stand alongside me, eager to make his mark. Nothing scared him. He'd never back down or run from trouble—or hesitate to blab about what we had done, no matter how many times I yelled at him to keep his mouth shut. He was sure everyone would think our antics were funny—but I knew better.

Heavily loaded wagons and pickups bounced across the uneven tracks, hurrying to get ahead of the next train. Sam and I would take turns lighting the fuses and launching the explosives at the unsuspecting passengers and then follow with eggs and water balloons. Though only seven years old, Sam threw like a rocket. Usually the explosives scared everyone so much they didn't think to duck.

One Saturday morning in late October, when Navajo farmers flooded in to sell their crops, we spotted a horse-drawn wagon bulging with hay and sheep. Three old guys squeezed into the back with the animals. The couple driving the wagon struggled to steady their load as the wheels groaned and the horses staggered under the weight. There couldn't have been a better target.

"Sam, let's loosen up the driver with eggs, water balloons, and cherry bombs," I said. "The Crow triple play."

Sam nailed the driver with an egg to the side of the head. I followed with a water balloon, washing off the egg yolk that dripped from his face. Against my orders, Sam dashed to the wagon and climbed inside, mounting one of the sheep like it was a horse, his arms waving in the air.

Seconds later, I tossed a cherry bomb into the wagon bed just a few feet from Sam, but he didn't flinch. The sheep bleated like crazy at the blast, and the horses reared, jolting the wagon off the rig. When the back gate popped open, sheep spilled onto the street and scurried across Route 66 and the railroad tracks. The three old guys struggled to their feet and chased after them. Sam had already stumbled out, laughing his head off.

Traffic stopped, including the trains. Pedestrians, motorists, and the confused owners of the sheep attempted the longest and wildest roundup I'd ever seen. It was a glorious sight—everyone shouting and darting here and there. No one noticed us.

I felt powerful and invisible.

We rarely got caught. When we set up our headquarters, we carefully mapped out our escape routes and always had a good head start on any would-be pursuers. Occasionally we attracted the attention of a fast, pissed-off teenager, who caught us and pounded us into the ground. We'd promise to stop, and the kid would rejoin his wagon or truck. Then we would go right back to the tracks and begin again.

By midmorning we had moved on to the bars. Dozens of them lined Coal Avenue and Route 66 beyond the tourist strip. All the doors were covered in blood and urine, and all the patrons were wasted by noon.

Before going inside, we'd harass the drunks in the parking lot like we did the ones in our front yard—a firecracker or two strategically placed. Most of them jumped, but a few didn't budge at all. They were stiff, their skin a scary bluish tinge. Dad said some of the drunks would pass out and freeze to death overnight when the temperature dropped. The police called them Popsicles.

Our first stop was Seig's Bar. It was so dark inside that we were hard to see. Racing in, I'd yell, "Kit Carson and the cavalry are coming. You better get out your tomahawks." I'd throw Black Cat firecrackers on the floor next to men who could barely stand while Sam swung his arm to knock off their hats.

Once in a while, angry patrons caught us, but

we usually wriggled free and dashed out the door, howling with laughter. When the owners chased us off, we moved to the next bar. There were so many to choose from.

For variety, we'd follow wobbly drunks to the filthy outhouses behind the bars. They walked like they had already taken a dump in their pants. Our favorite prank was to toss a cherry bomb inside after a patron took his seat. We pressed the door shut until it exploded. The drunk would stumble out looking like Wile E. Coyote in the Road Runner cartoon, smoke and paper floating like confetti around his head.

From the cliff carved out behind the bars, Sam and I rolled huge rocks down the hill into the outhouses. It was like bowling but a lot more fun. When we made a perfect strike, the flimsy, filthy wooden boxes would fall over with the drunks inside, and they'd scurry away with their pants down. Sam and I laughed for days.

According to Dad, Cherokees were superior to everyone, so it was okay for us to pull pranks on the low-life Navajos and Mexican merchants. None of us kids had met any other Cherokees, but Dad assured us they were all supermen, just like him. I felt proud, knowing how much better I was, even though I was still scrawny and not very strong.

• • •

On Sunday, I would return to the bars by myself after delivering newspapers. The town was always quiet. Sam wouldn't go with me, complaining that everyone was too hungover to react to our cherry bombs and firecrackers. But I got a kick out of watching all the angry Navajo wives hunt down their men. And there was always a big one-sided fight when they found them. After doing this for a few weeks, I recognized several women who came back every Sunday. And there were plenty of entertaining newcomers too.

One morning, I followed a heavyset woman who had a look almost as tight and ferocious as Dad's. She wove her way through the drunks sleeping it off in the parking lots and the bars. The men leaning against the outside of the bars had their hats pulled over their eyes to shade the sun. The woman went down the row, lifting one hat after another in search of her husband.

"You seen my **hosteen**?" she asked each one.

I chuckled as the men squinted up at her and slowly shook their heads, in no condition to lie convincingly.

She marched from bar to bar, her fists clenched, her face darker and angrier as she went along. Everyone knew her husband was about to get a vicious, well-deserved beating.

The loyal men shouted warnings when any woman approached. Some guys climbed out from under pool tables and bar stools and made a run for the exit. I rooted for them, but they never got far.

At last, the large Navajo woman found her husband lying flat on his stomach near the curb in front of the American Bar. She grabbed him by the hair and bounced his head on the hard pavement like a paddle-ball. Swearing in Navajo, she dragged him down the street and hoisted him into the bed of their wagon. The seat sagged under her weight as she flicked the reins to get the horses moving, signaling the end of another lost weekend.

The next weekend, and all of them after that, there would be just as many drunks and angry wives. Nothing ever changed in Gallup.

Watching these men get beaten somehow made me feel better about what went on at home. And I discovered that Mom wasn't the only sad woman. Gallup was full of them.

CHAPTER 13

Our life in the duplex came to an end one January morning when a worker from the health department banged on our door. The city would be there in two weeks to tear down the building, he said. Before leaving, he spray-painted "Condemned Property" over a pee stain on our front wall. When we packed up the Rambler and green trailer and took off, the drunks on South Second Street probably celebrated, the conscious ones anyway.

We moved about a mile away to 306 South Cliff Drive. Our new orange stucco house sat on a steep hill across from a huge gully the size of a miniature canyon. On the main floor, we had three bedrooms and a back porch enclosed by a cinder-block wall, and on the floor below, a basement and garage. Although not as nice as our house in Albuquerque, it was still a big step-up. No more trash in the front yard—and no more drunks. Sam and I shared a room in the basement away from the rest of the family upstairs.

We could sneak out through the garage without anyone knowing.

Dad started spending more and more time away from the house, even after he got off work. No one complained. As long as he wasn't there, we didn't have to listen to him fight with Mom. He pretty much ignored Sam and me until the day he burst into our room to tell us about the upcoming boxing match between Benny "Kid" Paret and Emile Griffith.

Dad loved listening to fights on the radio. The Rambler had the best radio we owned, so he'd sit in the car and ask us to join him. Sam was never interested, but I was happy to make Dad think I loved boxing as much as he did. He was always nice to me when he thought we agreed.

Dad studied the great boxers from the past, like Joe "the Brown Bomber" Louis and Jersey Joe Walcott, who barely kept his family alive on nine dollars a week before becoming heavyweight champion. His all-time favorite was Jack Dempsey, the "Manassa Mauler" from Colorado. The son of a miner, Dempsey fought as many as ten men a day for five dollars apiece before he went pro. He chewed on pine tar to toughen his jaw.

The "poor boy becomes a great fighter" stories were a big hit with Dad. He'd talk about these guys like they were members of the family, recounting moments of glory that were supposed to serve as life lessons. Boxing was the ultimate man's sport, he said, because it was the best way for a man to prove himself.

All I knew was that I was a puny kid with thick glasses, who didn't like getting hit. But Dad seemed to think that eventually I would become a true Crow man and love to pound the shit out of people.

It was chilly the evening of March 24, 1962, when he and I hustled to the Rambler. Dad opened the garage door but left the car inside, under the dim light of a single bulb. He brought sandwiches for us to snack on and glasses of iced tea to wash them down.

He leaned over and tapped my leg. "This is a special night. We're going to listen to history together."

The ring announcer at Madison Square Garden came on: "Ladies and gentlemen, main event. Fifteen rounds for the Welterweight Championship of the World."

"This is going to be a great fight. Griffith needs to kill Paret, that Cuban son of a bitch," Dad said, rubbing his hands together like he was warming up to kill the guy himself. "Paret called him a faggot, and Griffith has to defend his honor."

Was he serious? According to the boxing magazines Dad read, fighters taunted each other all the time, and this didn't seem any worse than lots of other insults he had spoken about.

"Paret won't die, will he? It's just a boxing match, right?"

His jaw tightened. "You don't call a man a faggot unless you want the ever-living crap stomped out of you. Surely even you understand that. Boxing is war with your fists, and all great fighters follow a warrior's creed. If you're disrespected, you have a duty to kill the bastard who did it. Otherwise you're not much of a man."

Dad shadowboxed over the steering wheel. "Paret needs killing. It's plain and simple."

The bell rang for the first round, and the fight began. Dad jabbed his fists harder at the air. All the usual explosive signs were there: bugged-out eyes, pulsing Y vein, and twitching lips. But that night, he also puffed himself up, growing larger than I'd ever seen him.

"Kill him, Griffith!" he yelled. "Kill the asshole. Kill him!" Sweat beaded on his forehead, and his body jerked from side to side, making the car sway.

Griffith was winning, but at the end of the sixth round, Paret fought back hard, knocking him down.

"Son of a bitch, man!" Dad yelled. "Get up and defend your goddamn pride. Get him NOW." His voice bounced around inside the car.

They had to give Griffith smelling salts, and if the bell hadn't sounded, Paret might have knocked him out. But by the end of the next round, Griffith was back on top again. Dad let out a breath. "Okay, that's more like it." He kept turning up the volume and fiddling with the station to get better reception. The crowd cheered both men's names in the background.

The bell came for the twelfth round. A minute into it, the radio announcer said, "This is probably the tamest round of the fight." But then he shouted, "Griffith has trapped Paret in the corner against the ropes! He can't defend himself. His head is snapping back again and again, but Griffith won't let him fall."

Dad pummeled the air with his fits. "Kill the bastard. Kill! Kill! Kill!"

"Paret has slumped to the mat, ladies and gentlemen," the announcer said. "He's been knocked unconscious, taking several unanswered blows to the head. I don't know how any human being could survive such a beating."

They switched to the ring announcer at Madison Square Garden. "The time: two minutes and nine seconds of the twelfth round. The winner by a knockout and, once again, Welterweight Champion of the World, Emile Griffith." The crowd roared.

Dad broke into a broad smile and relaxed his fists. His eyes returned to normal, and the Y vein receded into his forehead. He turned to me with a big grin and rubbed my head vigorously, as if we had both experienced a glorious outcome.

"Sometimes a man has to kill to make things right," he said, staring out the windshield. "You understand that Paret needed killing, don't you? They carried him off in a stretcher. Good. I hope the son of a bitch dies. I've beaten men to death, but we weren't in a boxing ring and I didn't get paid for it. No other way to even the score. I've gotten rid of a few richly deserving sons of bitches. No one misses them. I did the world a favor."

He switched off the radio and looked at me. "I'm crazy. Me and you both are. You gotta do what you gotta do. You understand?"

I nodded. All I wanted was to get out of the car and away from him. If he saw the disgust on my face, he'd want to hit me. My head swam with fear. How could I be his son?

I felt sorry for Paret. The referee kept pulling the fighters apart during the match—why didn't he do it after Paret was trapped on the ropes? He couldn't defend himself. The referee had to have known that Griffith wouldn't quit even though Paret couldn't raise his arms to stop him. I hated Dad and the referee.

We had just listened to a murder—and Dad loved it. I'd heard him say over and over that Cleo deserved to die, and Dad almost made that happen. How many people had he actually killed?

Was he right—was I crazy like him?

No. He and I were different. I wanted to be nothing like him. I was different from Mom too. Lonnie, Sam, and Sally weren't like them either.

But I couldn't deny that some of Dad's love for breaking all the rules had rubbed off on me, along with some of Mom's sadness.

Norman Mailer, the great sports writer who covered the fight live, said he had never seen one man hit another so hard and so many times. When I read that in the newspaper and in the boxing magazines, it made me feel worse. The picture of Paret's body slumped over the ropes was sickening. His eyes were swollen shut before the end of the twelfth round. He fell into a coma that would claim his life ten days later.

For weeks after that, all I could think of was how Benny Paret never regained consciousness because he was brain dead, probably while still standing, unable to fall to the mat. The more sickened I was by what I saw, the happier Dad was that justice had been served Thurston Crow–style.

CHAPTER 14

One afternoon later that spring, Sam and I walked along Green Avenue, looking for trouble. Our pranks had become more reckless and brazen. We threw rocks at signs in the middle of the day. We swung our baseball bats into mailboxes without checking to see if anyone was watching. Any pretense of normalcy had vanished.

Dinner would be ready soon, but we weren't in a hurry to get home. Dad would be there, and the less we were around him the better. Most of the time, he started yelling at Mom the instant he walked through the door.

After crossing South Third Street, we passed a large backhoe parked in someone's driveway, and in the carport next to it, I spotted an enormous truck tire partially hidden behind warped plywood.

"Hey, Sam, I bet we could have fun with that."

"You can't push that big thing out of there."

"Watch me."

It didn't look like anyone was home, but just in case, we ducked behind the truck and waited a few minutes. Nothing.

The tire reached my shoulders. The bolts were bigger than my fist. It had to be nearly two feet thick. I shoved aside the plywood, and the tire fell over. It took all our strength to set it upright. Sam steadied it while I rolled it into the street. I was surprised at how easily it moved.

"What are we going to do with this?" Sam asked.

"Just wait. You'll see."

We rolled it to the top of Elephant Hill, so named because of the White Elephant Storage facility at the bottom. Sam glanced down the steep slope and clapped his hands. He'd figured out my plan.

I studied the cars and trucks flowing through the intersection at rush hour. Sam kept trying to push the tire, but I told him we needed to wait until we knew there would be lots of traffic in the intersection when the tire reached the bottom. The timing had to be perfect.

After watching for several minutes, I gave the tire a gentle nudge. It rolled slowly and wobbled. The thick yellow rim wiggled from side to side.

"It's going to fall over!" Sam shouted, jogging down the hill alongside it.

"Don't touch it!" I shouted back to him. "It'll straighten out."

Within seconds, the tire righted and took off as if shot out of a cannon, a black streak screaming down the hill. It sounded like a high-pitched engine. The noise echoed all around us.

When the tire flew into the intersection, it drilled into a northbound Volkswagen Beetle, just behind the driver's door, smashing the car into a V shape. The windshield shattered, and the frame crumpled into a heap of useless metal on the sidewalk.

The tire kept moving, ricocheting backward, and slammed into a double-wheeled pickup truck loaded with hay. The wheel well crunched, bending the bed almost off the cab. Bales of hay exploded into the air. The truck screeched to a halt against the sidewalk, but the tire still didn't stop. A couple of drunks danced out of the way as it wobbled like a giant hula hoop and finally fell over.

Both drivers got out and circled their vehicles. The fat, middle-aged Navajo man driving the truck wore cowboy boots, a long jacket, and a big Stetson. He glanced up at the sky as if Coronado himself had delivered the blow.

I was more worried about the thin, young Volkswagen driver with the ponytail. He wore tennis shoes and looked like he could run fast, exactly the kind of victim we tried to avoid. The drivers and spectators gathered on the sidewalk, their eyes scanning for the source of destruction.

Sam laughed and jumped up and down. The blond bandits had struck again.

And once again, I felt powerful and invisible.

But I knew big trouble when I saw it. Along with destroying a monstrous tire and two vehicles, we had attracted a sizable crowd, and we needed to get out of there. My brother and I hadn't become Gallup's most successful juvenile delinquents by sticking around and laughing at our victims. But the enormity of what we had done was intoxicating. I started laughing too.

My sides ached by the time I noticed that the man from the Volkswagen was staring up the hill at us. I swear his eyes were glowing red.

I froze.

"What?" Sam asked.

The man lowered his head, yelled something warlike, and started sprinting up Elephant Hill. I pushed Sam ahead of me. "Run to the Baptist church and hide in the stairwell," I said. "Wait fifteen minutes and then go home. And keep your mouth shut."

I tore down Green Avenue, away from Elephant Hill, hoping the angry man with the ponytail would follow me and not Sam. If Sam was caught, he'd lead the guy to our house and spill his guts, including how much Dad hated men with long hair. Sam would think that what we had done was funny. He might even ask the guy in for dinner and show him our cherry bombs.

Three blocks into my escape, I panicked. Before me was the beginning of the S-shaped slopes that flattened into an open area. If I kept running, the guy would catch me.

Frantically searching for a place to hide, I saw a house with a yard carved into a hill. The dirt bank rose higher than the roof of a carport. I leapt over the bank and landed flat on a concrete block in the carport, knocking the wind out of myself and scraping my hands, elbows, and chin. A truck was parked there, and I dove underneath.

My panting pounded in my ears in the tight space under the muffler. I couldn't see the sidewalk, so I twirled my body around, ripping my jeans on the driveway, and then slid to the side of the truck and stared out. I forced myself to inhale and exhale slowly to quiet my breathing. Within minutes, I heard footsteps and saw a pair of tennis shoes shoot past the carport. I quickly moved deeper under the truck, held my breath, and closed my eyes.

He didn't come back.

As the sun sank behind the distant mountains, a blanket of darkness crept across the carport. Maybe Sam and I would get away with it after all—maybe he was scared enough to keep quiet. My hands and elbows stung as I lay on the concrete. My jaw had stiffened, and my T-shirt felt sticky with sweat.

When the streetlights came on, I crawled out from

under the truck. Silence. Worried the angry man might still be looking for me, I limped through the alleys to get home. Sam was waiting for me in our basement bedroom.

"What happened?" His eyes flicked to my various scrapes. "Did the guy catch you?"

"Nah, I jumped into a carport to hide." I glanced at my torn jeans. "I got busted up pretty good."

"Mom and Dad are real mad at you for being late."

"Did you tell?"

"No, but Mom said you'd get a good whipping."

"Has anyone talked to them?"

"I don't think so."

"Well, I better get up there before Dad comes down with the belt."

Mom and Dad sat across from each other at the kitchen table. Mom was whining that no one ever listened to her and that the kids never helped around the house.

When I entered the room, she looked over at me with teary eyes. "Where were you? It's been dark for hours."

Neither one of them mentioned my torn clothes and scraped chin. Dad stared at me in full anger mode, which meant that Mom had won him over to her side. It didn't matter to her where we were or what we were doing, but when she decided to get upset with one of us, she pushed Dad to deliver a beating—though he didn't need much urging. It was the one time he didn't get mad at her.

Eyes bulging, he stood and pulled off his belt. "You upset your mother, and I won't tolerate that."

I might have laughed if he hadn't been about to beat me—Dad didn't care what Mom thought about anything.

He wrapped the leather part of his belt around his hand so the buckle would hit me first, his most recent form of punishment. As if the two of them were following a script, Mom's tears disappeared and she beamed. Suddenly she had become important to him. It was the only power she had.

I focused on the living room floor to get ready for the pain. Then I raised my head, trying not to make eye contact. But I couldn't help it. Was that the way he looked at all the sons of bitches who had it coming? Eyes so full of hate. He'd hit me tonight until his rage subsided, but it would have nothing to do with me being late.

As he approached with the belt and the buckle, I pictured myself resisting torture at the hands of the Japanese after trying to escape. I did everything to pretend not to be me, but it never worked. I was stuck with being David Crow no matter how much I wished to be someone else.

Dad was in his trancelike state, talking to himself, lips twitching and eyes darting around unfocused. “My father beat me with a wet rope and damn near killed me,” he mumbled, as if a vicious beating was a rite of passage between Crow men.

The first blow was always the worst. It hurt the most, especially if my skin was still raw from the last beating—or if I was all scraped up from narrowly escaping an angry man with a ponytail. A few strikes in the same spot, and blood would flow down my pant legs.

I winced, fearing the hit of the buckle after the belt whizzed through the air, feeling like a coward. Dad said I should take my beating like a man, the way he always had. But how, exactly, was I supposed to do that? Feel proud that I endured it? Fight back? Was this how Cherokee men made their sons tough?

Or was this simply a case of two sick bastards taking it out on one of their kids before they turned on each other?

For some reason, he paused with the belt in the air. “Why were you so late, and why didn’t you let your mother know where you were?”

“I was at Joey Perea’s house reading their **Encyclopedia Britannica**,” I blurted out. It was the best lie I could come up with on my walk home. “We have a project due for school tomorrow. Mine is on Genghis Khan, the Mongolian warlord.”

Dad lowered the belt.

I talked fast, hoping to delight him with my knowledge of a brutal leader who perfected violence in a way he could appreciate.

"Genghis Khan pinned his own uncle on an anthill for three days in a hundred-degree heat and then tied his arms and legs to four horses that ran off in different directions. His uncle got yanked to pieces for challenging Genghis for leadership of the Mongol hordes. The great Khan tortured and killed all his rivals, not just his uncle. The carnage was amazing."

"**Carnage**? What does that mean?"

I hesitated, surprised he didn't know the word, but I recovered quickly. "It means the slaughtering of lots of people in bloody battles."

"Carnage," he repeated softly several times, as if the sound soothed his twisted mind. His eyes calmed and the creases on his forehead smoothed out. I'd triggered a complete mood change by praising a vicious, conquering asshole, someone like him. Genghis Khan was the Emile Griffith of dictators. I often won Dad over with the cleverness of my pranks, but that night, I had impressed his violent side.

He broke out in a broad smile. Mom pouted. By exciting Dad, I had knocked her complaint to the side.

"How's school?" he asked, lacing his belt back through his pant loops, as if he hadn't thought of beating me at all.

"Fine."

"Your mother says your paper route is growing." He nudged me toward the kitchen table. "Get David something to eat, Thelma Lou."

"But he deserves a whipping for being late . . ." Mom's voice trailed off when Dad glared at her, and she went to the fridge to pull out leftovers.

"Tell me more about Genghis Khan and the Mongolian empire," Dad said as I sat across from him eating cold roast beef, washed down with iced tea.

For close to an hour, I regaled him with all the details I could remember about the Mongol hordes and the great Khan's exploits. I even brought up Alexander the Great, who he wanted to hear all about another time.

Our class hadn't studied Genghis Khan, but I'd read about him at Joey's house the last time he had me over. It was always fun to read the encyclopedia. Dad would never call his parents to check.

Every day brought the possibility of a beating, so it didn't matter if I lied to get out of trouble. Lying was always preferable to the truth if it produced a good reaction from Dad.

He and Mom weren't hard to figure out. I could control Dad, unless his anger had reached a fever pitch. The trick was to catch him before that happened. It took split-second timing. That night it worked.

The way to control Mom was to make her feel important. All I needed to do was agree with whatever she said. Once she thought I was on her side, I didn't have to worry about her saying anything to Dad. That night, if I had gotten to her before she got to Dad, I could have convinced her she had allowed me to be late.

Easily the best form of self-defense was to stay as far away as possible from both of them.

For weeks afterward, Sam lay on the bottom bunk and kicked my bed above him, laughing about Elephant Hill. He loved to waddle around the room, imitating the tire. I laughed so hard my stomach hurt.

Both drivers' accounts in the newspaper said the rogue tire might not have been attached to a vehicle. That was code for "two little bastards rolled it down Elephant Hill." Sam and I had to be on the shortest of short lists of suspects.

On the local news, a reporter said, "A large, inflated tire from an industrial machine struck two cars, causing serious damage to both. One witness thought he saw the tire roll down Green Avenue, and it didn't come from a vehicle."

The next morning, after Dad went to work, Mom caught me as Sam and I were about to leave for school. "David, one of the neighbor ladies thought she saw you and Sam rolling a large tire on Green Avenue. Is that true?"

Anyone else would have nailed us, but not Mom.

"No," I told her. "I bet the tire flew off a truck."

"That seems right to me too." She turned and walked into the kitchen.

Secretly, I hoped the police would catch us and take Sam and me away. I'd dream that we were sent to live with a nice couple who couldn't have children. Our new family might get mad at us sometimes, but no one would get beaten, and we'd make up. Most of the time everyone would be happy. Our new parents would want Lonnie and Sally too.

In the morning, I'd wake to the cold reality of the Crow household.

CHAPTER 15

It was my tenth birthday and I was excited. The Gallup Giants, my Little League team, were about to start the first playoff game. Two weeks before, we beat the Dodgers, giving us a chance at the championship. I would be pitching. I was the only one on our team who could throw a slider and a curveball.

But that wasn't enough to save us. As the afternoon wore on, the Red Sox made one home run after another, and we never got past second base. At the bottom of the last inning, they were ahead 6–0. Two of our players struck out, and then I hit a hard ground ball right to the shortstop. Our season was over.

I dragged myself home, and when I came through the door, Mom still didn't mention my birthday. That was typical of Dad, but Mom usually wished me a happy birthday first thing in the morning and gave me a hug and something very small and inexpensive, like a pack of bubble gum. Not this year.

The turmoil in our lives had gotten so bad she'd forgotten.

That Saturday at breakfast, Dad thumped me on the arm. "Eat up," he said. "We're going for a ride."

Before we left, he wanted me to help him change the oil in the station wagon. We were almost done when I tripped and spilled used oil on the driveway. No one was clumsier than me unless I had a baseball or cherry bomb in my hand.

"Goddamn you," he said. I turned to say I was sorry, and he hit me in the stomach with his wrench, knocking me to the ground. "You have no mechanical ability at all. You must be dyslexic to the bone. Let's go before you screw up something else."

He didn't say much as we drove into the hot desert, his usual pulsing Y vein and bulging eyes working overtime. Today, he was extra angry—his chest puffed out like he was getting ready for a fight. It had to be about Mom.

On a lonely strip of highway, he pulled over, stopped the car, and stared out the windshield. For several minutes, his lips chattered and his head twitched, bobbing around on his shoulders. My hands got sweaty as his face grew darker and his frown deeper.

"You're the reason we didn't get rid of your mother ages ago," he blurted out. "The other kids don't care what happens to her." He leaned toward me, his eyes blazing with rage. "You're a momma's boy. My father died when I was twelve. I had to become a man. Now you need to do the same."

I shrank back against the door. "Please don't hurt Mom."

"No one wants her around. Why can't I count on you for the simplest thing?"

Dad went back to staring out the windshield. I had been afraid of this moment since that first car ride in the blinding snowstorm. After Mom hid the mail in Albuquerque, I knew she would be gone soon, as much as I'd hoped otherwise. Lonnie and Sam had been ready for a long time. Who could blame them?

But she was my mom and I loved her—even though she was far more helpless than five-year-old Sally. I needed to protect her from Dad and the world. That was my job. It wasn't right to hurt her or leave her behind.

Dad didn't wait for an answer. He started up the car and headed back as if all had been resolved. My stomach hurt worse than ever, and I got dizzy thinking Mom might not last the day. At home, Dad stood behind me as I opened the door. That was strange—he usually disappeared or drove off again. The curtains were drawn and the house was dark and quiet.

"Happy birthday, David!" my friends shouted as Sam turned on the lights.

A Cowboy Bill birthday cake sat in the middle of

the coffee table. Gifts were piled on one side of the cake, and paper cups filled with Kool-Aid were on the other. Ten candles stood in thick white frosting inside a chocolate lasso. Mom lit them as I walked into the living room.

Joey, Billy, Tinker, Benny, and six of my buddies from the Gallup Giants blew whistles in my ears. They patted me on the back and teased me about a home run I'd hit in our last winning game—a grounder the shortstop missed, followed by three overthrows. The worst home run ever.

Violet was there too. She hugged me. I liked to think of her as my first girlfriend, but Joey claimed they kissed every day. The liar.

As my friends clapped and laughed, I wanted to freeze the moment. Everyone smiled at me, but Mom's face glowed with a happiness I had never seen.

"Make a wish," she said.

I blew out each candle, wishing to be anyone but David Crow. Dad had taken me for a drive to bully me into helping him get rid of Mom while she set up this wonderful surprise—it was the meanest trick he had ever played on me. I hated him almost as much as I hated myself for not sticking up for her. I didn't deserve the cake or the gifts.

Forcing away the tears, I couldn't wait for everyone to leave. I wanted to run through the streets so no one could see me cry.

With Dad, fun was always mixed with pain and suffering. All allegiance had to be to him alone.

Two months passed without any discussion of getting rid of Mom, but I carried the weight of it everywhere. In the middle of October, my fifth-grade teacher walked to my desk and put a gentle hand on my shoulder. I liked Mrs. Garcia—she let me be funny in front of the class without getting too mad. Sometimes she even laughed at my jokes. "Mr. Rodriguez wants to see you in his office," she said. "The school secretary will be here to take you in a minute."

Every bad thought raced through my mind. I'd done so many things that could have gotten me into trouble. Maybe the principal found out I'd stomped on a carton of milk and soaked one of the cafeteria ladies a couple of days before. Maybe the recess teacher saw me kick the ball at Violet again. She always complained about me, but I told myself she didn't really mean it.

When the secretary came into the classroom and called my name, Violet pointed at me. "You're going to get it, brat," she said. "I bet Mr. Rodriguez gives you a paddling and sends you to jail. You deserve it for being the worst boy in school."

On my way to the door, I tugged on her ponytail for the second time that day, and she stuck out her tongue again. That's how I knew she liked me, maybe even more than she liked Joey.

I dragged my feet down the hallway, and the secretary pushed me in front of her toward the office. "I'm really sorry for whatever I did," I whispered, practicing to myself. "It won't ever happen again. Honest. I mean it this time. Just please don't tell Mom and Dad. Please."

In the principal's office, I glanced out the window at the sign—"Eleanor Roosevelt Elementary School, Home of the Raiders"—and braced myself for the worst. Mr. Rodriguez, a balding man with a narrow band of gray hair above his ears, sat behind a big wooden desk, talking on the phone. A college diploma from the University of New Mexico hung on the wall to the right, and a picture of him, his wife, and two daughters sat on a table along the wall. Official-looking papers sprawled out in front of him, probably listing my terrible deeds.

When he hung up, he asked, "Do you have any idea why I called you in here?"

I shook my head. "No, but I won't do it again. Honest."

"Hmm?" He tilted his head, puzzled. "Your mom says you love baseball, especially the New York Yankees. So why don't we sit here together and watch the last few innings of the final World Series game?"

My jaw dropped. Mom knew I loved baseball more than life, especially the New York Yankees: Mickey Mantle, Roger Maris, Clete Boyer, Bobby Richardson, Yogi Berra, and Whitey Ford. The Yankees were playing the San Francisco Giants in the 1962 World Series. I'd memorized the Yankee lineup and all the statistics, and I listened to Dizzy Dean announce the games on my tiny transistor radio.

I imagined myself as the great Mickey Mantle. I'd throw baseballs high in the air, positioning myself to catch them, or hit balls across the street and retrieve them. Sam would play with me, but even he got tired of it. Following a major league game, I'd provide a complete blow-by-blow account to anyone who would listen. Lonnie and Sally closed the door to their room when they saw me coming.

Mr. Rodriguez brought over two chairs, turned on the small TV set on the side table, and told the secretary to hold his calls. "I loved baseball as a boy too," he said. "Nothing excited me more than the World Series. My favorite team is still the Los Angeles Dodgers. I love to watch Sandy Koufax, but the Yankees are very good also."

How had Mom pulled this off? I couldn't believe that she'd had the guts to call my school and ask if I could watch the World Series during school time, and I couldn't believe that Mr. Rodriguez had agreed.

For the rest of the afternoon, I was the luckiest

kid in the world. We watched the last four innings of game seven on October 16. I never wanted it to end. The Yankees won, 1–0, clinching the series, a close game until the last out.

After thanking Mr. Rodriguez several times, I ran home and burst into the house. Mom was sitting with Sally at the kitchen table. She jumped up and I hugged her for what seemed like an hour. I described every pitch, hit, and out. Smiling, she went over to the couch to lie down and asked every baseball question she could think of, including how many bats Mickey Mantle hit.

I felt like a normal kid with a normal mom. But then I remembered my tenth birthday party, the horrible ride with Dad, and his plot to get rid of her. Before she could see my tears, I escaped down to the basement and darted out the garage door. I ran for as long as I could, doing the only thing that could dull my sadness and guilt.

That night, I woke up crying after another nightmare, soaked in sweat.

"What's wrong?" Sam whispered. "Are you sick?"

"No, but something bad is going to happen to Mom. Dad might kill her. And it might be soon."

I waited for Sam to say something, but he didn't. My brother always kept his thoughts about Mom to himself unless we were plotting to trick her or trying to get out of trouble.

• • •

Right after the World Series ended, the country was thrown into a crisis. For the next two weeks, Dad stayed riveted to the television and radio. Soviet Premier Nikita Khrushchev was going to nuke the United States into oblivion, Dad said, because that silk-panties-wearing President John F. Kennedy was afraid of him. Dad sprang into action, burying gasoline, water, canned food, and batteries in the yard, preparing to survive a nuclear holocaust.

On a Saturday morning, Dad drove us to a nearby warehouse and led us down into the basement, where we spent most of the weekend in what would be our bomb shelter when the nukes hit. Mom flitted around, not knowing what to do, until she saw a couch and some beds set up for people staying overnight. She immediately made herself comfortable. Sam and I helped Dad and Lonnie carry a hundred-pound bag of dry beans into a cool, dark corner near where we would sleep. We also had powdered milk, jugs of fresh water, and canned corn. Dad said we might have to live off the provisions for months, waiting for the radiation to clear.

Other families were there, as well as a handful of Gallup's newly formed volunteer security team. They fiddled with flashlights and tried out some donated pocket knives, talking about what to do if we were invaded. No one came up with anything other than staying in the basement.

As we lay in our sleeping bags, Dad loudly told us that the Communist bastard Nikita Khrushchev had no respect for the pansy President Kennedy. He yelled into the dark, "After the Bay of Pigs, the Commies knew they were dealing with a pathetic blue-blooded dipshit!"

I could hear people moving away from us. At least two families climbed out of the basement and drove away. We took off the next afternoon but left our supplies and marked everything with our name. Dad said we'd keep coming back to practice because the time of doom was near.

When the US reached an agreement with the Soviets and they dismantled their missiles, Dad told me they would try to nuke us again, so we needed to continue the drills. But as the days passed, he lost interest, and I went back to the shelter with him to pick up our stuff. His superior survival skills would have to wait. For the duration of the crisis, though, Dad was busy and content, a model husband and father protecting his family.

CHAPTER 16

I stood outside our house watching Mom and Dad walk down the sidewalk. It was a Sunday afternoon in early November, and they were going to the Gallup hospital, only a few blocks away. Mom would be having her hemorrhoids removed, which seemed the least of her problems. Dad yelled at her to hurry up and pulled her by the elbow, almost making her fall.

He returned in less than an hour. "I want everyone in the living room for a family meeting," he said. We huddled together on the red couch, staring at the TV.

"Your mother will be gone for good soon," Dad said. "So get ready to move and forget about her." His eyes didn't bug out, and the vein was asleep inside his forehead. "When she's released from the hospital, she'll take a bus to California to recuperate at her mother's house. By the time she gets back here, we'll be in Fort Defiance. She'll never find us."

Two days later, I came home from school and

found Mom packing for her trip. I wanted to warn her, but it wouldn't have changed anything.

"I'll see you kids in a couple of weeks," she told us on the way out the door. "I love you."

I ran to hug her. My brother and sisters had already disappeared, but she didn't seem to notice. Dad picked up her bag and they got into the Rambler. How could she not know what he had planned for her?

After they pulled out of the driveway, I sprinted through yards and side streets to the bus station, hoping to catch a glimpse of Mom before she was gone. I stopped a block away so she wouldn't spot me. There she was, standing alone in front of the station buying a ticket in her thin cotton dress and flimsy sweater. When she turned in my direction, her face was contorted in a deep frown. She didn't see me or appear to see anything.

The bus pulled up to the curb, and she climbed the steps, disappearing from sight. If I knew she was going to a better place, I would have been okay. But I didn't think Mom could be happy anywhere or with anyone.

And no one wanted her.

It was almost Thanksgiving, and we hadn't heard anything from Mom. Dad kept telling us we were going to move before she got back, but day after day, he would pace the kitchen floor and yell into the phone, "Goddamn it, can't you find us a place to stay in Fort Defiance?" Slamming down the receiver, he'd say they were all a bunch of idiots.

As it started getting dark on Thanksgiving Day, Mom called collect from a bus station in Flagstaff, Arizona, and told Dad she was on her way and would arrive in Gallup in about three hours. He stomped around the house and then ordered everyone into the living room for another talk.

We never made it to the couch. "I don't want your mother coming into this house," he said, intercepting us in the kitchen. "When she gets here, all of you need to be in your rooms, except David"—he flashed his eyes at me—"and make sure all the lights are off. I'm leaving in the next few minutes, and after I'm gone, lock all the doors, including the garage. Remember the dead bolt on the front door so your mother can't use her key."

He jabbed me in the chest. "I want you to sit by the front door and wait for her. Don't turn on the porch light. Tell her she doesn't live here anymore. If she asks where I am, say you don't know. All you know is that this is no longer her home."

I pulled back. "Me? Why me? It isn't fair not to let her in. It's freezing outside, and she'll want to come in and get warm. It will almost be time for bed. Where can she go?"

"That's not your problem. She'll know this isn't her home when **you** tell her to go away. It's your job."

Lonnie, Sam, and Sally stood next to Dad, staring at me. At that moment, I hated them all.

He drove off in the Rambler. Lonnie, Sam, and Sally went to their rooms, and I sat by the door in the dark. It seemed like forever before I heard her key jiggle in the lock. When that didn't work, she knocked.

"Open the door!" Mom called out. "I'm freezing. Your daddy didn't pick me up. Where's Lonnie? She knew to come help me carry my bag. I'm mad at her."

I jumped up and looked through the peephole. I could barely make her out in the streetlight. She dropped her suitcase with a thud and pounded on the door with both fists. "Where is everyone?" she shouted. "Somebody let me in!"

"You don't . . . you don't live here anymore." I choked on the words.

"David? What are you talking about?"

My eyes burned with tears, and I swallowed hard. "I can't let you in."

"I'm your mother. I live here. Get me out of the cold right now."

The desperation in her voice nearly broke me. As

Mom pounded, yelling at me to unlock the dead bolt, I fell to the floor shaking.

Finally, she walked away as I sat crying, my head in my hands. A good son would never have done such a terrible thing to his mom.

When I was certain she was gone, I hurried downstairs and out through the garage into the cold night in my T-shirt. I pumped as hard as I could down the side streets and onto Route 66 until my legs hurt and my lungs were about to burst. By the time I got back to our house, my body was soaked and my arms and hands were frozen.

The streetlight shone on the chrome rear bumper of the Rambler in the garage. Dad was home. The porch light was on, but the rest of the house was still dark. I closed the heavy wooden door in the garage and crept into my room. Not a sound came from Sam in the bottom bunk as I climbed up to my bed.

As I lay there, I kept hearing Mom pounding on the door and the helplessness and despair in her voice. Where was she? Would she freeze to death?

I picked up a Hardy Boys mystery, turned on my flashlight, and tried to escape into their lives until sleep took over. The Hardy Boys always solved their mystery and defeated the villains and then returned to a home where they were loved. That could never happen to me.

In the middle of the night, I woke up to sliding

and swooshing sounds. I crawled up the basement stairs to see Mom's silhouette entering through the living room window. How did she do that? The window was at waist level from the front steps, so it wasn't hard to reach, but she had to pull herself through without falling backward. How did she even open the latch? It wasn't easy to turn. She had always seemed so helpless.

Her tiny birdlike steps trotted to the bedroom. When I heard my parents' door close, knowing Dad was inside, I couldn't help but sneak down the hall to listen. My heart thumped hard and fast.

Mom's voice was muffled, too soft to make out the words. Dad rumbled an unintelligible response. Worried he would kill her, I strained to hear more, but soon they were both quiet.

It was light when I woke up. As I climbed the stairs, I heard Mom talking with my brother and sisters. Everyone was sitting at the table. Dad was there too, drinking coffee and reading the newspaper.

"Why didn't you let me in last night, David?" she asked, as if I'd made a minor mistake, like forgetting to pick up my socks.

"It wasn't my fault, Mom. I just couldn't."

"Why not?" She scowled at me. "You knew it was cold out there, and I needed help with my suitcase."

She looked down at her plate and moved the eggs around without eating them.

I glanced over at my sisters and brother. Lonnie and Sally left the table and disappeared into their room. Sam took his bowl to the living room and sat in front of the TV, spilling his cereal and milk on the carpet.

Dad folded up the paper and took off, as though nothing had happened. Maybe I'd gone crazy too and dreamed the whole thing.

Throughout the day, I kept telling myself that everything was back to normal. Mom had come home from visiting her mother. Her hemorrhoids were better. We would all continue just as before.

On Sunday morning, Dad told all four of us to get into the car, and we went for a ride into the desert. Outside of town, he pulled over. "We're going to make your mother's life a living hell," he said, "so she'll want to leave."

I knew only a couple of kids whose parents had gotten a divorce. The moms kept the house and the kids, and the dads gave them money and visited. Our dad would never agree to any of that. He wouldn't give Mom anything—ever. He wasn't going to let any judge make him fork over good money or give

Mom a house or let us see her. He wanted her to simply disappear.

What could we possibly do to make Mom's life worse? It was already a living hell. She would never leave. In fact, Dad's plan might actually backfire—Mom might feel more important since she would be the center of attention all the time.

Dad turned to Lonnie sitting next to him. "I want you to ignore your mother. Don't help her in any way. Ninety percent of the work that happens in the house comes from you. She will completely fall apart without your help."

Then Dad looked over his shoulder at Sam and me in the back seat. "I want you two to be purposely destructive," he said. "That shouldn't be hard for you little bastards."

For the next couple of weeks, the instant Dad left for work, our house turned into a scene from **Lord of the Flies**. Sam and I used our glasses and bowls as weapons, hurling them at each other. Milk, juice, and cereal flew everywhere. Sam stood on a chair and flung the blender on the floor, smashing it to pieces. Even five-year-old Sally threw her silverware.

Mom ran in circles, wailing, as she did in every crisis. She banged on Lonnie's door. "Come out here and help me. I can't take care of the kids and house without you. Why are you doing this to me?"

Lonnie stayed in her room, which was the worst blow of all.

Each day I wondered if it was possible to be any crueler. When Dad returned from work, he'd berate Mom for "losing control of the children." I hated what we were doing, but I feared Dad's wrath more than I wanted to save Mom.

Our destruction knew no bounds. Sam and I ramped up our pranks all over Gallup. Somehow, hurting other people made me hurt less.

One afternoon, as we walked along a busy street, Sam threw a brick at the windshield of a parked car, putting a large crack in it. No one came after us. Another day, we tossed a cherry bomb through the half-open window of a pickup. The two drunk Navajos in the cab jumped out and threatened to drag us to the police department.

We both shrugged. "Go ahead if you want," I said.

Going to jail would have been better than going home.

When we got tired of damaging vehicles, we went inside the El Morro Theatre to watch **The Magnificent Seven** again. This time, we were armed with a few hard snowballs hidden in our coat pockets. Soon after the movie started, we both launched shots from the balcony, ripping a hole in the screen.

The room lit up as Sam and I ran down the stairwell to escape. We were about to blast through the emergency exit when a vise grip closed on my wrist, practically pulling me off my feet. "I caught you, you little vandals. You two aren't going anywhere." The manager was built like a tree stump, with massive arms that stretched his shirt.

I promised him that Dad would pay for the damage if he called our house. He pulled a pen and piece of paper out of his pocket, and when he loosened his hold to write down the fake phone number, I yanked my arm away, and we bolted out the door.

Later that afternoon, at the local bowling alley, Sam heaved several balls one right after another down a single lane, breaking the pin-clearing device. We easily outraced the fat manager through a side entrance as the emergency buzzer sounded. On the way home, Sam threw a rock at a neon sign in front of a trading post, shattering it. The shop owner came out screaming and chased us down the street. We laughed and dashed through the alleys to our house. Half of Gallup was after us.

We were doing more than breaking Mom. We were destroying any sense of civility and decency the four of us still had.

We were no longer brothers and sisters. We were members of a gang.

CHAPTER 17

Dad's heavy footsteps and shouts jolted me awake. Lonnie was crying. I jumped to the floor and ran upstairs. The bright light of the bathroom spilled out into the hallway. Lonnie's feet dangled in the air as Dad bear-hugged her around the stomach and leaned her over the sink.

"Throw up as hard as you can!" he yelled. "How many did you take?"

"All of them," she said, vomiting into the sink.

"Jesus!"

An empty bottle of Bayer aspirin lay on the floor by the toilet.

"It's a damn good thing I heard you," Dad said. "Keep throwing up. Get it all out!"

Lonnie made several gagging noises, and a flood gushed out into the sink and onto the floor. Dad filled a large glass with water and forced her to drink all of it, and she threw up again.

Sally and Sam came up behind me, both of them

staring, wide-eyed. Mom's bedroom door remained closed. She took something to help her sleep, but the racket in the bathroom was loud enough to wake the neighbors. Even so, she never appeared.

Dad saw us and waved us away. Sam went back to the basement, and Sally ran into the bedroom she shared with Lonnie and closed the door. I started down the stairs but stopped, turned off the light, and leaned against the wall to listen.

In between sobs and gulps, Lonnie said, "I don't help Mom anymore . . . She begs me, but I walk away . . . I tell her we want her to leave." She blew her nose. "And . . . when you come into my room and talk to me the way you do . . . it's like you want me to be a grown-up. I can't. Don't make me."

My mind flashed to all the times I saw Dad whispering in Lonnie's ear and leaning over her on her bed, close to her face, holding her hand. She would shake her head hard and say no.

But what did he want from her? I didn't understand, but I knew Dad was pushing her to do things no kid should ever have to do.

Lonnie spurted out, "You tell me I'm a better mother than she is . . . I'm only fourteen. Mom is always screaming at me and saying she hates me."

"Don't worry," Dad said softly. "This is all her fault. She'll be gone soon, I promise. But no more swallowing bottles of aspirin, do you hear me? You could have died. C'mon, let's walk around the block and get you some air."

Dad helped Lonnie put on her coat and they went out the front door. Crouching by the living room window, I watched them walk up the street and then followed them out into the cold drizzle. Lonnie was still having a hard time catching her breath.

Afraid Dad would see me, I hurried home and climbed under the covers to wait for them. When the front door opened, I sneaked up the stairs and stayed hidden at the top.

"Go to sleep, Lonnie," Dad said. "We'll be rid of the crazy bitch soon, and we can have our own lives."

"What life!" Lonnie screamed, slamming her door.

I returned to the basement and crawled into bed. Dad had saved Lonnie, but he was the one who had driven her to swallow the bottle of aspirin. It was all his fault. And what if there was still a lot of aspirin left in her body? She could die. When I slept, I had visions of her sinking under water and never coming up.

By the time I woke up the next morning, Sam was already upstairs eating his cornflakes. Mom's bedroom door was closed, and the Rambler was gone. Lonnie and Sally were gone too.

Sam and I went to see Mr. Pino and greet the

Saturday visitors crossing Route 66. But nothing seemed funny, not even the drunks stumbling down the street. Most of our cherry bombs stayed in the paper bag, along with our firecrackers. Sam helped me deliver my afternoon papers, and we stayed out until after dark, throwing rocks on the outskirts of town until we couldn't see them land. We were freezing and hungry, but neither one of us wanted to go home.

We slipped inside the house and found sliced roast beef in the refrigerator. We ate it like wolves and then grabbed a couple of spoonfuls of peanut butter. It was long after dinnertime, but no one noticed.

On Sunday afternoon, Dad pulled me aside twice. "Why haven't you gotten your mother to leave yet? You sure as hell know what to do. Wreck everything in the goddamn house for all I care, but get after it. Don't worry about Sam and Sally—they'll follow your lead. Lonnie is doing her part. Your mother can't function without her help. The rest is up to you. I better see some results tomorrow."

I was jittery the next day, thinking about what I had to do. When I got home after school and paper deliveries, Lonnie was in her room, and Sam and Sally were watching TV. I had about an hour before Dad would walk through the door.

Mom was in the kitchen fixing dinner. I stood behind her, watching her slice roast beef. The okra was sizzling in the frying pan, and a pitcher of iced tea sat on the counter, ready to be poured into glasses.

The house was nice and calm, but I couldn't let it stay that way. Dad would be furious and beat me. I had to do something right now.

I went into the living room to gather my nerve and motioned Sam and Sally to come toward me. As we whispered back and forth about what I wanted them to do, Mom heard us talking and called out, "How was school today, kids?"

"It's none of your business!" Sam yelled. Sally laughed.

Sam and I picked up two of the Melmac plates off the dining room table and threw them against the living room wall like they were Frisbees, smashing both of them. I picked up a chair and threw it into the couch. It hit Sam on the way, so he grabbed another chair and threw it at me.

Mom hurried into the living room, the knife in her hand. "I want you to stop this—NOW!" she yelled.

"You're not in charge of us anymore!" I yelled back at her.

The knife sat loosely in her palm, but then she tightened her grip until her knuckles turned white. "David, I count on you to be my big helper," she said, sobbing. "My oldest boy. Look at what you've done. How could you do this to me? Sam and Sally are acting like animals. And Lonnie won't help with anything."

"I'm not your helper anymore either," I said. "Dad said you're not going to be our mom much longer."

She didn't move. Her eyes turned glassy as she stared straight ahead at the living room window.

Sam picked up a spoon and threw it at Sally. Sally raked her arm across the table, and the remaining plates, silverware, and glasses crashed to the floor. I flew on top of Sam and wrestled him to the ground, knocking over the coffee table.

Mom screamed.

Startled, I jumped up in front of her. The knife sailed past my face, striking the living room wall just below the picture window. A chunk of plaster fell to the carpet, leaving a white gouge in the beige wall.

Her hands flew to her mouth, muffling a loud gasp, her eyes wide with horror. "I didn't mean to do that. It . . . just slipped out of my hand."

We were still standing frozen when Dad walked into the living room and saw the mess.

"Mom threw a knife at David's head!" Sally yelled. "She just missed him."

"Goddamn it, Thelma Lou," Dad said. "What the hell did you do that for? You really are crazy."

Sally ran down the hall and closed her door, and Sam and I retreated to the basement. The house became quiet again. There was no dinner that night. Trying to calm myself, I went out through the basement door and ran as hard as I could down Route 66 until the lights in Gallup were a dim spot against the desert sky. I had never run that far out of town.

The next morning, when I came upstairs, Lonnie, Sally, and Sam had already left for school. I raced out the front door before Mom or Dad could see me. The Rambler was still in the driveway.

After finishing my paper route that afternoon, I came home to find my brother and sisters sitting around the kitchen table. Dad sat on the couch, and Mom slumped beside him in her nightgown. Her tiny overnight bag sat near the front door.

"What took you so long?" Dad said. "We've been waiting for you."

"I didn't know I had to be here."

"I stayed home from work today. Sit down—we need to have a family talk. I have some things to say to all of you."

He looked down at Mom. She stared vacantly, her eyes dark and sunken, like the POWs I'd seen in war photos.

"I'm taking your mother to the Nazareth Psychiatric Hospital in Albuquerque," Dad said quietly. "She needs help for her nerves, and I'm going to make sure she gets it." He told me to take her overnight bag to the station wagon.

What the hell was he up to now? There was no way he wanted her to get well. Either he would take her to the funny farm, as he called it, hoping they would keep her for good, or he'd dump her out in the desert after hitting her over the head.

As Mom stumbled to the car, I ran over and threw my arms around her. "I'm sorry for being so bad."

"It's okay, honey," she said. "You didn't mean it. When my nerves get fixed, everything will be better."

The Rambler backed into the street and I waved to Mom, but she sat motionless, looking out the window dazed and unfocused. I felt empty inside, unable to imagine that Mom could ever forgive me—or that I'd ever be free of Dad's death grip.

Lonnie made us dinner and told us to do our homework after we washed the dishes. The upstairs was neat and clean, showing no evidence of the terrible events of the day before. For a moment, I pretended Lonnie hadn't swallowed the bottle of aspirin and I hadn't wrecked the house and the last of Mom's nerves.

Dad would be home soon. I dreaded hearing the Rambler roll into the driveway.

CHAPTER 18

On the Friday before Christmas, my class had a party with cookies, punch, and games. Everyone was smiling, talking about what they would do during their vacation. Some of them planned trips to see their grandparents.

With Mom gone, the fighting at home had stopped, but Dad was still as angry and unpredictable as ever. He talked a lot on the phone to the housing office at the Bureau of Indian Affairs and to the staff at the hospital, always yelling before he hung up.

I'd been spending more time with my paper route customers, and a few of them invited me in for hot chocolate. A nice lady gave me a globe for Christmas, and others gave me nickels, dimes, quarters, and even a silver dollar.

Most of our neighbors had put up lights and filled their yards with plastic Jesus statues and Santa Clauses. After delivering the Sunday paper, I rode my bike by the East Aztec Baptist Church, where Sam had hidden during the Elephant Hill escape. Families and friends greeted each other warmly with "Merry Christmas" and "God bless you" as they hurried inside to get out of the cold. Violet went to church there, but I didn't see her.

Dad never had anything to do with the holidays, railing against the Jews and their scheme to spread the false myth that Jesus was God so they could get rich off our stupidity. If Mom had been there, we would have put up a small tree and then exchanged one gift on Christmas.

But that wouldn't happen this year.

When Dad got home from work on Christmas Eve, Lonnie fixed dinner from the canned food we had reclaimed from the now-abandoned bomb shelter. Corn, Spam, and black-eyed peas. After Dad left the table, the four of us leaned in close, whispering, and then we joined him in the living room.

"Can we go see Mom . . . please?" I asked him.

"She's somebody else's problem now." He looked up from the newspaper to see all of his children standing in front of him. For once, Lonnie, Sam, and Sally took my side, everyone pleading with Dad to take us to see Mom.

"Okay." He exhaled an impatient sigh. "We'll go see her, but just this one time. Grab your coats and get in the car."

As we drove out of town, we passed Stearns Sporting Goods Store, still open for Christmas shoppers. I stared at the shiny bikes in the window, shifting around in my seat to keep them in sight as long as possible.

"I wish we had one of those," Sam said.

"Me too."

"There's no reason for Christmas or gifts since there is no God," Dad said. "Christ faked his death and tricked the Jews into accepting blame." His head jerked, and he mumbled to himself. "Where's the bastard now? Dead. And he'll stay dead. Mary was no virgin. They nearly killed Joseph for knocking her up without marrying her. No one is saved. We just die. Rich people worship money, and poor people worship Jesus. It's all they've got. The poor dumb bastards. Do-gooders pretend that giving gifts makes us better. It ain't so."

Dad glanced at Lonnie in the front seat and then over his shoulder at Sam, Sally, and me. "And don't encourage your mother by telling her she'll be part of this family again because she won't."

The knot in my stomach got worse. I couldn't remember a time when my stomach didn't hurt or when my palms weren't sweaty.

Maybe giving gifts didn't make people better, but it felt good to get them. And I liked making gifts in school for the family. My mind shifted to watching the end of the World Series with the principal and then to doing all those horrible things to Mom in return for her kindness. How could I be okay if she wasn't?

After two long hours, we pulled up to the Nazareth Psychiatric Hospital, a three-story building ten miles outside Albuquerque on Rattlesnake Hill. A few snowflakes fell as the five of us paraded in. Near the entrance, I picked up a brochure that said the hospital was run by the Dominican Sisters and specialized in psychodramas. I didn't know what that meant, but it sounded bad.

We followed Dad into the warm lobby and passed a small, plastic Christmas tree covered in lights. Peppermint sticks and Santa Claus and reindeer ornaments hung from the limbs, and a mound of perfectly wrapped gifts sat underneath. For just a moment, I relaxed, surprised that the place was so quiet and peaceful. But that ended the second Dad opened his mouth.

At the reception desk, an older woman with gray hair and glasses asked, "Who are you here to see?"

"Thelma Lou Crow," Dad said. "She's in the nut ward."

"We don't use terms like that here, sir," she said, shuffling papers on the desk.

"Do you prefer fruitcake factory?"

The woman ignored him. "Visiting hours end at nine," she said, looking at her watch. "So you only have about a half hour."

Dad grunted. "We won't stay one second longer than we have to."

She picked up a phone, but he kept talking. "People here are missing a few marbles, including the doctors and nurses," Dad said.

The receptionist adjusted her glasses on her nose. "Please wait here, and someone will escort you to Mrs. Crow's room." Her voice was calm, but her tight mouth gave her away. Dad had rattled her.

Soon a pretty nurse in a white uniform and cap arrived. "Follow me, children," she said. "Let's go see your mother. She'll be happy to see you."

The lobby and hallways had the shiniest floors I'd ever seen. Christmas pictures were pasted on the patients' doors. Old men and women sat in wheelchairs outside their rooms, staring. Their faces and shoulders drooped, but they perked up when they saw us, probably hoping we were there to visit them.

"Is my mom okay?" I asked the nurse.

"She's getting the best treatment available," the nurse said, leading us into Mom's room. "Seeing you will be the best medicine of all."

"I'll be down the hall," Dad said, walking away. "Don't stay too long."

Mom was asleep, and we stood by the door while

the nurse woke her with a gentle nudge on the shoulder. "Thelma Lou, your children have surprised you on Christmas Eve."

Mom barely raised her head and then turned on her side, motioning us toward her. I got to talk to her first.

"I know what a bad boy I've been." I put my hands in my pockets and stared at my feet. "I'll always mind if you'll just get better." Dad's voice played in my head, warning us not to make her think she would ever come home, but he wasn't there.

"Merry Christmas," Lonnie said. "How are you feeling?"

"I'm so drowsy." Mom put her hand to her mouth and yawned. "The medicine is strong, but my nerves seem better."

Sam and Sally moved forward and took Mom's outstretched hand. I reached over and placed a card and wooden Santa Claus I'd made in school on her blanket.

She gave me a sleepy smile. "I'm so proud of my oldest boy who didn't forget me at Christmas." Her gaze shifted slightly. "Thurston."

I whipped around to see Dad behind us, his arms crossed and the Y vein pulsing on his forehead.

"I'm getting better, Thurston." Mom opened the card and read inside: "'I love you and hope you come home soon.' How sweet." She closed her eyes. Lonnie shook her head at me, knowing I was about to get into trouble.

Dad pressed his hands into my shoulders. "Time to go now."

As we turned to leave, Mom tried to rise but slumped back on the bed. "I love you all," she said. "I'll be home before you know it."

I looked back at her. How could she be proud of me? I was the biggest liar of us all.

Down the hall, Dad grabbed the collar of my coat and shoved me against the wall. "What's wrong with you?" he said, his face in mine. "Why did you write that you hoped she'd come home soon? We'll be long gone to Fort Defiance when she gets out."

CHAPTER 19

As the gray, dreary weeks of January passed, we still hadn't moved. One night, I overheard Dad screaming into the phone. "I don't want her back, you dumbass. That's why I left her with you. I've put up with the crazy bitch for sixteen years, and I've had enough. Keep her in your permanent rubber room for locos."

After the call, Dad did his usual stomping around the house, yelling and swearing, and we did our best to stay out of his way. Eventually, he summoned us for another family meeting. We sat on the red couch, and Dad turned off the TV.

"The stupid loony bin won't keep your mother. My insurance won't pay for all her treatment either. They want more money. Lots of it. From me. I don't want to pay to tranquilize her, and I don't want to go get her, but I have to. Our housing in Fort Defiance was supposed to be ready by now, but it won't be for a few more weeks, and I have to bring her home tonight."

He marched out of the house and left in the Rambler. Since Mom couldn't stay in the hospital, and we'd already made her life a living hell to make her leave, I worried again that Dad would think his only option was to kill her.

But the station wagon pulled up with two people in the front seat. Mom got out in a robe, shuffled up the stairs, and went straight to bed. She was so calm she was practically sleepwalking. Every few hours, she called me into the room to get her a glass of water, and then she'd take a large pill and turn over to go back to sleep. The medicine would steady her broken nerves, she said. Dad called them horse pills.

For brief periods, she stopped crying, but she still didn't have much energy. Each night, after dinner, I went to their bedroom and listened.

"You've got to get a job, Thelma Lou," Dad told her. "I'm tired of footing all our bills and paying for your psycho medicine."

Mom begged him not to make her work. Dad left want ads on the breakfast table each morning and told her to interview for jobs. A month or so later, she came home and called everyone to the kitchen. "I got a job at Winn's Variety, working the ten-to-two shift on Tuesdays and Thursdays. That means you kids need to mind and help with the housework and cooking. Your daddy is money crazy, and this'll make him happy."

Lonnie returned to helping Mom with dinner and getting us to clean up and do our homework. And things went smoothly, meaning we didn't throw dishes, knives, or other utensils at one another. After her first two-day workweek, I found Mom alone in the kitchen, making dinner. "How's the job going?" I asked.

"I hate it. I want to quit," she whined, opening a can of okra and dumping it into the frying pan. "They give you only two fifteen-minute breaks. You guys need me more."

"Sorry you don't like your job." I paused. There was something else on my mind. "Could you use part of my paper route money to buy a speedometer for my bike?"

"Sure," she said. "I'll pick one up at Gallup Sporting Goods."

That was easy enough. Mom and Dad kept the money I earned and let me pocket the tips for spending money. But several days went by and Mom still hadn't bought the speedometer. Every time I asked her about it, she said she'd forgotten.

"Please get it tomorrow," I said.

When I got home after delivering my papers, I found a speedometer sitting on the kitchen table. "I hope that's what you wanted," Mom said.

"What about the cable and the box it came in?"

"They sold it to me just like that, honey. Won't it work?"

"No, Mom. I'll go back to the store and get the rest of the parts you must have forgotten." I picked up the speedometer and ran out the door.

Mom followed me outside and yelled something I couldn't understand as I sped off on my bike. At Gallup Sporting Goods, I told the high school kid behind the counter I needed to talk to the manager.

A short, fat Mexican man came toward me from one of the aisles. "I'm the manager. Can I help you?"

"My mom bought this for me." I held up the speedometer. "But she forgot to bring home the cable."

The man grabbed my upper arm and pulled me toward the counter. "So you're the one who stole it." He pointed at a box that had a coiled cable and a round hole where the speedometer had been. "You little thief. I'm calling the police."

I jerked my arm free, dropped the speedometer, and bolted out the door. When I pulled pranks, things got broken and sometimes people even got hurt, but stealing crossed a different line. Being called a thief felt terrible.

Dashing into the kitchen, I said, "Mom, how could you take the speedometer without paying?"

"Honey, I put money on the counter." She sliced

the roast beef and arranged it on a platter. "The man must not have seen it. I'll straighten it out tomorrow."

"But I saw the box it came in and—"

"No one loves me, not my husband, not my mother, not even my children." Her eyes welled with tears.

Poor Mom. It was pointless to be mad at her. Besides, she'd been through enough lately, and I didn't want to make her feel worse.

"I love you," I said, putting my arms around her. "It'll be okay."

On a Wednesday afternoon in early March, Dad got home from work while Mom was at a friend's house, which almost never happened. Again, he gathered all four of us kids into the Rambler and drove us into the desert.

None of us spoke. I sat in the back seat behind Dad, my throat dry with dread. I could only assume he had another ditching plan.

He pulled the car over on a sandy shoulder and turned off the engine. Little Sally's wide eyes went from me on her left to Sam on her right. He shrugged. In the front seat, Lonnie stared at her lap. I could tell she knew what was coming.

Dad gripped the steering wheel and looked straight ahead. "We're moving tomorrow while your mother is at work. Go to school and pretend like it's just another day. When I pick you up, you'll have fifteen minutes to pack." He turned to glare at Sam, then Sally, then me. "And I better not hear that any of you blabbed."

My stomach lurched, and I thought I'd throw up all over the seat. Mom would come home to an empty house. How could he do that to her? Muttering to himself, he started the car and turned around. Watching the rocks and cactus along the highway, I kept telling myself that Dad had been promising to get rid of Mom for years, so maybe it wouldn't happen this time either.

That night, she served the usual okra, roast beef, and iced tea, complaining about her job and our lousy behavior while Dad read the paper—like every other dinner in our household. Sam and I hit each other under the table and threw Sally's doll down the stairs. Lonnie retrieved it and told us to leave Sally alone.

"Knock it off, goddamn it," Dad said.

"You kids need to help more around the house," Mom said as Lonnie washed the dishes and put them on the rack to dry.

When it was time for bed, we went to our rooms, pretending everything was normal.

"Do you think we can get all our stuff in a box in fifteen minutes?" Sam whispered.

"We don't have that much," I said. "It probably won't take more than five minutes."

Sam turned over and went to sleep. Not me.

Reading about the Hardy Boys couldn't distract me. I shone my flashlight at the cracks in the ceiling. Would I be sleeping in a different bed tomorrow night? Or would I wake up and find out this was all a nightmare that hadn't come true?

Before school started the next morning, I played kickball in the parking lot, punting the ball at Violet as usual. She ducked and stuck out her tongue at me. After lunch, Mrs. Garcia told me to go to the principal's office.

I stared at her. I couldn't move.

"Don't worry," she said. "Your dad came to take you somewhere. You're not in trouble."

"Uh . . . okay."

I glanced around the classroom for the last time and forced myself to get out of my seat. As I walked down the aisle, Violet said, "You're probably being kicked out of school, you big brat."

I pulled her pencil out of her hand and dropped it on the teacher's desk on the way out of the room. When I looked over my shoulder at her, she stuck out her tongue and then smiled.

In the parking lot, Dad stood next to the Rambler tapping his watch. He yelled for me to hurry up. Lonnie, Sam, and Sally were already in the car.

"Are we really leaving?" I said. "We're not going without Mom, are we?"

Dad didn't answer. We pulled up to our house, quickly packed our belongings into cardboard boxes, and put them in the Rambler. Dad had already loaded the furniture, curtains, towels, sheets, and dishes into the green trailer. My shoes squeaked as I stumbled through the echoey house in a daze.

"The water, gas, and electricity will be shut off today," Dad said. He dumped Mom's clothes on the dirty mattress he'd dragged into the bare living room. "And I disconnected the phone. The landlord has our last check. I told him he could rent the place to someone else."

"I think that's everything then," Lonnie said.

"Empty the refrigerator," Dad told her. "Hurry, we don't have much time before she gets home."

Lonnie ran to the kitchen, and Dad taped a note to the front door:

Don't look for us. We don't want you.

As we drove down South Cliff Drive, my arms and legs felt numb. Before we got onto Route 66, I turned around to see the top of the Winn's Variety sign in the distance. Mom would arrive home to find that cruel note and everything gone. She'd be cold, hungry, and tired, with no food, no heat, no warm bed, and no one to ask about her day. Soon the landlord would kick her out.

"She has almost two hundred dollars—and I let her keep the car," Dad told us once we'd gotten onto the highway.

Yeah, like that was some big prize. The Ford station wagon he bought her had a broken heater, an oil leak, a rusted-out muffler, bald tires, a huge crack in the windshield, and an engine that coughed thick black smoke. When Mom drove faster than twenty-five miles an hour, the car shimmied so badly it almost shook apart.

As Dad drove the Rambler out of Gallup toward the northern edge of the Navajo Indian Reservation, my mind filled with questions I couldn't answer: What would Mom do? Where would she go? How would she survive? If Dad had paid for her to keep getting help, could she have become a good mom someday?

I stood a better chance of making it on the street than Mom did. How could we do this to her?

And what would become of us?

PART 3

Fort Defiance
1963

A well-built hogan in Fort Defiance, Arizona. 1965.

CHAPTER 20

It took us less than an hour to reach the city of Window Rock, the entrance to the Navajo Indian Reservation, where you can see the sky through a giant hole in a wall of red sandstone. On the left, we passed the tribal headquarters in a long building flanked by six flagpoles. What I knew about the reservation I had learned in our enclosed EPNG compounds and my trips to the Hubbell Trading Post, and it didn't occur to me that life in Fort Defiance would be any different.

By then, I had stopped crying, but my insides felt raw and shaky. None of us kids had spoken since we left Gallup. Dad kept muttering something about "the useless bitch."

He turned right and headed north to Fort Defiance and the Bureau of Indian Affairs Headquarters, where he had been working since we moved to Gallup.

"What's the matter with all of you?" He looked at Lonnie next to him and in the rearview mirror at Sam, Sally, and me. "We finally got rid of that no-good mother of yours. You kids should be thanking me."

I stared at the scenery and tried not to think about Mom. Ahead on the left, a long black rocky ridge jutted out of the flat desert and rose high into the sky. Soon after, we came to a small run-down village, like something you'd see in **National Geographic**. There were no traffic lights, stores, or big buildings. A gas station sat next to a small diner on one side and a ramshackle laundromat on the other, located in what appeared to be a temporary storage unit.

Navajo women exited the laundromat carrying mountains of clothes in woven baskets and climbed into dented pickup trucks. Kids ran around without shoes, and men lay passed out in the parking lot. Mangy dogs drank from oily pools of water.

From the front seat, Lonnie glanced over her shoulder at me and widened her eyes. This was far worse than Gallup—we were taking another huge step backward.

Hogans, five-sided adobe mud-and-wood structures with sheepskin doors, were scattered everywhere. A lot of the Navajo shoppers in Gallup and at the Hubbell Trading Post lived in them. Dad said they had small chimneys and dirt floors with no running water, electricity, or bathrooms. He laughed. "They sure are primitive bastards."

As we drove by, Navajos milled around outside their hogans collecting sheep dung and mesquite wood for fuel. At one place, a sheep was hoisted on a spit over an open fire. Women sat at rickety looms weaving rugs while skinny sheep and horses stood there lifeless and children ran around in ragged clothes.

The remaining families lived in small, rusted-out trailers. With each one we passed, I felt relieved that Dad didn't expect us to live there, but nothing ahead looked better.

He slowed and took a right off Kit Carson Drive onto Eighth Street, a dirt road with enormous craters. Sally grabbed onto my leg to keep from sliding off the seat. The Rambler jolted so hard I thought the axle had broken.

Dad parked in front of a tiny wooden box. Sam and I could have toppled it with a couple of hits from a hammer. All four of us went stiff. I would have welcomed 709½ South Second Street, even with the drunks in the front yard.

"This neighborhood is called Mud Flats," Dad said. His voice strained the way it always did when he was embarrassed. We stared at the shack in front of us. "I convinced the BIA to let us live here until other housing becomes available."

The Navajo kids running around the neighborhood stopped and stared at us in the car as if we'd gotten lost and would soon be on our way. There wasn't a single friendly face. No one smiled.

I never wanted to get out. Ever.

"Unload—now!" Dad yelled.

As we reached for the door handles, a pack of feral dogs exploded onto the car, barking and clawing at the windows. We all jumped back in our seats. Sally screamed.

"Ignore them," Dad said.

But when we opened the doors, the dogs snarled and nipped at us, attacking anything they could latch onto. On my way to the house, one of them charged me on the wooden steps. His ugly fur barely covered his ribs, exposing scabs and open wounds. My calf burned as he bit my leg, tearing a hole in my jeans.

I kicked the dog in the head and yelled, "Go away!" He whimpered and took a few steps back but then joined several others, all of them growling and poised to strike. I bolted through the door.

While Dad, Lonnie, Sally, and I unloaded boxes from the car, Sam threw rocks at the dogs, but that didn't work. Even after Dad kicked them hard, they kept coming.

Inside, the drywall had large cracks and stains. Sheets of shiny pink-orange insulation hung from the ceiling, and beams of sun filtered into the living room through holes in the roof. As we walked into a small hallway, we stirred up clouds of dust from the thick layer of dirt coating the floor. In some places, water had mixed with the dirt, and our shoes left footprints in the semi-dried mud. The flimsy plywood floor buckled under my feet.

The heater didn't work, and it was cold enough to see our breath. We would have been warmer in a tent. There were three tiny bedrooms, and you could hardly turn around in the bathroom. Spiders ran out of the drain in the tub when I turned on the light.

A puny kitchen with peeling linoleum led to the back door and our backyard: a large pit filled with rocks, whiskey bottles, wine jugs, and weeds. Our wooden box didn't have a number. Mail was delivered to PO Box 82. The tribal ledger listed it as house 231.

The ground on Eighth Street was harder than concrete when we arrived, but within days, I learned "Mud Flats" was the right name for the neighborhood. Rain turned the ground into a goopy stew of red clay, garbage, wine bottles, urine, and feces. If Mom had come with us, she would have changed her mind about the sorriest place she'd ever lived.

For the first time, I didn't want to explore. We didn't have anywhere to go except for the school about a mile behind us. Whereas Gallup had expanded my world, Fort Defiance shrank it. Our previous neighbors on South Cliff Drive might not have liked Sam or me, but we had so many fun stores, alleys, and streets to roam through. And, of course, there was Ray Pino.

Here, there was no escape.

Most of the men milled around by the side of the road talking to one another, not working. Endless lines of small children, old men, and women carrying heavy loads shuffled along Kit Carson Drive, their cheeks sunken and their skin chafed by the wind. The older men and women bent over as they walked, weighed down by a sadness that mirrored my own.

The sides of the road were littered with wagon wheels and car parts damaged by all the deep ruts. Gallup seemed rich by comparison, and Albuquerque was a wealthy fantasy from the past. Our part of town had no public facilities except a shuttered aluminum shed with a padlocked garage door and weeds covering the front. Neatly printed on the door in red paint was "Ft. Defiance Fire Station No Parking."

Dad loudly claimed his Cherokee heritage had brought him there to serve his Navajo brethren, but nothing about this poverty-stricken, hostile place made me feel that way. And I'm positive my brother and sisters agreed.

The following Monday, Sam, Sally, and I reported to Tse'hootsooi Elementary School, a Navajo word meaning "the valley between the rocks," an accurate description of Fort Defiance. Lonnie enrolled at Window Rock High School and acquired driving privileges when the BIA gave Dad an old brown Ford sedan to do his safety officer's job. It had a cracked windshield and no hubcaps or front fender, but it had official US government license tags.

Lonnie drove Sally to her kindergarten class in the Rambler and then drove a quarter mile to the Window Rock High School parking lot. Sam and I walked. It never occurred to Lonnie to offer us a ride, and it never occurred to us to ask. We had to get used to living in Mud Flats, and this was the only way to get started.

First came the dogs. As soon as we stepped out of the house, they barreled into our yard and snapped at our legs. We threw rocks at them and kicked them away, scuffing up dirt. Within seconds, our shoes, socks, and pants were filthy. We walked backward to keep the dogs from sneaking up behind and biting us, and they finally took off.

Then, about halfway to school, as we navigated the broken, weed-filled sidewalk on Kit Carson Drive, a stream of Navajo kids left their hogans and trailers. In jeans and cowboy boots, their black hair slicked back with gel, the boys surrounded us in no time. A few walked directly in front of us and slowed down. Others got right behind and bumped into us. They laughed and spoke in Navajo with their mouths full of chewing tobacco. We didn't understand them, but their tone wasn't friendly.

"Let's get out of here," Sam said, breaking through and racing ahead.

I kept walking. If we ran away every day, they'd think we were chicken. Besides, they would eventually catch up with us.

Two older boys jumped in front of me while the others stood at my back. The biggest one shoved me in the chest, and I fell over the guy who had dropped to his hands and knees behind me. I got to my feet and started down the sidewalk again. Taunting me in Navajo, they blocked my path all the way to the flagstone entrance to the school. I had to go into the street to get around them. They shouted in English, "See you after school."

I didn't say a word.

As my tormentors scattered, I looked at the school for the first time. It was much nicer than I expected—shiny corrugated steel walls painted orange, glass doors, and a big blue sign that read "Home of the Papooses." Across the gully was the even nicer high school. They were the only modern buildings around except for the teachers' apartments next door, which were enclosed by a barbed-wire fence similar to the one on the EPNG compounds.

Stumbling into a brightly lit office, I asked where to go for the fifth grade. A large Navajo man stood by the front desk. "I'm Mr. Lee, your principal," he said. "What's your name?" He was a burly guy built like Dad, with the same mean eyes.

When I answered him, he said, "A boy who looks just like you reported for third grade, and a young lady by that last name walked a little girl to her kindergarten classroom."

I nodded. "My brother and sisters."

"I thought so." He didn't smile. "One of our assistants will take you to your class."

The young Navajo woman said, "Welcome, David."

Welcome? That was a joke. As she and I walked down the hall, kids peered out every door with hostile stares, like they all knew I didn't belong in Mud Flats or Fort Defiance.

My new classroom had a blackboard on one side, and on the other were three rows of windows looking out to the rocks and weeds on the playground. Twenty-five Navajo kids gawked at me, two of whom had knocked me down on the way to school, but I spotted a few Anglo faces too. Many of the Navajos slumped down in their seats, their eyes dull and angry. They were too thin, and their clothes were dirty and torn. But a handful of them wore clean, pressed shirts and sat up tall, well-nourished and happy.

A kind, lanky Anglo man got up from behind his desk. His eyelids drooped and fluttered, as if he'd just woken up from a nap. "Welcome. My name is Mr. Aday," he said with a thick Southern drawl. His pants were pleated like a girl's skirt, and he wore the wing-tip shoes I saw on people in newspaper car ads. No one else spoke to me except the cafeteria lady who asked if I wanted a sloppy joe sandwich.

I ate as far away from everyone as I could. And outside during recess, I flattened myself against the building, wanting to disappear.

In the bathroom, on the playground, and in the cafeteria, whenever I left the sight of a teacher, boys pushed, shoved, and punched me. While I used the urinal, a kid crept up behind me and peed on my pant leg. Then he stuck a plug of Red Man chewing tobacco in his mouth, yelled "**bilagáana**" in my face, and strolled out the door.

On the way home, four boys jumped us. Sam dodged them, but they were on me before I had a chance to fight back. They threw me down on an anthill and sat on my arms and legs, pinning me so I couldn't move. My ears and neck burned as big red ants sank their pincers into my skin.

Sam ran up behind the boys and pushed them off me. They wandered away, looking over their shoulders, watching me strain to get to my feet, their laughter echoing in the valley.

• • •

"We have to move back to Gallup," I told Lonnie later that evening when she asked how the first day went. "I can't make it here."

Shrugging her shoulders, she closed her biology book and put it on her bed. "We can't move back," she said. "Dad doesn't want to. He gets housing as part of his job. It's not so bad. At least Mom and Dad aren't fighting."

"I guess you had a better day than Sam and I did."

"Some of the high school boys are nice—and some of the girls too," Lonnie said. "A couple of the girls told me that the meanest boys drop out by ninth grade. When you and Sam get to high school, your life will get better."

"If we live that long."

My escape had always been to roam around town, throw cherry bombs and firecrackers, read and sell newspapers, and talk to people. That was impossible in Mud Flats.

Lonnie made friends quickly and took off to see them whenever she could. Dad wasn't around much either, coming and going at random times. He stockpiled powdered milk, Spam, canned corn, potpies, and cereal for us, so we weren't going to starve. Our tiny shack was the only safe place in town.

In those first days in Mud Flats, Sam, Sally, and I huddled together like scared mice, often under a blanket watching television. Everyone in the shows looked like they were in a snowstorm because the reception was terrible. We had just two channels, but they represented our only outside view of the world.

Mom was always on my mind. I missed her okra and roast beef dinners and her watery iced tea. I missed trying to take care of her too.

I didn't realize how sad Sam, Sally, and I had become until one afternoon when Lonnie and Dad were out. Sam and Sally watched TV in the living room, eating peanut butter sandwiches, while I put a potpie in the oven and turned on the gas. Forty-five minutes later, the oven was still cold and the potpie still frozen. Lighting a match, I opened the oven and reached for the pilot light.

A flame shot out and blasted me to the back of the kitchen and flat onto the floor. The house shook and the windows rattled. Smoke erupted from the dirty oven along with the thick smell of burning gas.

Trying to stand, I fell backward, snapping the screen door off its hinges, and rolled off the stoop and into the ditch in our backyard. I got to my feet and fell backward again. The world kept spinning, my stomach with it, and a million bees buzzed in my head. I gasped and wheezed, but air wouldn't fill my lungs. My face burned.

Sam and Sally flew out the back door, their mouths wide open when they saw me.

"Are you okay?" Sally asked. "Is the house going to blow up?"

I raised my hand to let them know I wasn't going to die. They were quiet for a moment, and then Sam walked over and rubbed my head, pretending to get cut by the sharp edges of my newly frizzed hair. "Ouch," he said, shaking his hand. All three of us started laughing and couldn't stop.

"Your hair looks like a rusted Brillo pad," Sam said. "And your eyebrows are all gone."

Back in the house, he kept yelling "BOOM!" and running through the living room making loud noises that sounded like an explosion. We cracked up again and again.

It was the first time the three of us had laughed together in a long time.

CHAPTER 21

At the end of our first week of school, I walked into the house feeling relieved I didn't have to face the bullies or the dogs again until Monday. Dad stood inside the door, home early from work. "Get in the car," he said to me. "You and I are leaving for Gallup."

The urgency in his voice made my stomach churn. He had promised us we'd all go with him to Gallup the next day when he shopped for groceries, so what was this about? He was agitated and angry, pushing me outside. After telling Lonnie, Sam, and Sally we would be gone for a few hours, he and I got in the Rambler and took off in silence, his eyes bugged out and the Y vein pulsing on his forehead. As his chest puffed, he began twitching and arguing with himself.

I asked repeatedly why just the two of us were headed back to Gallup, but he didn't answer. He acted like I wasn't in the car.

The sun hung low in the sky when he parked on

South Cliff Drive across from our old house. Where was Mom now? Surely, she would have left after coming back to the empty house.

Dad pulled out a pair of binoculars and slowly scanned from one corner of our old living room window to the other. He continuously adjusted the knob, studying the house for what seemed like an hour, though it couldn't have been more than ten minutes.

"Sneak in and see if your mother is there," he said. "I need to know. And don't get caught."

Dad obviously thought she was inside, but how? Did he think she was dead? I didn't want to find out.

"Get moving." He shoved me against the passenger door.

Scurrying across the street, I hoped no one would see me. My friend Billy lived next door, but I never wanted to see him or his family again. Through a side window, his mother had watched us slink away like burglars in the night. I'll never forget her angry eyes. She hated Dad, and I didn't blame her. I hated him too.

The heavy wooden garage door was ajar, and I pulled it open. My heart sank at the sight of Mom's broken-down brown Ford station wagon inside. She had to be there, and if she was alive, she'd be in terrible shape, trying to make do in the cold, empty house.

What would I say if she saw me? Sorry for ditching you? If I found her dead, I knew I'd have killed her by breaking her heart. I wanted to run at full speed through the streets of Gallup away from all of it. Maybe Mr. Pino would let me live in his storage room.

I opened the basement door and waited for my eyes to adjust to the dark. When I could see the familiar green-and-black checkerboard tiles on the floor, I slowly tiptoed up the stairs, trying not to make the steps creak. As I crept softly into the living room, I prayed it was empty, but I knew better.

The late-afternoon light through the window gave me a clear view of Mom slumped in the corner, her clothes piled where Dad had left them on the dirty mattress. Her face was contorted in pain. She raised her head but didn't seem to see me, her vacant eyes showing no emotion. Until that moment, I hadn't known the look of complete hopelessness.

My arms and legs felt too heavy to move. I fell to my knees, crying.

Her eyes came alive when she realized I was there, and she struggled to her feet. I forced myself to stand and walk toward her, stepping around the mattress and pile of clothes.

She put her arms around me. "Don't leave . . . me . . . this . . . way," she said, holding my shirt and neck tight. "You're my oldest boy . . . protect me . . . I need you!"

"I'm . . . mm . . . so . . . so . . . sorry," I blubbered into her shoulder.

Mom's tears soaked my shirt as we stood holding each other.

Suddenly the hair rose on the back of my neck, the same way it had in Albuquerque when Dad found Mom with his hidden mail. I turned to see him standing inches behind me, his face swollen with fury. For once I didn't care. Nothing he did to me could be worse than what I had just experienced.

"Shit, you couldn't even do the one simple thing I asked," he said, yanking me from Mom's arms. He shoved her aside, but she didn't fall. She grabbed my shirt to pull me from him, but he jerked me away harder, tearing my shirt.

"Thurston, let me at least have David. Please."

"Thelma Lou, get out of this house. Now. Go to the nut house or to your whore mother, but get the hell out of here. We don't want you."

Dad dragged me to the front door. Mom tumbled to the floor, crying and shaking, her arms and legs sprawled. If grief could have killed her, she'd have been dead. I wondered if she might be better off dead and hated myself for the thought.

Still gripping my arm, Dad marched across the street and shoved me into the Rambler. He went around to the driver's side, started the engine, and whacked the side of my head with his fist. A ringing jolt rattled my ears as my head bounced off the passenger window. I was too numb to feel it.

"You'll never be much of a man. I should leave you with her, you goddamn coward."

Dad had that right: I **was** a coward. What else would you call a son who wouldn't protect his completely helpless mother? I lacked the moral fiber to stand up to him—and to help her. A better son would have stayed.

When we got home, my siblings didn't ask where we'd been, and I didn't tell them.

Something broke inside me that day.

Many nights afterward, I dreamed of Mom. She would beg me for help, but Dad would smash her face to pieces before I could save her. In other dreams, Dad would hit Mom and she'd fall to the floor. By the time I reached her, she would be dead from the blow. Then I'd look up, and Dad would be pointing a gun at my head.

Dad didn't believe in God, but I did. The most frightening nightmare of all was hearing God say, "You won't be forgiven for hurting your mother. You're a lost cause."

Waking up, I'd always ask for a second chance.

When Dad was around, he often had whiskey on his breath and told us about the women he'd been dating. He was shopping for our new mother, he said. I couldn't imagine who would want that job.

If Dad was happy working with his Navajo brethren in Fort Defiance, he didn't show it. "Most of those morons couldn't find their ass without two maps and a compass," he said, shaking his head.

"Why don't you get another job?"

He shot me one of his ugly looks. "Get it into that thick skull of yours—we're staying put."

I didn't think he paid attention to our physical appearance, but one night when he came home for dinner, he stared at me across the table for several minutes. He had long been used to seeing my glasses reshaped by electrical tape—he refused to buy me a new pair no matter how broken they were—so I knew he was fixated on something else: the bruises and bumps under my eyes and on my lips and the scrapes on my ears. "You're getting the crap beat out of you on a regular basis, aren't you, boy?" he said. "Come over here."

I kept my eyes down as Dad pulled my head up and rubbed his thumbs over my cheeks. He wasn't trying to comfort me. He was taking measure of how many times I'd been hit.

Puffing up his chest, he grabbed me by the shoulders. "Look at me," he said. "You better figure out how to defend yourself because we aren't going anywhere."

He didn't have to say more. I saw it all over his face: How could the son of a full-blooded Cherokee be such a wimp?

Dad had taught me to probe for weaknesses and find an advantage in any situation. Nothing so far. Most of the trailer and hogan kids dipped snuff, smoked cigarettes, drank whiskey, and got at least one girl pregnant before dropping out of school after eighth grade. Some kids in my class were one or more years older than I was and as tough as Dad had been at the same age. They roamed in gangs at night, fighting rivals over territory or a girl or whiskey, sometimes killing one another.

There was no way to intimidate them or turn them into friends.

Except for Henry. At lunch on my third day at Tse'hootsooi Elementary, as I sat in the corner of the cafeteria trying to be invisible, one of the well-dressed Navajo boys in my class had come over to me.

"Hey, you're the new guy. What's your name?"

He was big and strong and had a warm smile. I had spotted him on the playground laughing with everyone. Even the meanest hogan kids seemed to like him. Still, I'd felt nervous. Why would he want to be my friend? I didn't have much to offer him.

"I'm Henry," he said, motioning for me to join him at his table.

Since then, we'd been walking to class together

and telling each other jokes. He said I could come over to his house in Window Rock sometime. When I was with him, the other kids left me alone.

But when Henry wasn't around, I didn't have a single protector. Though Sam had been my fearless ally in the pranks we pulled in Gallup, he had no desire to do anything in Mud Flats other than outrun the bullies and survive.

"At least Sam isn't getting his ass kicked," Dad said. "Why don't you fight back? Beat their asses one at a time?"

"These kids roam in packs. They shoot BBs and pellets at us that sting almost as bad as the dog bites." I winced inside—Dad wouldn't care.

"Do something. Stop being a coward," he said, as if the abuse was my fault. "I'll buy you a .22-caliber rifle, and the next time they give you shit, just shoot them."

I didn't know how to turn the Navajo boys into friends, but trying to kill them didn't seem like a good solution.

When we heard a soft knock late one afternoon, I thought I was hearing things. But then it happened again. Sam, Sally, and I looked at each other on the couch, our eyes wide. No one had come to our house since we moved to Mud Flats. I opened the door slowly and saw the friendly face of an elderly Navajo woman.

Nothing could have surprised me more. Heavyset, her gray hair in a tight bun, she wore a traditional red velvet full skirt and black blouse and lots of turquoise jewelry on her wrists and fingers. I recognized her as the woman I'd seen coming and going from the rusted trailer across the street.

"I been watching. Think you need help," she said. "I Evelyn." She smiled and leaned forward, scanning the living room behind me. "Where your mother? Why you here?"

It took a while to understand her broken English, but I felt her concern from that first instant. Her bright brown eyes exuded greater warmth than I'd ever seen.

"I help make dinner." She walked into the house and moved from room to room like part of our family. "You do homework."

If there was a God, he must have sent this angel of a woman to us. For the first time in forever, a blanket of calm fell over the house.

Sam, Sally, and I saw her every day after that.

"What learn in school?" she would ask.

"The bullies beat me up, and the dogs keep biting us," I said, showing her the holes in my pants and the cuts on my face.

"I wash off blood, shoo dogs and bullies," Evelyn would say with a smile.

One afternoon, she held me in her arms, stroking my hair as I told her things I'd kept bottled inside. "We ditched Mom, and Dad beats us with a belt buckle . . ."

I rattled off all kinds of dirty Crow secrets and then felt ashamed.

Every day at school, I'd get attacked on the playground and punch and kick back, but I never won. It seemed like all the tough kids knew they'd found an easy mark. As I walked to class with fresh cuts and bruises, fighting the tears, I'd think about Evelyn and her smiling eyes and the way her tongue clicked when she pronounced English words and I'd start to feel better.

Sometimes in bed at night, I worried she might not come again. But each day, the second we got home, Evelyn appeared. She was the first adult who truly loved me—she cared for me without wanting anything back. I knew that whatever happened, she'd be on my side.

Sally and Sam loved her too. The tension drained from our shack as soon as Evelyn walked inside. I never told her I loved her because I was afraid she wouldn't say it back, but I think she knew.

Evelyn would tell us stories about the Long Walk,

known as the "fearing time," after the Navajos lost the war against Kit Carson.

"When Grandma little girl, she live near here. Soldiers round up Navajo people, force them walk many miles. Can't walk fast enough as soldiers on horses. They fall. Soldiers shoot them. Food full of maggots and worms. Many starve. Apaches kill many too. Navajo people prisoners for four years. Walk home to sacred place. Everything in God's plan."

How could she forgive what had happened to her people? And how could she be so kindhearted? I didn't understand. She filled the house with noisy laughter. She told us to have **hozhoni** (harmony) and show **ajooba** (kindness) because those things will return to you. She even offered to walk us to school.

"I beat up bullies," she'd say. I think she might have really done it.

On our way to school one morning near the end of March, an older, muscular Navajo boy strode alongside me as I was being bumped and shoved. Everyone moved away immediately.

"I'm Tommy," he said with a smile, towering over me. "What grade are you in?"

"Fifth."

I figured I was about to get the crap stomped out

of me. I braced myself, keeping my body between him and Sam so my little brother could make a quick getaway.

But Tommy continued talking as if we were old friends. Other hogan and trailer kids deferred to him, and no one bothered Sam or me.

When we arrived at school, Tommy said, "Come by my trailer anytime. I live on Seventh Street." He took a couple of steps toward his classroom and then stopped and looked over his shoulder. "Hey, what's your name?"

"David Crow."

"**Gáagii**." He nodded. "That's a good name. See you, **Gáagii**."

"What's **gáagii**?" Sam asked before we had to go in opposite directions in the hallway.

"I don't know. Henry will tell me." By that time, he and I had become good buddies.

Mr. Aday was at his desk, the roll book open and ready. He reminded me of Ward Cleaver, always calm and patient.

Henry came into the room right behind me. "What does **gáagii** mean?" I asked him.

"It means 'crow' in Navajo. Why?"

I told him about Tommy walking to school with Sam and me.

Henry's eyebrows shot up. "Tommy? He runs the

toughest gang in Fort Defiance. He can beat up anybody, and no one messes with him." Henry slapped me on the back. "Cool. I'll call you **Gáagii** too."

"It sounds better than **Bilagáana.**" I sat at my desk next to Henry's. "What does that mean?"

Grinning, he said, "**Bilagáana** is a bad word for white man."

"Yeah. **Gáagii** is way better." We both laughed.

With Evelyn, Henry, and Tommy on my side, life seemed a little brighter.

CHAPTER 22

"Get in the car, boys."

Somehow Dad had figured out where to find us. Without a word to anyone, Sam and I had grabbed our jackets and taken off that Saturday morning, running up the dirt road that zigzagged to the big silver water tower overlooking Canyon Bonito. My brother liked to throw rocks against "Fort Defiance" stenciled in black letters near the top, making a dull thud that echoed around us.

Sam spotted Dad's brown sedan in the distance, the exhaust billowing white in the cold air, and I groaned. We were in trouble or Dad needed something. Either way, our fun was about to end.

"David and I are going on a special trip," Dad said as we got in the back seat and he turned the car around.

"Can I go too?" Sam asked.

"No. Not this time."

"Why not? It isn't fair. I never get to go." He crossed his arms and thumped back against the seat.

"When you're older."

That was a lie. Dad was up to something, and he knew Sam would blab about it, even if he threatened him with a beating. I would have gladly let him take my place.

After we dropped Sam off at home, I moved to the front seat next to Dad. At Kit Carson Drive, he took a right and headed north.

"I need your help," he said. "And no one can know what we're doing, especially your brother and sisters."

He didn't elaborate, switching to a lecture about avocados and how they could cure any disease. "Only the Cherokees are aware of this," he said, slicing the air with his large hand. "And sugar and salt are the deadliest killers. The sons of bitches doctors know all about it, but they make so much money off idiots that they keep their mouths shut."

Dad ranted on, lowering his voice while his head shook and lips twitched. I could make out only a few words. His arms bulged and his forehead vein popped out, but he seemed more excited than angry.

What was he going to make me do?

In an hour or so, Dad turned onto a long dirt road that ended at a Quonset hut. A fat padlock hung from the door next to a small sign: "US Department of the Interior, BIA." No one was around, and an endless landscape of rock and cactus stretched in all directions.

"Why are we here?" I asked.

Dad looked at me with a smile. "Because this is where the loot is stored." He backed the car up to the door.

"The loot?"

"Tools—expensive tools—that we're going to sell for some folding green. Since the white man stole this land from the Indians and gave them a little bit of money and the worthless BIA, we're going to steal some of the power tools and sell them to greedy Mexicans who can find buyers. It's quite simple really, and no one will ever know."

"Why do you need me?"

"To be my lookout man. And I want to teach you how to make some easy cash."

He scanned the horizon. "How long since we've seen someone?"

"Huh? I don't know. I think a truck might have passed us before we turned down this road."

"What color was it? How many people were in it? Did they look like police, BIA workers, or Navajos that might live nearby?"

I shook my head. "I don't remember."

"When I ask you these things, boy, you better have answers—it might mean the difference between swiping enough to make a good profit and going to jail. You don't want to go to jail, do you?"

I knew not to challenge Dad. He'd just call me stupid and stay mad at me a long time. Being in the car with him when he was angry was like getting beat up in a phone booth—there was no escape.

"You stand next to the car while I go inside," he said, leaning over and sticking his face in mine. "And don't get any bright ideas about following me. Watch the road, and if you see anyone, throw a large rock close to the door. If I don't come, pelt the building as hard as you can. It will make a hell of a racket against the aluminum. We're far enough away from the highway that this will work."

Dad checked the horizon again. "Okay, we're good. Let's go." He hurried out of the car, removed the padlock with a key from his bulky key chain, and opened the door.

I lined up a few rocks on the hood and then stuck my hands in my pockets and stared at the vast scenery. I would much rather have been fighting the Navajos at school. I shivered, sweat trickling down my back.

Within minutes, Dad came back to the car with electric saws, screwdrivers, and crescent wrenches and tossed them into the trunk. "See anything?" he asked.

I shook my head, and he hustled back to retrieve as many tools as the trunk would hold. It seemed like an eternity before he closed the door and locked the padlock. He slammed the trunk and we sped off.

"Won't the workers miss the tools?" I asked.

"No, they won't even notice they're gone. I left lots of them behind. The BIA idiots buy these tools in mass quantities and don't keep good records. And they move them from warehouse to warehouse. I'll meet some of my Mexican partners in Gallup on Monday after work. They'll sell them to gas stations and construction crews who don't ask questions about where they come from. There's a big market for that in Gallup. I'll bring you on those trips in the future, but for now we need to hightail it home."

On our way back, we stopped at a gas station, and both of us went inside to use the bathroom. Two men were arguing, and their voices got loud.

"You bumped me, you little Mexican bastard," the big guy said.

The short guy shook his head. "It was an accident."

"Let's take it outside, and I'll kick your ass."

"Look, I didn't mean to bump you. Forget it, will you?"

The big guy got in the short guy's face. "You have a big mouth. I need to teach you a lesson." He raised his fists.

The short guy stepped back, put his hands in the air, and hurried out the door.

When we got in the sedan, Dad asked me, "Which guy do you think was right?"

"The short guy. The big guy just wanted to start a fight."

"You're right. The guy who left should have killed him."

"**Killed** him? But he was smaller and not as strong. Besides, it was a stupid argument."

"That's why a man should always carry a gun. That bigger bastard would be no match for Smith and Wesson. When some asshole gets too loud, the smaller man needs to find a way to shut him up. I've never met a man I couldn't beat, but sometimes there's more than one."

"Who are Smith and Wesson?"

He threw his head back and laughed. "Only the makers of the most powerful handguns in the world. They are the great equalizers."

"Would you have shot him?"

"Hell yes. I love ridding the world of assholes. I've been doing it ever since I was in the navy."

"But don't you worry about getting caught or even getting shot?"

"No one will ever get the drop on me. I've beaten a few bastards to death. When I was in New Orleans at the end of basic training, I got into a fight with some loudmouthed son of a bitch who said he was a better boxer than I was. After the bar closed and everyone was gone, we settled it in the alley."

"What do you mean?"

"I beat the living shit out of him. They found his body the next day. None of the guys squealed. Nobody cares about these bastards, but after that, I made sure there were no witnesses—someone's liable to pop off and finger you. Like when I was in the Q and put a shiv in the lifer cons who had it coming. No one ever saw me."

Dad's head twitched, and he talked to himself nonstop until we got home.

CHAPTER 23

As the weeks passed, the poundings at school continued. They usually began with a kid knocking books out of my hands or kicking or tripping me. I had to fight back or the bullying would only get worse. And Dad expected me to retaliate, warning me that if I didn't learn how to defend myself, he'd beat me harder than the Navajos did.

The nice Anglo missionary kids got the crap stomped out of them too. I felt sorry for them. But I was different. I was a Cherokee. When the Navajos realized that, they would stop fighting me.

I thought back to the Navajo families I used to watch at the Hubbell Trading Post. The shy kids would cringe and stare at their feet when anyone talked to them, like many of the hogan and trailer kids in Fort Defiance. It occurred to me that if I embarrassed the biggest, strongest Navajo hogan kid in my class, maybe everyone would leave me alone for fear they'd be next.

I found the perfect target: Gilbert Blackgoat. He had started school late and was three years older, four inches taller, and twenty pounds heavier than me. His English was poor. He shoved me whenever he had a chance. A girl in my class said he had a wife and would drop out of school after eighth grade to raise sheep with his dad.

Gilbert had to be the shiest kid in Fort Defiance. His eyes never left his feet. If I took him on, everyone would respect me.

Every day I tried to figure out how to embarrass him, but nothing came to me. Then a gift of gigantic proportions arrived at school—a brand-new **bilagáana** to replace my sick homeroom teacher.

"Hi, I'm Miss Smith," she said, a short, plump Anglo woman in a flowered dress who didn't look much older than Lonnie. She was from Arkansas and wore too much makeup and perfume.

"This is my first time on an Indian reservation, and I'm excited to be here. I'll study this chart to help me learn your names." She held up a sheet with squares representing our desks. "Please raise your hand and correct me if I pronounce your name wrong."

The class snickered as she butchered most of the names—Begay, Yazzie, Deschine, Todacheenie, and Wauneka, among others. When she finished roll call, she said, "Now we're going to have a contest to select the class princess. Write down your favorite girl's name on a piece of paper, and I'll pass around a cigar box. I'll announce the winner on Friday."

Our naive new teacher gazed at the silent faces, her eyes hopeful as she tried to connect with her students. "This will give me a chance to learn more of the girls' names. I'll work to get to know the boys too."

Her last comment got my attention. I knew what to do. When the bell rang and everyone left for the next period, I raced out with the other kids and then sneaked back in before Miss Smith returned. I had about five minutes to remove a majority of the names from the cigar box and replace them with just one: Shirley Gilbert Blackgoat.

By that time, I had gained a reputation for my pranks, having upped my game from Gallup. In between periods, when the classrooms were empty, I rummaged through the teachers' desks and took test answers, markers, BIC pens, glue, tape, chalk, rubber bands. I'd squirt glue in girls' hair, run markers down their arms, and yank their ponytails. They would make faces at me and giggle. I even picked on boys who could beat the crap out of me.

Sometimes I'd hide an eraser in my pocket to save for later. Throwing a chalk-filled eraser at someone's head was always good for a laugh. It was also lots of fun snapping rubber bands through the air into a girl's hair. I would launch paper airplanes too, often choosing the teacher's head as my target. "You brat, keep it up and I'm sending you to the principal's office," they'd say, and the class would crack up.

For variety, I used my peashooter and fired tiny pebbles at the kids' ears. No one had better aim. If my shooter wore out or was confiscated, I replaced it with a straw. Other times, I pulled out a small water pistol and squirted my classmates in the neck.

Of course, the principal and I got to know each other very well. But nothing he said or did ever deterred me. I was on a mission, constantly looking for ways to cause some mischief, get a few laughs—and ease the sadness I felt all the time.

When Friday came, Miss Smith counted the ballots at her desk. Smiling, she scanned the class. "Which one of you is Shirley Gilbert Blackgoat? I don't see her on the seating chart." She waited for a proud Navajo girl to raise her hand, but the class burst out laughing instead.

Gilbert's head dropped to his desk, and his shoulders hunched. Suddenly he jumped up from his chair, his fists clenched. He knew who did it. No one else would have pulled something like that. I braced myself as Gilbert turned red and erupted like a volcano. He flew over to my desk and knocked me to the floor.

"Kill you, **Gáagii**. I pound you."

He straddled my scrawny chest and punched me like a jackhammer, getting in some good hits before I managed to get my hands in front of my face. Henry laughed the hardest, as did my new friend Jim, a Menominee Indian whose father worked for the BIA in Window Rock.

"Stop!" Miss Smith yelled.

Gilbert froze midswing.

Our teacher stood over us with her hands on her hips. "Apologize to David. There seems to be a misunderstanding."

Without saying a word, Gilbert got to his feet and walked back to his desk, his fists still clenched. His head looked like it had sunk into his chest. Miss Smith knew enough not to force him to say he was sorry. When class ended, he chased me down the hall, but I was fast, sliding into my next class before he could catch me. Students began calling him Princess Shirley.

Classmates, even guys I thought hated me, came up to me and said, "Did good, **Gáagii**."

But not everyone found my humor amusing, and most of the hogan and trailer kids still jumped me on the walk home from school. I had a long way to go before the bullies left me alone.

• • •

That afternoon, when Dad got home from work, he asked about the dried blood on my purple cheek. I told him how I'd made Gilbert the class princess.

Dad shook his head. "No son of mine is going to be the butt of Navajo beatings just to get along."

After dinner, he sat next to me on the old red couch and draped his arm around me. It was the first time he had touched me without hitting me since we moved to Fort Defiance. Sam plopped down on the floor to watch television, and Sally joined him.

"Instead of making fun of Gilbert," Dad said, "why don't you fight him like a man? It's the only thing that works with bullies. I'll teach you to box so you can defend yourself. You know, we have papers that prove we're Cherokees. If you stood up for your heritage, the kids would respect you. You act like you don't believe you're an Indian."

I knew we were Cherokees—Dad had told us from my first memory. But I was a defective one. Sam was already two inches taller than I was and a lot stronger. Boxing lessons might help, since embarrassing Gilbert wasn't enough to stop me from getting clobbered. "I want to beat up the bullies, Dad. I want to be tough like you."

"Good. I'm glad you're finally figuring out how to survive here. When we're finished, you'll be able to outbox Gilbert—or anybody for that matter." He puffed out his chest and raised his fists, the way I'd seen him mimic boxers many times. "Gilbert doesn't know how to fight. All he's doing is hitting you, and you're a sitting target."

He stood and removed his shirt to get ready to spar with me. Flexing his chest muscles, he pulled up his fists and punched into the air. I stared at the cold glow of his blue eyes below the crisscrossed lines on his forehead and couldn't believe he was my father. He was powerful and mean. I was weak and spineless.

"You're scared, and bullies sense fear," he said. "Throw the first punch so hard, the bully will run away. No one will expect it—not from you."

We walked into the backyard and cleared some weeds and rocks inside the crater. Dad kicked a dog in the throat when he lunged at him. Sam followed behind, throwing rocks at the other dogs to keep them away, and Sally watched through the newly repaired screen door.

"Jab with your left and punch with your right," Dad said, demonstrating with his fists in the air. "Move your head back and forth so it isn't an easy target. You want to keep your opponent off balance."

For two weeks, the lessons continued daily in the backyard while Sam looked on, laughing most of the time. I grew more confident, trotting to my right, swinging at Dad's palms. My blows were getting more accurate, making him smile and nod.

"Tell the bastard you're the superior Indian," he

said. "I want to be proud of you, damn it, but I can't. Your little brother is bigger, stronger, and faster than you. Sam would whip your ass if he wasn't afraid of what you'd do to get even."

For sure, I could trick anyone and tell funny stories. But that wouldn't help me with Gilbert, no matter how determined I was.

After each lesson, I imagined myself in a canvas ring, wearing Everlast shorts and boxing shoes, fighting for a large purse in front of all the pretty girls in the arena. As I took off a silk robe, the fans cheered and chanted, "Crow, Crow, Crow." In every dream, Violet sat ringside waiting to give me a kiss.

Believing in Dad and in myself gave me new courage. Before long, my footwork got faster and more varied. "Move to your left, now to your right, drop your head, step into the punch," he shouted. I started surprising Dad with my punches, nailing his chest or gut before he could block me. When he'd try to punch me back, I'd block his arm. I worried he'd get mad, but he praised me instead. Our boxing lessons were the closest I ever felt to my dad.

When Lonnie watched the boxing lessons, she said, "You can't beat up everyone who bullies you. You need to make friends with them."

"It won't work," I said. "The kids in my class don't believe we're Cherokee, and they crush Anglos. Dad's right—I have to prove myself."

CHAPTER 24

About a month before school ended for the summer, Dad pulled Lonnie and me into his bedroom and closed the door. He was as angry as ever.

"Your crazy mother got help from my asshole boss at Woodmen in Albuquerque. He gave her money and got her a room and a job as a waitress at a truck stop. And then the do-gooder son of a bitch helped her get a lawyer to fight me in court."

So Mom was okay. I was careful not to let Dad see how relieved I was. In fact, it sounded like she was a lot better off than if she'd stayed with us. Maybe her broken nerves were getting fixed. At least she was fighting back against Dad and trying to make a life for herself.

"I'll bet she whines constantly about having to work. I need you both to testify that she's an unfit mother." His deep-set eyes narrowed at me. "David, you need to tell the judge she threw a knife at you and it barely missed. That'll finish off the crazy bitch.

You won't ever have to see her again, and I won't ever have to give her a goddamn nickel."

Hurting Mom again wasn't what I had in mind.

I wanted to make things right. I wanted to tell the judge that Mom wasn't to blame for throwing the knife and that she could be fit if she got a lot of help for her nerves. My testimony wouldn't bring her back to live with us no matter how many good things I said, but I wanted to show her I loved her.

On the morning of the trial, Dad, Lonnie, and I got into the Rambler and took off for the courthouse in Gallup. Under any other circumstances, I would have been grateful to miss school. Not that day.

Dad and his attorney escorted Lonnie and me into a large room, where Mom waited with her attorney and the judge. She wore a new dress, and her hair was combed and sprayed into place. It stunned me to see her so ready to defend herself against Dad, even though she didn't stand a chance.

Mom held her composure under questioning—at first. She sat up straight in her chair next to the judge and held her head high, promising to tell the whole truth and looking more confident than I ever remembered. I wanted to go hug her and tell her she looked nice, but I didn't dare while Dad was watching.

Mom's attorney asked Lonnie if Dad tried to make Mom leave by being mean to her. She didn't answer. "If your mom had the proper financial help," he continued, "do you think she could handle the four Crow children?"

Lonnie sobbed and shook her head.

The judge asked Mom to leave the room, and her attorney started questioning me. The judge must have realized I wouldn't say anything in front of her. But I never did answer the questions. I stammered a few unintelligible noises and nothing more. If I said Mom was good and could take care of us, the judge might make Sam, Sally, and me live with her. Mom couldn't handle that. And Dad wouldn't allow it. My brother and sister didn't want to go back with Mom either. And they'd never leave Lonnie—neither would I.

I couldn't put us all through another fight that would end like the final days on South Cliff Drive.

When Dad's attorney asked about the knife-throwing incident, I told him I'd been terrible that day. "I pushed her over the edge," I said. "All of us tried to break her down—it wasn't her fault."

He stared at his white pad, furiously taking notes. Then he asked if Mom could take care of us.

I shook my head and cried. I might as well have stuck that knife into her heart.

He stopped the questioning.

The judge said he would make a final decision the following week. I knew he would rule against Mom.

As we walked out of the courtroom, I wondered how I could ever face her again. I hoped she had already gone home, but when we entered the hallway, there she was with her attorney.

She stared straight at me. Her expression morphed into a deep sadness, and she sobbed so hard I thought she'd collapse. Mascara streaked down her cheeks. She slowly walked outside, shaking and crying. Before getting in her attorney's car, she turned back to me.

"Your daddy did me dirty," she said.

And I'd done her dirty too. Nothing she or the courts could do would change that. Dad's law was stronger.

A week later, the trial still weighed heavily on me. But in my day-to-day life, survival was my immediate problem. Summer vacation would start soon, and I wanted all the bullies to see me beating Gilbert before then. Worried about losing my nerve, I flicked his ears when walking by his desk in homeroom. "Gil-l-l-l-l-l-bert . . . bah . . . bah . . . Blackgoat . . . Navajo princess."

He jumped up to go after me, and everyone in class started laughing—except for Miss Smith.

"Stop that right now," she said. "Get back to your seats or I'm sending you to the principal's office."

Gilbert and I stared at each other with narrowed

eyes and slowly went to our desks. After class, he bumped me in the hallway, and I shoved his shoulder hard.

"I'm Cherokee, and I can kick your ass."

Gilbert grinned. "See you after lunch, **Gáagii**."

Even though making Gilbert challenge me is what I wanted, my stomach felt queasy the rest of the morning. What had I done? Could I really beat him? Dad said I had mastered the basic skills, and once the fight got going, my superior Cherokee breeding would kick in. "Trust me," he said. "I'm always right."

At recess, I went to the far corner of the playground where all the fights took place. Arriving first, I shadowboxed to get ready. Moments later, Gilbert walked up with most of our classmates behind him. He looked angrier and more powerful than I'd remembered. His brown eyes glowed as he curled both hands into tight fists and waited for me to make the first move.

More and more people gathered around us. Soon most of the school had shown up to watch.

I put up my fists, moved my head from side to side, rolled to the balls of my feet, and said, "Let's go." Circling Gilbert, I puffed my chest, flexed my arms, and shadow punched. A few of the girls giggled and the boys laughed. Gilbert broke into a broad grin. I think he thought this was another **Gáagii** trick.

I bobbed my head, moved to his right, and stared

him down. His smile fell, and his face got serious. Maybe I scared him shitless after all. I shuffled my feet and swung hard for his outstretched chin. Gilbert blocked my right hand easily with his left. As I pulled my arm back to get ready for my next punch, his right fist whistled through the air like an arrow to a bull's-eye. Both lenses popped out of my glasses, my nose spurted blood, and I looked up at him from the dirt. Shaking off the hit, I got to my feet and punched him on the shoulder.

His next blow crunched my jaw. I went down like a fat kid on a seesaw. Pain blasted through my skull. The coppery taste of blood flowed down my throat as I stumbled to my feet. Before I could regain my balance, he knocked me down again, falling on top of me, pinning my arms under his knees.

Staring upward, I spotted the fuzzy outline of Sam's white face in a sea of brown ones. His grin turned into a frown. Now I understood why he laughed at Dad's boxing lessons. He knew my strength and size were no match for Gilbert. I struggled to get free, but it was useless.

"You little shit . . . not Indian."

"Am too."

"You lie."

He held his fist in the air, ready to strike, the way Dad had held his belt in Gallup when I told him the Genghis Khan story. As blood continued to flow out of my mouth, I could tell Gilbert didn't want to hit me again.

"Okay. I'm not Indian." I would have agreed with anything he said, even if he had called me a girl.

"Told ya." He climbed off me and walked away.

The crowd dispersed.

"You're crazy, **Gáagii**." Henry grabbed my arm and helped me to my feet. Jim shook his head and turned toward the noon-duty teacher rushing over.

"What happened?" asked the stocky Navajo woman. "There's blood all over you. Did Gilbert do this?"

"He didn't do anything."

She placed her hand on my shoulder. "I can't help you if you won't tell me the truth."

"I'm fine."

"Go to the school nurse and then tell the principal. He'll punish Gilbert for this."

What total bullshit. No one would have taken my side, nor should they have. I walked toward the bathroom. She yelled behind me, but I kept going.

Leaning over the sink, I squinted into the mirror. My right eye was swollen shut. My face throbbed so much I thought I'd see it pulsing. Blood oozed from my lips and dripped from my nose, and a purple bruise outlined my jaw. With a wet paper towel, I dabbed at my nose, mouth, and lips, every touch bringing fresh pain.

Though Gilbert was wrong about me not being an Indian, he sure as hell proved I was no boxer.

By the time the bell rang, I had cleaned off most of the blood and dirt, but I still looked like Frankenstein. I popped the lenses back into my glasses and carefully slipped them over my nose.

It took every ounce of courage to go face my classmates. Forcing my feet to the door of my room, I paused in the almost empty hallway before walking inside. Everyone's eyes followed me to my seat, except for Gilbert's. He kept his head down.

"Are you all right?" the teacher asked.

"Yes." I smiled gamely, but, no, I definitely wasn't all right.

"Tell me who did this to you."

"No one," I said.

When I glanced around the room at all the hogan and trailer kids, I couldn't believe what I saw. Their expressions were full of admiration. They respected the effort, while others probably thought I was a complete idiot.

No one bothered me on my walk home that afternoon.

When I entered the kitchen, Sally's mouth dropped. "What the heck happened to you?"

"Gilbert," I said.

Sam chuckled. "Dad's boxing lessons didn't help. I saw the whole thing."

"Not a bit," I said. We all laughed hard, though it hurt my face.

"You barely got in a punch before he creamed you."

Sally handed me a glass of water and put her arm around me. We heard the front door creak and turned to see Evelyn coming into the house. She froze when she saw me. Her big brown eyes looked frightened. Sally scurried to her room, and Sam went into the living room to turn on the TV.

Evelyn let out a heavy sigh. "Come with me, David." In the bathroom, she wet a washcloth and gently wiped away the remaining dirt on my face. "You should not fight bad boys." She kissed my forehead. "Why you fight?"

I didn't answer—I didn't know how else to survive in Fort Defiance.

When Dad came home, he looked at me with disgust. The two of us sat at the kitchen table, and I waited for him to say something. Sam and Sally sat on the couch and watched us out of the corners of their eyes. Lonnie soon joined them.

"Why didn't you teach Gilbert a lesson?" Dad said to me. "I taught you how to fight. What's wrong with you? How do you expect to grow up to be a man?"

I didn't answer as tears rolled down my cheeks.

"I told you to swing hard and first."

"I . . . I . . . did," I stammered. "But he hit me hard and knocked me down again and again."

Dad's serious face broke into a wide grin. "I knew that once Gilbert swung, you'd drop like a sack of shit."

Lonnie, Sam, and Sally had heard every word. They all broke out laughing, and I laughed too, though it wasn't funny to me.

After that, life in Mud Flats got a little better. Some of the high school boys still gave me trouble, but the kids in my class left me alone. Gilbert and I had come to an understanding.

And I never picked another fight.

CHAPTER 25

Most days that summer, Sam and I escaped into the hills. We would peer out the front window to make sure none of the older hogan or trailer kids were nearby, and then we'd dash out, fill our pockets with rocks to fight the dogs, and run. We played catch or tormented the snakes and lizards. Sometimes we wandered into the arroyos.

Occasionally a rock or a shot from a BB gun would whiz by our heads, or a Coke bottle with thick glass would hit hard. It always meant we hadn't looked around carefully enough. We started walking backward to check if we were being followed. I eventually got better at detecting pursuers despite my poor eyesight and hearing.

By that time, Dad was ordering me to get in the car almost every Saturday. "We need to run some errands," he'd say after breakfast, using his code phrase for stealing and selling. Lonnie, Sam, and Sally had no idea what we were doing.

As we drove off one hot morning in July, he said, "You and I are going to requisition tools from Uncle Ulysses S. Bia in Shiprock today."

That was Dad's running joke—playing around with the USBIA letters—as though everyone stole from the United States Bureau of Indian Affairs and it was no big deal. We were common thieves, and it made me feel dirty to help him and listen to how unfair the world had been to him and his red parents.

After stopping to gas up his sedan, Dad drove down Kit Carson Drive and then north on Indian Route 12 toward our destination, a full BIA warehouse. He always knew when a new shipment of tools had arrived. Since warehouses were spread all over, we were often gone most of the day.

We drove for an hour in silence while I watched for roadrunners to dash through the desert. Without warning, Dad pulled over to the shoulder of the two-lane highway. At first, I thought we had car trouble. It was over ninety degrees, and heat waves shimmered off the asphalt. As far as I could see, the landscape spread out in a rugged, gigantic, uneven table.

Dad went around and opened the trunk. He pulled out two towels, a water jug, a plastic bowl, and beef jerky. "Follow me," he said.

We walked about two hundred yards into the desert, the sun pounding on our heads.

"See that coyote?" Dad nodded toward a limp

creature lying on the ground several feet ahead of us. "It's caught in a trap set by the Navajos." Dad handed me the jug, bowl, jerky, and one of the towels. He wrapped the other towel around his left forearm. "Walk behind me—slowly. Don't make a sudden move."

He crept behind the coyote, took the towel from me, wrapped it around the animal's jaw, and gently lifted its head. With his left foot and right hand, he opened the trap, releasing the heavy coiled spring and the sharp steel teeth. His strength was amazing. The coyote shook its injured front paw, nearly cut in two, and growled.

"Fill the bowl with water and place the jerky next to it." Dad never took his eyes off the animal. "Now slowly back away and stay behind me."

He carefully lowered the coyote's head and removed the towel. The animal bared its teeth and snarled, staring at us as we walked backward. When we stopped about thirty feet away, the coyote dropped its head, lapped up the water, and tore into the jerky. Then it limped into the desert, out of sight.

"His paw will heal," Dad said, his voice soft as he unwrapped the towel from his forearm. "I don't think he was trapped long. His ribs didn't show, and he had energy to spare." He paused. "I've been freeing coyotes for as long as I can remember. They don't do anything wrong—they need to eat like any animal. The Navajos are wrong to trap them. It's cruel. They die a slow, awful death. I'll free every trapped animal I find."

Dad always had more compassion for animals than he did for humans. I was almost jealous of that poor coyote. Why couldn't he show the same kindness toward his four children and their mom?

I squinted across at Shiprock, a mountainous rock standing alone on the horizon. Evelyn told me it was once a sacred giant bird that carried the Navajo people from the cold north to their lands in New Mexico.

Dad took a drink from the water jug and followed my eyes. "The Navajos have a lot of legends about that rock, but it's actually the remains of an ancient volcano. Over twenty million years ago, during the Late Oligocene and Early Miocene periods, the tectonic plates underneath us shifted and lava erupted from below the earth's crust. The molten rock exploded through all kinds of sandstone and shale and landed on the surface, where it hardened. Erosion has removed most of the upper layers, leaving behind that massive shaft."

He started walking back to the car. "You need to understand the world around you, boy. Study science and math. Learn the importance of Avogadro's number and pi and the Pythagorean theorem."

I followed, astounded he was so smart. But he didn't act like other smart people. He loved violence as much as he loved knowledge, as if they went hand in hand.

"And you should learn the stories in the Bible—not as religion, but as history—along with the works of the ancient Greeks and English greats. You can't be ignorant about the world you live in or the origin of the universe or the laws that govern the planet. Otherwise, you're no better than that helpless coyote."

When we reached the Shiprock BIA warehouse, no one was around. I watched out as Dad filled the trunk with electric drills, saws, and various other tools. It was always a relief not to have to warn him. The previous two weekends, I'd had to throw rocks at the building when I saw someone coming, panicking that our luck had run out. But Dad reassured them by showing his USBIA badge and explaining that he was moving the tools to a different warehouse.

After he finished loading and put the padlock back, we took off for Gallup. Dad had arranged to meet with his Mexican buyers that day, not wanting to wait until Monday. The heat inside the car made it almost impossible to breathe, and I rested my head against the door for some air, though the hot breeze blowing through the window didn't help much. Dad was wearing a long-sleeved shirt, as he always did, to cover the scars from the EPNG explosion years before. I didn't know how he could stand it.

Driving along Route 66, we passed the usual parade of young and old Navajos walking by the side of the road. Just outside Gallup, Dad slowed down and thumped me hard on the shoulder. "See that old man over there?"

"Yeah." The poor guy was stooped over, and his clothes hung on him like rags. He shuffled along by himself carrying a crumpled grocery bag.

"If we killed that old man, where would we bury him? Where's the nearest—"

"Whoa!" I bolted up in my seat. "Why would we kill him? Why are you asking me that?"

"We're not going to kill him. That's not the point, goddamn it. Listen up. I'm teaching you something here. Do you see a place where we could dump the body so no one would find it? Where's the nearest police station? How many routes are there away from here? How many vehicles passed us in the last ten minutes in either direction? What color were they? How many people were in them? What were the license plates? State and number. What do you remember?"

Another one of his games. Okay, I'd play along. "Three cars and a truck have passed us. Two cars were blue and the third was green. The pickup was red, and three Navajos were in the back. But, Dad, it's not so much about how close we are to a police station. What really matters is how close we are to a car, or even a pedestrian, who might tip off the police."

He whipped his head around and stared at me, a smiling spreading across his face. "You're right, David. You're finally paying attention." He sped up and passed the old man. "If you don't know all these things, you can get caught. Murder is the easiest crime to get away with because you have no witnesses. Robbery, kidnapping, any of the other crimes—there are witnesses or people you need to depend on. The perfect murder will never be solved."

He muttered to himself and then said, "Most of the cons in San Quentin had committed several murders they didn't get caught for. They got picked up for botching a robbery, passing bad checks, stealing a car in broad daylight. You have to be smart about the world if you're going to survive in it."

I didn't respond. I was done playing his game.

"You've got to be observant and wary," he said. "Rules are for losers. If you don't believe it, look at the rules the Indians have to live by on this reservation while they're being forced to take rations from the white bastards who conquered them."

I couldn't imagine that other dads took their ten-year-old sons to steal tools from their employer or explained how murder was the easiest crime to get away with or insisted that rules were for losers. I closed my eyes to stop him from talking to me, pretending to go to sleep.

When we got to our rendezvous point with the buyers, Dad thumped me on the shoulder again and told me to keep watch. Standing several feet back from the dirt road, he talked with three fat, filthy Mexicans, their teeth badly stained, joking about making **fácil dinero**—easy money—by cheating **estúpido** BIA officials.

If I spotted trouble, I was to bang my hand loudly on the side of the car. At one point, I saw a vehicle approaching, the dust kicking up behind it, and I banged on the car and yelled. It turned out to be a pickup filled with Navajos who raced by without looking at us. Dad yelled at me for being a dumbass.

I was hot and tired and just wanted to go home.

Not far from Window Rock on our way back, the car jolted to a stop. Ahead of us were the Haystacks, a series of connected mounds of sculpted red stones, and a pickup with BIA license tags, squashed like an accordion into a rock the size of an elephant. Dad said the driver must have stopped off at the Navajo Inn after work and stayed too long.

As the safety officer, Dad inspected government accidents, and that included anything involving BIA vehicles. "Based on the condition of this pickup," he said, "the guy went to the happy hunting ground, the place where drunks go when they exit the surly bonds of Earth's grasp."

Dad chuckled at his witty use of the English language and opened the car door. I got out to follow him.

"Stay here," he said, grabbing a pen from the glove compartment. "You're not prepared for this." He reached into the back seat and picked up a clipboard, an accident report form, and cloth gloves.

I leaned out the window to get a better look, but I couldn't figure out what I was seeing. Seconds later, curiosity took over, and I jumped out.

Sneaking up behind Dad, I saw rivulets of blood shaped like an elaborate spider's web in the dirt near the front wheel. A bloody torso in a plaid shirt hung out the windshield like a headless scarecrow. Flies buzzed everywhere.

On the ground, Dad knelt next to a severed head. It had a smashed nose and deep gashes on both purplish cheeks, framed by a long braid of black hair resting on its right ear.

Dark brown eyes stared back at me.

When my brain could make sense of the scene, vomit surged through my mouth, violently emptying my stomach. My insides shook. I wiped my face with the bottom of my sweaty T-shirt.

Dad stood up. "I told you to stay in the car. Get your ass back there and wait for me. I'll be finished with the paperwork soon."

Several moments later, he opened the driver's door and tossed the clipboard onto the seat and then went back and picked up the dead man's head by the braid. It dangled like a tetherball that had come loose from the pole. He placed the head inside the smashed truck cab.

My throat burned, and vomit coated my mouth. I coughed several times, and Dad handed me the water jug. "Take a big swig, spit it out, and then drink some to clear your throat." He let out an exasperated sigh. "Toughen up, damn it."

Dad got on the highway, made a U-turn, and stopped in front of the Navajo Inn, a lone, nondescript bar. Drunks staggered in and out. Unconscious men cluttered the parking lot, and two guys lay facedown in the road. There were no streetlights, and at night the locals often ran over them in the dark.

"Navajo alcoholism is a terrible tragedy." Dad panned the parking lot and shook his head. "Selling alcohol on a reservation is a federal crime. Isn't it ironic that this guy got killed driving back to the reservation after drinking until he couldn't see straight? This little bar is only a half mile from the reservation and the Arizona border—and it's the largest liquor outlet in the entire state. The Mexicans running this joint have a license to steal. And the Navajo tribe helps them. They laugh all the way to the bank."

Two men teetered out of the bar together, leaning on each other to stay on their feet. "The driver probably never knew what hit him," Dad said. "Maybe he's better off than the ones who freeze to death in the parking lot or get run over."

He turned to me. "Half the PhDs in America study Indian alcoholism, but nothing changes because no one really gives a shit. And you're worried about stealing tools." He laughed. "Come on. Let's go home to get some grub. We've had a helluva good day."

Whenever Dad did something wrong, he told stories that made his actions seem acceptable, even reasonable by comparison—Mexican bastards killing Navajos with whiskey and white invaders stealing everything from Indians trapped on reservations. Examples of rough justice, as he called it, which included beating assholes who richly deserved it—and more often than not, I was one of those assholes.

CHAPTER 26

One Friday that fall, after playing catch with Tommy in front of his trailer, my brother and I came home for dinner to find Lonnie, Sally, and Dad sitting around the kitchen table. Dad's loud voice boomed, "Goddamn those bastards. I'll go to your high school and kick their asses."

Though only six years old, Sally listened in on most of our conversations. As Dad ranted on, she sat on her knees with her elbows on the table, her head resting in her hands, and took in every word. Lonnie mumbled something and then pushed back her chair and walked past Sam and me, her eyes shiny with tears. Soon we heard the Rambler's engine start and the car rolling down the street.

Dad waved for Sam and me to sit with him and Sally at the table. "David, tonight you're going to make things right for your big sister."

"How?" I asked.

"Some of her classmates are having a hayride, and they didn't invite her." Dad reached into the cupboard from his chair and pulled out plates for Sam and me to load with Spam and corn. "It isn't an official school event, but they're providing the chaperones, and everyone's meeting there. You're going to fix this hayride, but good."

He got up from the table. "You two eat while I get what you'll need."

Sam and I were on our second helpings when Dad came back from his car with a grocery bag and unloaded several potatoes onto the table, along with a bag of sugar. He kept his trunk filled with supplies, always ready for anything.

"Here's the plan, David." He took a tool from his pocket that looked like a short screwdriver but it had a notch instead of a flat head. "This is a valve core remover. It's easy to use. As soon as it's dark, you'll sneak into the high school parking lot and remove all the tire valves from the hayride trucks."

"How will I be able to find the valves in the dark?"

"You'll rub your hands along the rim of the tire until you feel the cap. Untwist it and reach for the core. It'll feel like the tit of a cow."

Sally poked at Sam's chest and they both giggled.

"The core has grooves that screw into the tire valve," Dad said. "Put the remover over the valve and turn it counterclockwise." He demonstrated with his little finger. "The core will twist out. Stick it in your pocket and don't forget to replace the cap."

Smirking, he handed me the tool. "Removing the valve will flatten the tire. You can't add air without the valve cores, and no one will have extras. It'll seem like the tire hit a nail and needs a patch."

"That makes sense." I smiled, happy to be the star in his prank. Who'd think the valve core had been removed if the cap was there? Dad was brilliant.

"Now, the next step." He picked up a potato and waved it at me. "You'll put one of these in the exhaust pipe on each truck. Use this to trim them." He pulled a penknife out of his pants pocket and handed it to me. "Push the potato deep inside and carefully wipe away the residue from the peel so nothing's visible. Understand? If you don't think you'll have time to get every valve core, put the potatoes in first."

"What do the potatoes do?"

"The exhaust can't escape if the muffler's clogged." His face beamed. "The engines will stall and won't restart."

"Then we won't need the potatoes and the valve cores," I said.

"You always need a backup plan." Dad tapped me on the shoulder. "And if you do this right, this'll be the worst hayride Window Rock ever had."

I nodded, filling a small paper bag with the tools and potatoes.

"What about the sugar?" Sam asked.

Dad stared at the bag on the table. "If David pours sugar in the gas tanks, it could clog the carburetor and disable the trucks, but it isn't a sure thing. Besides, it'll be too bulky to carry that big bag of sugar. Let's forget about it for tonight."

Sam jumped from his chair. "Let me go. I can help."

"When you get older, you'll be a big help," Dad said, "but not tonight."

Sam lowered his eyes and shook his head. Sally reached over and held his hand.

"I can handle this," I said, feeling a mixture of pride and fear. If I got caught, Dad would beat me and Lonnie would be embarrassed. But if I pulled off the prank, I'd be a hero.

Just after dusk, I threw on my coat and left for Window Rock High School, about four hundred yards beyond the elementary school. I could stay hidden in the dark, but the school grounds were lit to daylight status. Four hayride trucks lined the perimeter of the parking lot, and Lonnie's classmates milled around, going in and out of the auditorium, laughing and talking. It seemed impossible to get near the trucks unnoticed.

After studying the area for a few minutes, I realized that no one was in the trucks yet, and the passenger sides faced away from the lights—in total darkness. If I did this right, I could remove the valve cores on that side without being seen. And the tailpipes would be a cinch to reach.

In case I ran out of time, I started with the potatoes. Crawling under the first truck, I tried to shove a potato into the tailpipe but it was too big, and I had to use Dad's penknife to carve one to fit. Then I wiped the residue from the outside of the pipe with my coat sleeve and jammed the peels into the paper bag. When I finished plugging each tailpipe, I moved on to the first tire.

The valve core twisted off easily, and the tire whistled like an untied balloon. Everyone was too far away to hear, but to be safe, I slowed down the twisting to soften the noise. Each truck had a double set of back tires, so I worked on three tires before hurrying to the next vehicle, remembering to put the cores in my jacket pocket as Dad instructed.

I had just removed the valve on the last tire when someone shouted, "Let's go!"

Fumbling with the cap, I gave it a couple of quick turns and then dashed off to the edge of the parking lot and rolled into a gully.

My heart pounded in my ears. For sure, they were going to see me.

"Hey, the apple cider is over here," another kid called out.

I took a deep breath and rolled out of sight into

the dark field that separated the high school from the elementary school. Lying on my stomach, I watched high schoolers climb on top of the hay bales and their adult chaperones get inside the cabs. The engines fired up.

I felt powerful and invisible again.

When I got back home, Dad was pacing by the kitchen table, his eyes bugged out. "What took you so damn long?"

Sam and Sally clapped when I dumped out the potato peelings onto the table and then emptied my pockets, producing a dozen valve cores. A smile spread across Dad's face.

"Did anyone see you?"

"No. I got the tires on the passenger side, and there were double sets in the back, but I couldn't get the other side."

His eyes flashed with anger. "Why didn't you flatten them all?"

"There were kids and chaperones in the parking lot. I would've gotten caught moving to the other side of the trucks in view of the lights. But I jammed a potato in all the tailpipes. They won't get far, and half the tires are completely flat, so they won't go very fast."

"You're like a real-life spy," Sally said.

Dad smiled and rubbed my head. I sighed with relief that I had succeeded. No beatings that night.

"Those bastards needed to pay for not inviting Lonnie. It shouldn't take long for the potatoes and flat tires to do their magic."

Lonnie spent the evening with the other students who'd been left out of the hayride. She didn't know what we had done on her behalf and wouldn't have wanted it. But the rest of us believed a great wrong had been righted.

CHAPTER 27

"I'm taking the three of you to Gallup today," Dad said the next morning as Sam, Sally, and I ate our cereal in front of the television. "We'll be going with Vance and his two kids."

Dad had become increasingly restless. On the rare occasions he was home, he couldn't seem to sit still, his eyes darting here and there. He would close his bedroom door and talk on the phone, often yelling. This trip to Gallup would be the first time we'd do something as a family besides just shop for groceries. Lonnie had to stay home to work on a class project.

Vance had the same job as Dad but in a different BIA office in Navajo, New Mexico, twenty minutes from Fort Defiance. Dad called him the Drunken Kraut.

There wasn't much to like about the guy. He had beady eyes, pasty white skin, puny arms and legs, and the smell of cigarettes and whiskey on his breath. The sadness in his eyes made me think of Mom.

"David, you need to watch over Sam, Sally, and Vance's kids," Dad said. "They're the same age as Sam and Sally, so that won't be hard. We'll drop you off at the movies and pick you up later. Can you handle that without getting into trouble?"

I nodded, preferring to get into lots of trouble by throwing cherry bombs and Black Cats from what remained of the arsenal I'd bought from Mr. Pino.

Vance pulled up in a brand-new silver Buick Electra, the last person in the world you'd imagine owning such a nice car. Was he in the tool-stealing business too? Sam, Sally, and I squeezed into the back with his two silent kids, who stared out the window, clearly unhappy to meet us or to go to Gallup with their dad. As the Buick bumped over the ruts on our street, Vance pulled a bottle of whiskey from underneath his seat and told Dad to have a snort.

"I know where we can get some nice, tight Mexican ass," Vance said, retrieving the bottle from Dad and taking a gulp. His slicked-back blond hair didn't cover the big bald spot or the nasty scab on the back of his head.

"I didn't know there was any left." Dad laughed.

"Over at the Shalimar, there are lots of easy Mexican women, and drinks are half price. They have a live band too."

"Let's go." Dad reached over for more whiskey.

When we arrived in Gallup, they let us out in

front of the Chief Theatre, on Coal Avenue, a block from El Morro Theatre where I'd torn the screen with the ice ball. The marquee advertised a sizzling double feature: MEN IN WAR — TWO MEN WHO HATE EACH OTHER'S GUTS and POOR WHITE TRASH — SEE HOW THEY LIVE. I could have written both scripts.

The dads gave us enough money to see the movies and buy a hot dog and a drink. "We'll be back," Dad said. "Stay at the Chief."

The chairs were thick and fluffy, and the previews and cartoons were almost as good as the main movies. When the double feature ended and the lights came on, we went to the bathroom and returned to different seats. The ushers didn't seem to notice. By the time **Men in War** had begun again at seven o'clock, I'd been checking regularly for Vance and Dad. All I saw were loads of drunken men in pickup trucks weaving down the road.

Nine o'clock rolled around, but still no sign of the Buick. I went back to my seat as the curtains opened for **Poor White Trash.** The theater would close in a couple of hours.

We had eaten our hot dogs hours before, and our stomachs were growling. Sam had scrounged through the trash cans for food throughout the afternoon. Between films, the five of us walked through the seats, looking for half-empty bags of popcorn, bits of hot dogs, and candy spilled on the floor. Sam found a full box of Sugar Babies, but he wouldn't share it.

"Make him give us some," Sally whined at me.

"I found them," Sam said, downing the entire pack in one giant gulp. Brown juice ran down his full, freckled cheeks.

On one of Sally's many bathroom runs, I heard her crying and ran out to help her. An usher had her by the arm. "You've been here all day without paying for the extra movies," he said.

"Our dad dropped us off and hasn't come back," I said. "We have nowhere else to go."

The usher looked from me to Sally and released her arm. "Stay out of trouble."

Sally and I met Sam back at our seats. Vance's kids took the endless hours in stride, like they had lots of experience waiting for their dad. I wondered if they had a mom or if she'd gotten ditched like ours.

Minutes later, Sally left again and reappeared with a hot dog. "The man who was going to kick us out gave me the last one," she whispered.

When the movie ended at eleven, all the lights went up and the ushers swept the aisles and cleared the trash. We didn't budge, hoping to stay out of the cold night air as long as possible.

A young, skinny usher bumped our chairs with his broom. "You have to leave now. We're closed."

Dragging our feet, we shuffled through the door

as the lights went off inside the theater. The white-and-red neon Chief logo flickered out too. We looked up and down Coal Avenue before sitting on the curb. Drunks stumbled by without paying any attention to us. One peed on the nearby light pole.

Another full hour went by. Either Dad and Vance were in trouble or they were still having some Mexican ass and whiskey and had forgotten about us. Our teeth chattered and our knees knocked. Soon my ears and feet went numb. Sally and Vance's daughter cried softly. Sam and I each put an arm around Sally to try to warm her, and Vance's son did the same for his little sister.

"What happened to Dad? Is he dead?" Sally kept asking.

I told her no each time, but I wished he had died and someone would come along to rescue us.

No such luck. At almost one o'clock, first came the sound of squealing tires, and then Vance's Buick swerved to a stop in front of us. Dad jumped out of the driver's side. "Get in, goddamn it. We have to find the Navajo sons of bitches who beat the shit out of Vance." Dad glared at the girls slowly climbing into the back seat. "Hurry up!"

Vance slumped against the front passenger door. Under the glow of the streetlight, I could see that his tan jacket was covered in dirt and blood. A bruise ran the length of his cheek, his nose looked squished, and he had a bloody gash on his bald spot. His ear had a notch missing, as if a dog had taken a bite out of it. The smell of puke, whiskey, and stale cigarette smoke filled the car.

"Thurston, my jaw is broken." Vance's words came out garbled. "Shit, I just swallowed a tooth." He gagged with dry heaves. "My ribs feel broken too."

"Dad, we're hungry and cold," I said. "Can we go home now?"

"Please, Dad," Sam and Sally chimed in.

"Shut up!" Dad snapped his head around to give us a dirty look. "We have to get these bastards!" He hit the gas pedal. "We're looking for a pickup full of drunk Navajos."

By this time of night, that description fit every vehicle in Gallup.

"Vance, don't worry—we'll kick their asses." Dad raced down the street, dodging drunks, parked trucks, and curbs.

What had Vance done to get beaten so badly—and why hadn't Dad been with him?

Several times, Dad sped to a truck and said, "Vance, wake up. Are these the assholes who did this to you?"

"No, Thurston, it isn't them," Vance would say, not raising his head.

When Dad finally gave up and drove home, he told Vance to go to the nearest hospital. The guy stumbled out of the car and puked twice as his kids silently watched. It took him forever to walk over to the driver's side.

He nodded at Dad and drove away. How he maneuvered the car over the ruts on our street in his condition, I don't know, but I felt worse for his kids than I did for him.

It would be a long time before we saw any of them again.

Monday afternoon, I had to stay late at school to retake a math test I had failed, so Sam left without me. When I got home, Dad's brown Ford sedan was parked in front of the house. Bracing myself, I hurried inside.

Sally was crying. "Dad's hitting Sam in the bedroom." She grabbed my arm. "When he walked through the door, he told Evelyn to get out."

The belt strap whistled as the buckle snapped against Sam's skin again and again. I shook, knowing I was next. Sam didn't whimper. He never did. He's the bravest soul I've ever known. I'll never understand how he took those vicious beatings without uttering a sound.

The bedroom went quiet, and then Dad called out, "David, get in here. You would've gotten it first, but you weren't home."

He opened the door, and I looked into blue eyes filled with hate. If the eyes are windows to the soul, his had descended into hell long ago. The Y vein on his forehead was in full throb, and his eyes bulged like he was being strangled. Sam slipped past Dad through the doorway, his face scrunched in pain, tears quietly rolling down his cheeks. He limped into the living room without looking at me.

"What'd I do?" I asked. "Why am I . . ." I tried to dance away from Dad, but he yanked me by the arm. "Please. I'll do anything . . . don't hit me. I'm sorry . . . I won't do it again, whatever it was. Please. I promise."

Begging never helped. Fessing up to a mistake never did either. Lying would have been the best strategy, but I had no idea what to lie about.

He bared his teeth and wrapped the belt around his hand to get a tight grip. "You little bastard. Shut up and take your whipping."

Dad dangled the buckle and swung. I squeezed my butt, hoping that would make the blood vessels hide down inside my skin, but it didn't work. Spinning like a top, I tried to make the belt hit new areas. When it struck the same spot over and over, the blood vessels broke and the skin ached worse. It didn't take long for the hits from the buckle to turn into a deeper pain that penetrated my bones.

To block it out, I imagined being Mickey Mantle

hitting a grand slam in the World Series, but each hit brought me back to the belt. Then I visualized being strong enough to fight back against him like Superman, but that didn't help either. Fighting Dad was impossible.

When it was finally over, I collapsed on the floor. I knew I'd pee blood again.

"Get up!" Dad yelled. "Do you know what your idiot brother did at school today?"

"No," I croaked.

"The teacher asked the dumbass what he did over the weekend, and he got up in front of the whole class and told them everything, beginning with your little escapade in the high school parking lot. They heard about Vance, including the fight with the Navajo sons of bitches. I had to go to the damn principal and deny everything."

"What about the trucks?" I asked.

The Y vein had begun to fade, but now it was pulsing again. The belt fidgeted in his fist.

"Please don't." I put my hands in front of my face. "What about the valve cores and potatoes?"

"Yeah, you did one hell of a number on them all right." Dad threw his head back and laughed. "They didn't get a mile. Some of the trucks had to be towed." Distracted, he seemed to forget about the beating and put his belt back on. "I told the principal you're a mischievous little bastard, and it wasn't my day to watch you."

Later that night, Sam and I looked at each other's legs before going to bed. Mine were purple, bumpy, and swollen from my butt nearly to my calves. Sam's were no better. It hurt to lie in bed. It hurt to move.

I yelled at Sam for telling his teacher and class about what went on over the weekend. He didn't think he'd done anything wrong. Now nine years old, he always told the truth even when the consequences were painful. That would never change. It was the weirdest combination possible—Sam was devious but honest. He would do whatever I told him yet wouldn't hesitate to tell anyone if asked about it.

Though he and I were as close as brothers could be, I had stopped confiding in him about things that could get us into trouble. I had lots of secrets, not just the ones I needed to keep from Dad, but the ones I didn't want anyone to know—not even Lonnie—mostly how I hated being a Crow.

By the next morning, everyone at school had heard about Sam's confessions. At least Lonnie could honestly say she had no clue her brother ruined the hayride. But this was one prank I didn't want credit for.

None of the teachers asked questions, but if they had, they couldn't have gotten information from me if they'd put a stick of dynamite in my mouth.

At the start of gym class, I opened my locker and pulled out my shorts, but then stuffed them back in. I didn't want anyone to see my legs. When I walked outside in my jeans, my teacher, Mr. Jackson, said, "Go put on your gym shorts, David."

"No. I can't." I took a step toward the track where the rest of the kids had gathered.

Mr. Jackson stuck out his arm to block my path. "We're doing the fitness test today, remember?"

"Please leave me alone. I'll run in my jeans."

He marched me back into the locker room. "If you don't change, you and I are going to the principal's office."

Wrapping my arms around my chest, I stared at the ground. "I can't. I hurt myself . . . and I bruise easily."

"Take off your jeans, David. Now."

I slowly stripped down to my underwear. Mr. Jackson's jaw dropped and his eyes turned dark. I tried to hold back, but I lost control, an unforgivable crime in Dad's mind, and tears spilled down my face.

"Do you want to tell me what's going on?"

"No! Please, don't say anything. Dad will kill me if he thinks I snitched."

"Put your pants back on. You don't have to wear shorts today."

Relieved, I wiped my face with my T-shirt and joined the other boys outside. Getting Dad involved with the school was the last thing I needed. In my next class, though, my teacher asked me to report to the superintendent's office over at the high school. My classmates snickered. I felt their eyes follow me to the door. A couple of the kids whispered something about the hayride incident, but that wasn't what this was about.

I walked as slowly as possible to the high school thinking of what to say. Superintendent Martin and Mr. Jackson leaned against the desk, waiting for me. Mr. Jackson gave me a tense smile before he closed the door and lowered the shades.

"Would you please pull down your jeans?" Mr. Martin asked.

"Please don't do this. If Dad finds out . . ."

"Pull them down—now." His voice was kind but firm.

I turned around, loosened my belt, and let my pants slide down to my knees. Mr. Martin gasped.

"I told you," Mr. Jackson said.

"I fall down and hurt myself all the time." I managed to steady my voice, but I couldn't hold back the tears.

"We don't believe you," Mr. Martin said. "We think an adult is hurting you."

"No." I shook my head in panic. "No one is hurting me, sir. Please don't say anything."

Dad couldn't know about this. Pulling up my pants, I tried to get a grip on my crying, but couldn't. I focused on the blue Indian head logo on the carpet and the words underneath: "Window Rock High School, Home of the Scouts."

"David," Mr. Martin said, "if nothing is going on, it shouldn't be a problem for me to call home to find out how you got injured so severely."

"No!" I yelled. "Dad will think I ratted. We don't have anywhere to go. Our mom is gone. No one else wants us. I'll wear gym shorts if you want. I'll do anything."

Mr. Martin and Mr. Jackson studied me for several moments, and then Mr. Martin put a comforting hand on my shoulder. "If you ever want to talk, I'm here."

Wiping my tears on my T-shirt again, I nodded. From that day on, I changed into gym shorts. No one in class mentioned my legs, and Dad never got called.

CHAPTER 28

I had stopped reading the newspaper because we didn't get one, and I couldn't imagine being a paperboy in Mud Flats. At least our school had a library. But no one seemed interested in the news until Friday, November 22, 1963, when President Kennedy was assassinated. The teachers talked about his death like it was the end of the world. For the next two days, we sat in the living room watching TV almost every waking moment, but once the drama ended, everyone in Fort Defiance went back to ignoring the world outside the reservation.

By the end of the year, Mud Flats had become more tolerable. Kids still threw rocks and Coke bottles at me, but I avoided getting beaten up most of the time. Then after Christmas vacation, I had a new challenge: a **bilagáana** named Cal, who moved to Fort Defiance from Phoenix and transferred into my class. Instead of being frightened and bullied by the hogan and trailer kids, he got some of them to join **his** gang.

It didn't make sense. Cal looked like an easy bully target. He had blond hair, blue eyes, glasses, and the skinniest arms and legs I'd ever seen. But he smoked Camels, chewed tobacco, drank whiskey, and always had some combination of razor blades, brass knuckles, switchblades, and guns available to him.

"I cut up guys all the time and shoot them dead," Cal said on the playground. "And I've screwed most of the eighth-grade girls behind their hogans."

It didn't take him long to discover that the Crow kids didn't have a mom and their dad wasn't home much. One evening, after Evelyn left, we heard a voice from outside. "Open the door before I kick your ass."

Sam, Sally, and I had been watching television in the living room, and I ran to the front door just as Cal barged in. Since moving to Mud Flats, we didn't think to lock the door once we got home from school. He walked straight to the kitchen and within seconds found Dad's Old Crow bourbon under the sink and took a big swig.

"Hey—" Sam started, but I put my hand on his chest and shook my head. Cal had Dad's violent streak and loved being in fights with weapons. Trying to save Dad's liquor wouldn't be worth getting stabbed.

Cal left the bottle on the counter and went from room to room until he found change on Dad's dresser. I followed him but was afraid to say anything. He put it in his pocket and left. The next morning, Dad hit both Sam and me for the missing quarters. If we'd told Dad about Cal, he would have whipped us harder for letting an outsider take advantage of us.

Later at school, Cal cornered me in the bathroom. "Where does your old man keep his money? Give me ten dollars when I come by later or I'll hurt you bad."

Dad didn't keep cash stashed in the house, but it was only a matter of time before Cal would find Dad's rifles, rings, good clothes, and other bottles of bourbon. When Evelyn left that evening, I locked the door, feeling every bit a coward.

Soon after, Cal appeared and knocked, but I didn't let him in. He pounded the door and jiggled the knob. "I'll hurt you bad if you don't open up!" he shouted.

I put my finger to my lips to keep Sam from yelling back. The three of us stared at each another in silence and waited. Cal shouted again, then gave the door a couple of kicks and walked away.

The next morning at recess, he grabbed me by the collar of my shirt and pulled my face toward his. "I'm coming this afternoon. Let me in or else." He pulled a switchblade from his boot and held it up to my throat. "I'll kill you and your old man too."

When Sam and I got home, we told Evelyn.

"Tell your father," she said. "He know what to do."

I shook my head. "I can't. Dad would tell me to get the money and the whiskey back—and probably beat me besides. He'd want me to fight Cal."

After Evelyn left, I sat in the living room, barely able to breathe. When Cal knocked, Sam and Sally scurried to their bedrooms. Opening the door slowly, I pushed against it to block him from coming inside, but he swept by me like I wasn't there. A pack of Camel cigarettes and a lighter stuck out of one pocket in his jacket, and the other pocket bulged with something, but I couldn't tell what it was.

"Where does your old man keep his money? Not just his loose change."

I followed him into Dad's room, not answering. I couldn't think of how to stop him. None of my pranks and schemes had prepared me for someone like Cal.

"He leaves change on his dresser," he said, "but he has to keep more somewhere. Give it to me now."

"Get out, Cal." I tried to sound tough as I moved between him and Dad's closet where the guns were stored. "Dad and Lonnie will be home soon, so you better leave."

He reached into his pocket and whipped out a .22-caliber pistol.

I couldn't move.

Smiling, he stuck the barrel to my forehead and pulled the trigger.

I fell to the floor shaking, picturing my brain splattered all over the bedroom walls. Cal laughed and put the gun back in his pocket. "Next time it'll be loaded. Tell your old man my gang will kill him too."

Cal left the house, and I watched him slowly walk down the street through the living room window. Even the dogs left him alone.

"What are you going to do?" Sally asked. "He might kill you next time, and what about us?"

I didn't have an answer. I was still shaking, hearing the gun clicking over and over again in my head.

Lonnie came in the door moments later, and Sally burst into tears. "Cal tried to kill David with a gun. He stole Dad's whiskey and money," she said between ragged breaths. "He comes every day and scares us."

"Come over here, you guys," Lonnie said, and we followed her into the living room. "When Dad gets home, we'll tell him about Cal." She sat on the couch, and Sally snuggled next to her. "Dad will drive over to Cal's house and talk to his mother. She'll get him to stop bothering you, David. If that doesn't work, Dad will schedule a meeting with Mr. Martin at school, and he'll straighten this out."

Lonnie hadn't been home for any of Cal's visits. She didn't have a clue. "Those are the worst ideas I've ever heard," I said. "Dad will either kill Cal or beat me for not handling him myself. And the last thing I want is to get the school involved. Don't tell anyone." A thought occurred to me, and I was desperate enough to try it. "I have a better plan."

Gathering my nerve, I walked one block over to Tommy's trailer. When his mom came to the door, her dark almond eyes widened, no doubt surprised to see the frightened look on my face.

She smiled at me, but I didn't smile back.

"Is Tommy home?" I asked. "I really need to talk to him."

She stared at me for several seconds. "Wait here," she said. I heard her say something in muffled Navajo.

Tommy came outside right away. "**Gáagii**, what's wrong?"

"Cal pulled a . . . pulled a gun on me . . . in our house," I stammered. "Stuck it to my head . . . and . . . and pulled the trigger. Said next time, it'd have a bullet in it."

"I'll take care of him." Tommy smiled and put his arm around me. "It's okay." He went back inside and turned before gently closing the door. "Don't worry, **Gáagii**. I'll get him."

Walking home, I felt good for the first time since meeting Cal. Like Dad, Cal understood how to intimidate and threaten, but Tommy was tougher, stronger, and more intimidating. I'd finally found someone who would protect me, though I couldn't figure out why.

The next day, after Evelyn went home, Sam, Sally, and I crouched under the living room window, sneaking careful peeks, watching for Cal to arrive. We didn't have to wait long before he appeared at the front door. I looked out the window and saw Tommy come into view from around the corner of our house.

"You been messing with **Gáagii**," Tommy said to Cal.

"Mind your own business."

Tommy raised his fists. "**Gáagii** is my business."

Cal reached for a switchblade, and Tommy slugged him in the face. In one punch, Cal lay flat on his back, blood dripping from his mouth. Tommy put his boot on Cal's throat. When Cal tried to move, Tommy used that same foot to kick him in the ribs. Cal doubled over and groaned.

"Mess with **Gáagii** again, and we'll finish this," Tommy said. "Now get out of here."

Cal gingerly rolled to his feet and walked down the road without looking back. Sam, Sally, and I watched Tommy in awe. When Cal left, I opened the door and Tommy smiled at me, bright teeth and glowing dark eyes in his broad, powerful face. "Don't worry, **Gáagii**."

The next day on the playground, Cal formed his hand into a gun and pointed it at me. "Pow," he said, but he never came to our house again.

Except for Dad's beatings, nothing had ever frightened me more. Oddly, after Tommy stopped Cal, it was easier to face the hogan and trailer kids in Mud Flats. I knew they wouldn't try to kill me.

CHAPTER 29

With each passing day, Dad acted more like a coiled rattlesnake ready to strike anything in his path. During one of our weekend drives to Gallup for groceries, a guy in a pickup passed us and moved in front of the Rambler too close for Dad's comfort, so he raced in front of him and slammed on the brakes. The guy nearly crashed into our rear end, missing us by inches. Dad jumped out of the car and pounded on the driver's side window. "You Navajo punk, get out and fight me like a man."

Then when we stopped for gas, Dad claimed the attendant overcharged him and threw the money on the ground. "I'll kick your ass, you son of a bitch," he yelled, putting up his fists to fight as the attendant walked away.

A couple of weeks later, we had to stop for gas again, this time near where we used to live in Ganado. It was a bright, sunny Saturday, and Dad had rounded up Sam, Sally, and me to go with him to meet one of his BIA friends. He told us they needed to talk over some business in private, so we sat in the car and waited.

When we drove away, Dad noticed that the Rambler was nearly on empty. Bumping along on a narrow pockmarked dirt road, we found a gas station that amounted to a rusted-out trailer with a warped plywood sign that read "Black Bear Gas Station."

In front of the trailer, an adult black bear stood in a chicken-wire cage so small he could hardly move. The poor animal had matted fur, droopy eyes, and a sagging mouth—a hungry-looking version of the big black bear Dad brought back from his hunting trip years earlier.

Two pumps sat in the dirt several feet from the trailer. A Navajo family in a pickup was already at one of them when we pulled in. Four skinny kids huddled silently in the bed, their faces tired and bored, like they'd been there for hours.

As all of us piled out of the car, the owner—a fat Mexican man not much taller than Shorty John—scurried out of the trailer and stuck the nozzle into the gas tank and scurried back inside. Sally and Sam took off for the wooden outhouses behind the trailer. I walked around the pumps, stretching my legs, and looked over at Dad.

He was staring at the pitiful bear in an almost trancelike way and then jolted awake and in two strides was at the back of the car, rolling down the tailgate window, his eyes fixed on the bear. With a loud grunt, he pushed up his sleeves, leaned in, and rummaged through his toolbox.

When he straightened up and turned around, I broke into an instant sweat—he had all the signs of what he called pure, unadulterated fury: bugged-out eyes, pulsing Y vein, and puffed chest. I caught a few mumbled words: "chicken shit," "son of a bitch," "dead man."

He strutted like a prizefighter toward the cage, wire cutters in his hand. I flashed back to the trapped coyote—Dad was on a rescue mission. Like the coyote, the trapped bear was an animal being exploited by man.

Dad started clipping the wire.

The Navajo man in the pickup grabbed the nozzle out of his tank and sped away. I ran to the outhouses. "Sam, Sally!" I shouted. "We've got big trouble. Get back to the car. Now!"

Racing around to the front, we saw the bear stick its large paw through the opening Dad had just made. As we hurried into the back seat, the owner flew out of the trailer. "You no take bear," he yelled, his thick black glasses bobbing up and down. "I find him. He mine. Go away."

Dad laughed and continued clipping.

The guy shook his head and lunged at Dad, his arms flailing. "Leave bear alone. No . . . no bear."

What was he thinking? The little man stood less of a chance with Dad than I did with Gilbert.

Dad dropped the clippers, turned, and ripped a hard left hook into the guy's fleshy face, launching him into the air, his glasses in one direction, his body in another. He landed on his back with a loud thud. Blood poured from his nose as he lifted his head to see Thurston Crow glowering over him.

"Get up, you fat little prick, so I can finish stomping the shit out of you." Dad shook his fist. "You're a real chicken-shit son of a bitch, trapping a defenseless animal."

The Mexican picked up his glasses, dabbed at the blood on his nose with his fingers, and scrambled back to the trailer. The door slammed, and I heard the sound of a dead bolt sliding into place. Dad pounded on the door as he tossed out more insults, and the lights went off inside.

"I'll be back in one hour," Dad shouted. "If the bear's still here, he'll feast on your fat brown ass. **Comprendo**, dipshit?"

Dad tossed the wire cutters into the toolbox, rolled up the rear window, and then threw the nozzle on the ground and hopped into the car. The bear was tearing at the torn wire in the cage as the Rambler took off down the dirt road, the three of us bouncing in the back seat. The Mexican man had to be more afraid of Dad than of the bear, and both would certainly be gone before Dad returned.

After driving to Mud Flats and dropping us off, Dad went back to the gas station. When he got home, he told us, "The wire cage had been opened, the bear was gone, and the trailer was padlocked. That's the last we'll see of the useless sack of shit."

Later, we heard that the man moved the station, a wise decision on his part. As Dad often said, "I've killed for less."

The following weekend, Sam, Sally, and I were back in the Rambler with Dad driving near the Petrified Forest National Park. He visited a friend in Holbrook, who let us come inside his trailer and watch TV. On our way home, Dad pointed out a petrified log at the side of the road and pulled over. He got out of the car and looked all around. No other vehicles were in sight.

"David and Sam, let's rock this thing out of the dirt and load it into the trunk. It only weighs about a hundred pounds. But we need to hurry so no one sees us."

Dad loved rocks of all kinds but especially petrified wood. It was protected by federal law—signs along the road said so—but Dad told us that the law applied to Anglos, not Indians.

"You and Sam take one end," Dad said, "and I'll take the other. We'll put this in the house for decoration. Look at the red and black markings. They're beautiful."

We grunted, pushing and pulling until we broke off a five-foot chunk of petrified wood. Scorpions and lizards hiding beneath it scampered away. The three of us shoved the log into the back of the Rambler, scraping paint off the bumper as we jockeyed it into place. The chassis sank low to the ground.

Our prize stuck out, so Dad grabbed a rope and tied the trunk latch to the trailer hitch. "It's too heavy to fall out," he said, rocking the car to make sure. "It'll work if we nurse the Rambler home slowly."

On the horizon, a trail of dust appeared and moved swiftly toward us. Dad told us to get back in the car, and he quickly slid into the driver's seat. Soon a Navajo Police Department GMC pickup truck pulled up behind us. Two uniformed Navajo police officers got out and walked to our car, flashing their badges.

Dad rolled down the window. "**Yá'át'ééh**, **hosteens**," he said, greeting them in the familiar "Hello, mister" vernacular to show he was one of them. Without responding, the officer with salt-and-pepper hair pulled out a small notebook from his pocket.

"Show me your driver's license, sir," the younger officer said to Dad. He stepped aside and spoke into his walkie-talkie. "Bringing him in now for questioning," I heard him say.

The senior officer recorded the Rambler's plate number and peered inside the car. The three of us stared back at him. "You have in your possession a stolen artifact from the Navajo Indian Reservation," he said to Dad. "This is a federal offense. You'll have to follow us to the police station."

Pulling out his BIA identification badge, Dad jumped out of the car and thrust it into the surprised officer's face. "I am a full-blooded Cherokee Indian, an authorized officer of the US Bureau of Indian Affairs, working on my sister reservation, and I'm taking this log to my Navajo home where it will remain after we leave. We're all Indians here, so cut the crap."

The young officer looked at the badge and back at Dad. "Remove the log, sir," he said. "And follow us to the station."

Sam and I got out to help unload it, but Dad pushed us away. He pulled the log out of the back, yelling, "This is complete horseshit."

Driving behind the police cruiser, Dad muttered about having to stomp the crap out of these dumb sons of bitches. I'd never seen his head and shoulders shake so much. About ten miles down the road, we pulled up to a small building with a sign that read "Navajo Tribal Police."

"Go sit in the waiting area while I straighten out these idiotic assholes," Dad said to us. "They'll be sorry they ever messed with Thurston Crow."

Ignoring Dad, Sam walked behind the station, gathered a pile of rocks, and threw them into a ravine, stirring up weeds and lizards. I decided he couldn't get into trouble as long as he didn't try throwing rocks toward the police station, and I left him alone. With her latest library book in hand, Sally went to an empty office, escorted by the secretary, who offered her a cup of water and a quiet place to read.

I sat watching Dad and listening to the senior police officer. "A man living nearby saw you and your sons stealing the log. They called us to investigate."

When we had gotten out of the car to get the log, a truck appeared behind us, but he was on a dirt road at least a quarter mile away. I couldn't believe he saw what we were doing.

Both officers, along with a third who had been at the station when we arrived, stared at Dad. Were they waiting for him to confess or apologize and swear he would never do it again? That's what I would have done. I glanced behind me at the two empty jail cells. If Dad didn't do something, he'd get locked up in one of them. And maybe the three of us kids too.

"Your police department has no jurisdiction over

me or that log." Dad slapped the counter. "I'm as Indian as you are."

He flexed his muscles and leaned toward the officer. "We can take this up at BIA headquarters if you're stupid enough to mess with a Cherokee operating fully within his ancestral rights. Who was here first, we Indians or this Indian reservation?"

The three Navajo officers looked at one another, and something passed between them. Their intense body language relaxed into resignation. Either Dad's bullying tactics worked or they decided that arresting him would have been too much bother. In any case, they let him go, warning him not to steal any more artifacts from the reservation.

But as usual, he continued his attack.

"You haven't heard the last of this," he yelled. "We Indians own these rocks. It's our right to move them around. You have no authority over them or me. As Navajos, you should know that. I won't be intimidated by you."

Dad's face twitched the entire ride home. He'd had so many confrontations in recent weeks that I worried jail, or even death, wouldn't be far away.

CHAPTER 30

On a Saturday morning in May, Dad told Sam and Sally that he and I had to go run errands without them. When they complained, he waved them away and said, "Cut the crap."

As we pulled away in the brown sedan, Dad started mumbling to himself, the lines on his forehead bouncing up and down. He was in no hurry. He seldom told me where we were going or what we would be doing on our stealing trips. My job was to keep my mouth shut and be his lookout man.

When we reached Yah-ta-hey, New Mexico, Dad turned south on Highway 666. That meant we would be going to Gallup first before heading north to the BIA warehouses—and that meant we'd probably stop at the post office, get some food, and visit one of his "lady friends."

Dad always had several young women he strung along, usually waitresses or hairdressers making very little money. "A man's got to have some fun," he would say. If he had enough time, he would take me inside where they worked. I could tell Dad wanted to kiss them, and they'd let him. It was disgusting. My siblings and I didn't have nice winter coats and warm shoes, but he would buy them all kinds of things, like turquoise necklaces and rings.

I'd have to sit there listening to Dad trying to impress the women with wild tales, as I expected him to do today. It was embarrassing, and we both pretended it never happened when we got back in the car.

When we got to Gallup, we went to the post office on Second Street, where Dad kept a number of boxes for "special mail." Before getting out of the sedan, he surveyed the parking lot and counted on me to do the same. Dad thought I had a talent for spotting out-of-town cars and trucks that didn't belong to tourists. Vehicles from Arizona, New Mexico, Utah, and Colorado were probably safe, he said, but if I saw a Kansas license plate, I needed to get his attention immediately, no matter what he was doing. And I always had to watch for a man who seemed out of place, especially if he was staring at Dad.

I figured he meant George. He'd met George and Mom in California, but it was likely that his partner in crime had come from Kansas. Or maybe the man was someone else Dad had double-crossed. He was good at making enemies.

Dad directed me to stay put and watch every car, truck, and person. If I thought anyone might mean trouble, I needed to honk the horn three times, and he'd come running. That day, the parking lot had only half a dozen other vehicles, so it would have been easy to spot something suspicious.

When Dad returned to the car, he was carrying a couple of small packages wrapped in brown paper, no doubt containing messages and supplies from his fellow crooks. He threw the packages into the trunk and drove over to Route 66, where he found a place to park near the Eagle Café, about two blocks from Mr. Pino's. Mostly locals and truckers ate there.

"David, check out the cars."

I walked up and down the street, scanning license plates for a block in both directions. No one would suspect an eleven-year-old kid. "We're good, Dad," I said.

When we went inside, he asked for a table near the rear exit and sat facing the front. He never ate at places with only one exit. And he never sat near a window. During one of our stealing trips, he told me that when he worked at EPNG, someone took a shot at him through a window at a restaurant.

A young Mexican waitress came to our table, and Dad winked at her and smiled broadly. The bright look in her eyes told me they had met before, so she must have been the reason for our stop.

"What can I get you two gentlemen?" she asked.

As he placed his order, Dad touched her arm. She couldn't have been more than sixteen.

When she brought our drinks, she stayed a few minutes and flirted with Dad. He told her we were on our way to visit his hundred-acre spread in Cibola County. He'd show it to her sometime when they were alone, he said. I almost spit out my iced tea.

The burgers were huge. We were about to eat when Dad hunched down in his seat. "Son of a bitch," he said under his breath, staring straight ahead.

I followed his eyes. "What?"

"We have to get out of here!" He grabbed my shoulder. "Move it!"

We flew out the rear door into the alley. Dad turned around and walked backward for a few strides to watch behind him and then took off running for the sedan. He was pulling away from the curb before I even closed the door.

"Goddamn you, David. I saw a guy in the restaurant who wants to kill me. That means you missed his car, you careless little bastard."

"But I checked, just like you told me. I didn't see anything."

He was too busy driving to hit me. We raced down Route 66, our tires screeching, narrowly missing trucks filled with Navajo families. Then we turned onto Highway 666 and sped north, away from Gallup. Dad's eyes were about to explode out of his head. He kept checking the rearview mirror.

Several minutes later, when he was sure we weren't being followed, he slowed down to the speed limit. "I'm not afraid of the asshole, but it's impossible to protect yourself from an ambush. You have to pay more attention, David."

"Sorry, Dad, I won't let you down again."

"You better not." He shot me a hard glance. "You need to understand what San Quentin does to a man. First of all, it doesn't make him sorry about a damn thing, except that he got caught. He simply gets smarter. But mostly, the Q makes a man mean. The guy after me blames me for going to prison. Something we did went wrong. He was an idiot and told the cops and judge he wasn't sorry. You have to say you're sorry even though you don't mean it. He has a violent felony on his record, and he's probably too stupid to lie about that and get away with it. The son of a bitch wants revenge."

It had to be George. Dad didn't say anything more about him other than the guy would try to kill him—and probably both of us if I was with him. But I had no idea what he looked like. How would I be able to spot him?

"From now on, you make sure when we go into any public place that no one is watching us, that there's no eye contact."

He got quiet. Sweat trickled down my back.

I thought he was done, but then he started up again. "There are things I need to teach you, things you need to know to survive in a harsh world full of assholes. That means you need to keep secrets. You're pretty good at that most of the time, but not always. You think the things I ask you to do are bad, but they aren't. You have to get a lot tougher and smarter about helping us not get caught. You understand me, boy?"

"Yes, Dad."

"Someday, I'll write down all the stories about the Q—the cons, the screws, the punks, the stoolies, the lifers, the warden, the chief psychiatrist. You wouldn't believe the stories I heard in the yard—tons of unsolved murders committed by the cons. They'd laugh about how easy it was. Hell, mine are unsolved too. You'll be able to read about them in my book—**Murder Eight.** After I die, you can publish it and make a lot of money. But for now, you need to learn how to steal without getting caught, how to keep secrets, how to be a good watcher, and how to help me when I really need it."

"I'll fight anyone who tries to hurt you. I promise."

"That's my boy," he said, rubbing my head with his powerful right hand.

I was learning to be the son Dad wanted and hating every part of it.

The rest of our day was uneventful. We loaded the

trunk with expensive tools and drove back to Gallup to meet Dad's compadres, as he now called them.

After he spotted George, or thought he had, Dad took side streets in Gallup, staying away from Route 66. It was always busy with tourist traffic and too easy to miss vehicles and people. But as spooked as he was about the possible George sighting, he continued taking chances, visiting his lady friends who worked in businesses lining the street.

One time in a restaurant in Gallup, he strode right over to a waitress and kissed her without checking around first. I went to him and said he wasn't being careful. He punched me in the chest, his face full of disgust. But later in the car, he reached over and gently squeezed my knee. "You were right," he said.

I had to save Dad from himself.

On our way back from Shiprock on another stealing trip, Dad kept going south at Yah-ta-hey, and when we arrived in Gallup, he turned left on Route 66. It was extra crowded that day, Navajos and tourists everywhere. If I reminded him about being careful, he'd probably punch me again, so I stayed quiet.

Crawling along the street in the heavy traffic, he glanced in the rearview mirror and yelled, "Shit!" He took a fast right on Fourth Street, driving over the curb, and then the first left on Coal Avenue, one block over from Route 66, and hurried to park. Dad pushed my head down as he hunched over the seat. We didn't move for a long time. I was afraid to make a sound.

When he finally sat up, he told me to go into every business from Fourth to Second and look for an Anglo who might be asking around for somebody. And double-check the license plates. I walked into all the places twice, my heart pounding. I couldn't make a mistake. But I didn't see anything other than the usual mixture of Mexican merchants, local shoppers, and Navajo families. I told Dad it was clear.

We drove to a truck stop on the edge of town, Dad's eyes in full bulge. After we ordered food, he calmed down some. I asked him what was wrong, assuming he thought he saw George again.

It took a while for him to answer, his face going through a series of familiar contortions. When he spoke, he rambled on about screws, cons, the injustice of prison, and why a man sometimes needed to kill to make things right. Suddenly he pounded on the table. "The bastard will never get me! I'll kill the son of a bitch first."

After lunch we left for home. Dad was silent the whole trip, deep in his own world. Later, I asked him if he was okay.

"Why the hell wouldn't I be?" he said, as if nothing had happened.

CHAPTER 31

In June of 1964, the Navajo BIA compound finally had a place for us. Apartment 251-4, a flagstone unit in a fourplex, with three bedrooms, a living room, and a fenced yard, became our new home. Within days after we moved, the BIA tore down the Mud Flats house due to asbestos contamination, probably the least of its flaws.

Our new part of town buzzed with activity. People walked in and out of two small trading posts, a deli, a post office, and an Indian hospital. Down the street from us was a twelve-unit apartment complex for the additional BIA support staff and their families. Doctors, Indian health service officials, and senior BIA employees lived in scattered flagstone apartments, log cabins, and modern houses in a tight area up against Canyon Bonito.

There were no hogans, rusted-out trailers, feral dog packs, or roaming Navajo kids throwing rocks and shooting BB guns. Though only a mile from the condemned shack in Mud Flats, this neighborhood was a world apart.

Our living situation greatly improved, but I missed Evelyn's daily visits. Shortly after we moved, I took over the local paper route from an older boy and stopped by to see her as often as I could when I passed Eighth Street.

Having a paper route meant I could read the **Navajo Times**, the **Gallup Independent**, and **Arizona Republic**. I loved keeping up with politics and events, just as I had in Albuquerque and Gallup, and most important, I now had a diversion from my life in the Crow household. Like my former customers, my new customers in the compound area let me into their lives with daily conversations and good tips.

But some of my customers lived in Mud Flats and in the nearby hills where trailers were spread out among the hogans. As soon as I turned down Kit Carson Drive toward Mud Flats and passed the two trading posts, the vicious dog packs appeared, along with the Navajo kids shooting BB guns and throwing rocks and Coke bottles. Their attacks were bad enough when we lived there, but now the heavy canvas paper bag made it even more difficult to maneuver out of harm's way.

One afternoon I complained to Dad about the dogs. He smiled and said, "On Saturday we'll drive to Gallup and get the tools to solve the problem."

After buying a machine-gun replica squirt gun from Tom's Variety Store, where Sam and I bought water balloons, we made our way to Jay's Super Market and bought a few bottles of ammonia. It cost me two weeks of tip money for the purchases, and I couldn't believe a squirt gun full of smelly liquid would stop the dog packs from tearing into me.

The next day I had my first opportunity to test Dad's solution. It was the toughest delivery day because the Sunday papers were full of thick packs of advertising and my bag groaned under the weight. It bounced against my legs, and I could hardly turn the bike.

When the first pack charged, two dogs bit into my legs before I could get off the bike and point the gun. Usually I would have ridden as fast as possible while kicking them. Stopping made me an easy target.

The second time they charged, I fired a long squirt into the lead dog's nose and then another into the next dog's eyes. They froze and ran away howling in pain, their tails between their legs. New dog packs charged on every street. My aim got better along with my confidence, and I emptied the gun into their faces, hitting them over and over. By the end of the day, they followed behind, fearing me.

I felt powerful and invisible again.

Dad understood violence and pain, and he was never wrong about what would work. But I still had to contend with the hogan and trailer kids. When I told Dad, he handed me a .22-caliber pistol with hollow-point shells. "This will stop the bastards. A few rounds will quiet them like the ammonia squirt gun did with the dogs."

"I can't do that. Using a gun that can kill isn't the answer."

"Suit yourself, but don't complain to me if you won't do anything to protect yourself. Their weapons are just as dangerous as a .22."

His solutions were drastic, as I had known since our first car ride together. I found my own way out of the problem. When I collected for the paper, I told the customers who lived where the kids were hitting me that I'd quit bringing their papers if they didn't get them to stop. Within days, the assaults had ended.

Whereas my customers in the compound were fun to talk to, many of my customers in Mud Flats and the surrounding hills were barely functional, especially the Anglos. Instead of hoping for good tips, I used my mental energy to create what became the Crow craziness index—a one-to-five rating system based on hygiene, physical appearance, strange outbursts, alcoholism, and unusual fetishes. I especially loved the customers if they were paranoid and I could get them riled up.

I gave our justice of the peace a five. He typically came to the door in boxer shorts caked with shit and urine and a stained T-shirt full of cigarette holes stretched across his mountain of a belly. He'd have a .38-caliber pistol in one hand and a bottle of whiskey in the other. Rarely sober, he often made a loud whooping noise and fired his gun in the air as I rode away, sometimes just missing me. I never wondered why there wasn't a Mrs. Bowman.

Another customer kept sheep penned in a small yard surrounding his trailer. With a fat, disgusting grin and chewing tobacco dripping down his chin, he explained that a sheep's vagina and a woman's vagina felt exactly the same. Laughing, he'd slap himself on the thigh as though he'd discovered some great truth and needed to share it. He also had pictures of small boys to show me if I was willing to go inside his trailer. He fell into a special category of weirdness that no number could capture.

The missionaries told me my soul could be saved if I renounced Satan. The instant I said I was there collecting for the paper, they would launch into a sermon about Jesus and suffering. I generally stood silent for a moment, but then temptation would take over.

"Yes, I repent!" I'd yell. "I renounce Satan. Save my worthless soul." Then I would pause and say, "The Lord wants you to tip me."

It never worked. Missionaries were tighter than a

tick when it came to money. Sometimes it took them a half hour to round up enough pennies to pay me.

The oldest missionary was a man who smelled like moldy cheese and always looked like he'd just woken up. His socks didn't match, his shirt was missing buttons, and his pants made it only to midcalf and were held up by a rope he must have found. He'd tell me that the Lord had sent him on a mission to Fort Defiance to help Navajos renounce their pagan gods and prepare for a glorious afterlife. I gave him a four.

My craziest customer became my favorite. A large, red-faced trucker, he moved from Texas to get away from the feds. His trailer sat off by itself a half mile from the road, the windows covered with newspapers to keep anyone from seeing inside. He buried boxes of ammo in his yard and planted yellow flowers on top so he wouldn't forget where they were. At all times, he wore a Stetson, a flak jacket, camouflage, a gun in his holster, and ammo belts. The cab in his truck was loaded with rifles.

Stacks of **Guns & Ammo** magazines piled high on his front stoop. He wouldn't allow me to take down his address because that Communist bastard Lyndon Johnson was after him. He'd ask if anyone followed me. I'd tell him that federal troops were coming from Albuquerque to lock him up, that he needed to prepare because I could see them on the horizon. He vowed to fight until the end. He was a perfect five.

Customers who refused to pay were on a different list. I always wrapped their final paper tight, put rubber bands around it, and taped a well-tucked cherry bomb on the outside. A perfect throw exploded as it hit the front door. The bastards had it coming.

My world expanded again and would continue to do so as I befriended more people in the compound. Earl Ashcroft, the Anglo owner of the Fort Defiance Trading Post, let me listen to him speak to his customers in fluent Navajo as they bartered and swapped goods. When the trading post was empty, he dragged out photos from his father and grandfather and told me stories about the history of Arizona and New Mexico. I listened to him for hours and studied the Navajos up close just as I had done at the Hubbell Trading Post years earlier.

The biggest luxury was riding the school bus safely past Mud Flats into the secure, fenced-in school grounds.

CHAPTER 32

We'd lived in apartment 251-4 just over a month when Dad did his customary summoning of the four of us to the living room for a talk. While we sat on the couch, he paced the floor, staring at the carpet. My stomach churned. He never gathered us to deliver good news.

"Mona Tully and I have been dating and we're going to get married," he said with no emotion. "She's twenty-eight with a bachelor of science degree and nursing degree from Duke University. She works at the Fort Defiance Indian Hospital, is an officer in the Navy Public Health Service, and owns property in Hatteras, on North Carolina's Outer Banks." He acted like he was reciting from her résumé rather than telling us about someone he wanted to spend the rest of his life with.

Sam and Sally fidgeted. Lonnie and I stared at each other. A plump widow would have been a more likely candidate or a divorced nurse whose children behaved better than we did. We knew Dad went to some woman's apartment in the evenings, but he'd known her only a couple of months.

"Mona has never been married. You'll meet her soon. She wants to provide you with the discipline and rules you so badly need. Who can argue with that?"

I didn't understand. Was Dad turning us over to her? He didn't believe in discipline and rules. And there was no way he loved her. So what the hell was in it for her? Why would this woman want to be a mother to three heathens and a girl who was only twelve years younger than she was? She had to be a psycho.

The next night, Dad herded the four of us into Mona's place, a flagstone apartment nearly identical to ours. She had a record player with opera music playing and furniture that was nicer than any we'd ever seen. She even had a painting on her wall of the North Carolina beach near her parents' home.

When we first entered her apartment, she didn't smile or look at us. She moved aside and pointed toward the living room. Lonnie perched on the edge of a stiff orange chair, and the rest of us sat on the matching couch like wooden soldiers.

Dad disappeared into the kitchen, leaving Mona standing alone in front of us. Her beady green eyes, taut face, and thin, rigid body gave her all the appeal of an officer at a concentration camp, like the ones in the World War II movies we watched.

"I love your father," she said, her voice flat. "We'll be a team. You'll follow my orders. I'm your mother now. You need strong discipline, and you're going to get it."

She marched a few steps across the floor as if she were collecting her thoughts for a speech. "There will be consequences for breaking my rules. I'll put a chart on the kitchen wall listing the punishments for your offenses and the dates the punishments are executed."

She abruptly walked into the kitchen. We were dismissed.

Any hope that life would be better for us vanished. She and Dad were getting married the next weekend in Gallup with a one-night honeymoon in the Shalimar Hotel, where Dad and Vance had gone to meet Mexican women with tight asses.

"Maybe she's just nervous and wants us to behave for her," Sam whispered. "We need someone to give us rules, and it'll be nice to have a mom, especially one who makes Dad happy."

"No one can make Dad happy," I said. "She doesn't smile, she doesn't hug, her eyes are cold, and she has a nervous laugh like she's hiding something." I stood and crossed my arms. "This is bad."

Sam looked at Sally, frowning on the couch next to him. "Mona's been to college and everything," Sam told our little sister. "It'll be okay."

"I'm glad I'll be graduating in two years," Lonnie said.

I didn't blame her for wanting to get out as fast as possible. But the rest of us had a long way to go before we could leave.

Mona barely spoke during our first dinner as a family. In fact, the whole table was quiet as her disapproving eyes watched us. Lonnie and Sally mostly pushed their food around their plates.

When Dad ate his last bite, Mona told us it was time to clear the table. "You will have a set of punishments for a multitude of offenses that are already apparent," she said as the four of us took our plates to the sink. "You're like a bunch of orphans who've taken over the institution. That will change shortly."

The day after Mona moved in, she called Sam, Sally, and me into the kitchen. "I want to show you something," she said.

On the wall next to the refrigerator, she'd taped a large piece of heavy white paper with our names written in red marker across the top. "This is where I'll enter punishments and execution dates for you. We will review it daily."

The next morning, Mona yelled for us to come into the kitchen. Under Sam's name on the punishment board, she had written, "Didn't brush teeth—cod liver oil." Sam had to swallow a large mouthful of the stuff. It looked like motor oil and smelled like a wet dog.

For the rest of the summer, Mona's rules and punishments grew, whether it was washing out our mouths with pumice soap for disobeying orders or pushing Dad to hit us for not calling her Mom or making us stand in the corner for talking back.

The day after school started, Mona came into our room just before bedtime. She looked at Sam. "You're stupid," she told him. "You didn't take out the trash, so now you get to sleep in it. Maybe next time you won't forget."

Dad appeared next to her with the metal garbage can from outside. "Get into bed, Sam," he said.

My brother pulled back his bedspread and climbed under his top sheet. At first, he burst out laughing when Dad upended the can, dumping coffee grounds, eggshells, cooking grease, potato skins, meat scraps, and dirty napkins on top of him. The putrid gray liquid from the bottom of the barrel poured onto him. He stopped laughing.

I seethed at the humiliating treatment. My rage was stronger than any feeling I'd ever had. How could they think up such a cruel punishment? How sadistic could Mona be?

She pointed at me. "Your turn. Last night you fell asleep in your shirt, so tomorrow you'll go to school in pajamas. Maybe you'll remember to take off your shirt next time."

Dad looked at Mona and smiled. "So this is how to get them to follow rules." He roared with laughter. They walked out of our bedroom and into theirs, content with their day's parenting.

The anger smoldering inside me kept me up most of the night. Sam didn't sleep either, thrashing under the stinking garbage. The reeking liquid saturated his sheets and pajamas and began leaking onto the tile floor. In the morning, the stench and the sight of my brother climbing out of the garbage made me cry.

Sam took a shower but couldn't get rid of the stink. Mona demanded we clean our room before school, as if it were our fault, but the rotten smell stayed. While we stripped Sam's sheets and swept and scrubbed, Mona sat Sally down in the kitchen and cut her long hair nearly as short as mine. Then Mona made a show of replacing all of Sally's dresses with boys' clothing, mostly jeans and T-shirts, as if to remove any vestige of being a girl. Lonnie's mouth dropped when she saw seven-year-old Sally looking like a third little brother.

Wearing my faded cotton pajamas to school that day hardly bothered me. Sam had it so much worse.

The following week, Mona handed me a letter addressed to Miss Brezina, my seventh-grade homeroom teacher. After class, she read it to me:

Dear Miss Brezina,

I am adopting the Crow children in order to give them a Christian home and discipline, which they sorely lack. Would you please outline David's behavioral problems that require attention? From what I have already learned, I feel certain he needs a great deal of guidance. I look forward to hearing from you.

Sincerely,
Mrs. Crow

"You must be so happy, David," Miss Brezina said, lightly touching my arm. "I'll write Mrs. Crow a letter."

There could have been nothing worse for me than having my strict Franciscan teacher spilling her guts to Mona. Still, I hoped that Miss Brezina wouldn't outline all that I'd done wrong.

The next day she beamed as she handed me a

sealed envelope addressed to Mona and Dad. "You may not think so now," she said, "but this might save you from a world of trouble. Your father and stepmother will help you work on serious problems with your behavior. I'm proud to have played some part in this. Give this letter to them and return the bottom sheet tomorrow."

When Miss Brezina was out of sight, I ripped open the envelope and read:

Dear Mrs. Crow,

I have interviewed David's teachers and am sorry to report that he has been a consistent troublemaker. Teachers have complained frequently, but Mr. Crow never responded. I've prayed for this day. God bless you and Mr. Crow for taking this step. Please sign this letter acknowledging receipt, and let me know if you wish to have a conference. We have much to discuss.

With warmest regards,
Miss Constance Brezina

There was no way I would allow Mona to get her hands on that letter, so I forged Dad's signature using a technique he'd taught me years before. Since our days in Gallup, I'd forged every report card and letter from the school by placing his signature under clear glass and then copying it by tracing the letters with a felt-tipped pen. I watched him do the same thing many times. The duplication had been so perfect, even he wouldn't have been able to tell the difference.

The next morning, I handed my teacher the return envelope.

She opened it, and her eyebrows gathered in concern. "Your father signed the letter, but there's no comment from him or Mrs. Crow. I thought they would ask for a conference so we could work together on your behalf."

"Dad signed it and told me to do better," I said calmly.

That might have worked if I'd left it at that—but I couldn't.

The next morning, I got to class early and brought a tube of wood glue I'd taken from Dad's car. After carefully spreading a thin layer on Miss Brezina's chair, I waited for her to sit at her desk to take roll. She sat for several minutes, reviewing the class roster and explaining the day's assignments, before lifting her enormous ass off the chair.

As she rose, the chair rose with her, and the dress made a long, steady ripping noise. She spun around like a clumsy figure skater, with the chair following.

The class exploded into laughter. Even Gilbert grinned and gave me a thumbs-up. Miss Brezina didn't need to ask who was responsible. She pushed the chair away, gathered the back of her torn dress in one chubby hand, and grabbed my upper arm with the other.

"I don't believe Mr. or Mrs. Crow read the letter I sent home. I'll call Mrs. Crow at lunch to discuss your behavior, including the insensitive thing you did today. Do you think what you did was funny?"

I sure as hell did. So did my classmates. When I got to the cafeteria, Henry was spinning between tables, imitating Miss Brezina. To duplicate the sound of her dress ripping, he made fart noises with his mouth. Henry swore he saw some meaty flesh, "like a Brontosaurus drumstick."

Miss Brezina and Mona would have a lengthy discussion, but I told myself I didn't care. There wasn't much else Mona could do to make my life worse. Besides, Dad would be impressed with how well I forged his signature.

That afternoon, I walked into the kitchen and saw "Forged letter" and "Brezina dress" written in separate boxes on the punishment board.

Mona caught me reading the new entries. "Your father and I didn't receive a letter from Miss Brezina. She brought her letter to me at the hospital this afternoon and told me what you did to her today. Do you have an explanation?"

I wanted to tell her how much I hated her and her

Nazi rules and that I had decided to have as much fun as possible at the expense of every idiot in Fort Defiance, including her, but I didn't say a word.

That night at dinner, Mona put the letter on Dad's plate. He'd already heard about my day. He held the letter in the air, staring at his perfectly duplicated signature.

"You'd have made a damn good counterfeiter." He smiled, stealing a glance at me while holding the paper up to the light. "You could've taught some of the cons in the Q a thing or two." He put the letter next to his plate. "What was the expression on the old battle-ax's face when she realized you'd glued her ass to the chair?"

I stood slowly, bringing my chair with me, and mimicked Miss Brezina's jerky spin and the furious look on her face. I copied Henry's ripping noise as I lowered the chair. Dad and I both laughed, but he laughed harder.

Mona ignored Dad and glared at me. "What you did today was reprehensible," she said. "The poor woman was trying to help you."

I sat back down, still laughing. "I knew Dad wouldn't care. He never has before."

Letting out an angry breath, Mona jumped up, clamped her bony fingers around my arm, and dragged me to the punishment board.

"You're grounded for the next nine weeks from

all activities except for delivering newspapers. You'll pay for Miss Brezina's dress out of your paper route earnings and apologize to her in front of the class."

The next day, apologizing was the most fun of all. It reminded everyone of how ridiculous Miss Brezina had looked, and wide grins broke out around the room. The hard part was keeping Henry from cracking up, which always made me do the same, but we managed.

My rage toward Mona grew. In a fit of fury, I threw a cherry bomb in her purse while she was in the bathroom. Mona and Dad rushed into their bedroom under a haze of dark smoke and brown and white confetti, which used to be her Benson and Hedges cigarettes. Dad's neck and eyes bulged as he yanked off his belt and pushed me down the hall into my room.

"Why did you do it?" he boomed.

"It was an accident."

"That was no accident. Don't lie, don't beg, don't dance, and don't cry, you little bastard. I'm going to beat the living shit out of you."

Every ounce of Dad's strength went into smashing that belt against my butt and legs. He swung until he was exhausted, breaking a record number of blood vessels. Not a single nerve ending below my waist was spared.

But the pain didn't stop me. I immediately began plotting a way to get back at her without getting caught. Dropping a cherry bomb in her purse was stupid. My emotions had gotten the better of me.

"Thurston, I know you dislike corporal punishment," I heard Mona tell him afterward, "but it's the only thing that will make him become a responsible adult. In time, he'll thank you."

Mona reveled in satisfying Dad's need for taking out his aggression on his sons' asses. I couldn't have hated her more, but I tried.

CHAPTER 33

I obsessed over how to use the short, precious hour between the time I finished my paper route and Mona got home. One day, I stopped by to see my friend Richard Kontz, who lived with his parents and eight siblings in the small house attached to the post office.

His father, Rex Kontz, was the postmaster. He invited me to join the 4-H Club, which he led in their backyard, and penciled me in on the Little League team he coached. Our first 4-H project called for raising a sheep. When I told him about the grounding, he said, "I'll reserve a sheep for you to feed, clean, and shear in our yard before your parents get home. You can keep the profit you earn from the sale."

That hour went by so fast. It seemed like five minutes. I couldn't wait to return the next day. When the Kontz children and I made mistakes, Mr. and Mrs. Kontz didn't yell, hit, or write outlandish punishments on a board. All they had to do was show disappointment in their loving, dark eyes. I wanted to please them, trusting they had my best interests at heart.

When I did well, like hitting a home run, Mr. Kontz's face lit up, and he gave me a huge smile. Over time, I learned from Richard that his dad had fought the Japanese in the Pacific, including the bloody Battle of Guadalcanal, but he never talked about it. That would be bragging, and Mr. Kontz would have no part of it—the complete opposite of my dad.

Mrs. Kontz couldn't have been kinder to me. One afternoon, she took me aside and held my shoulders. "If you follow the rules, and I know you will, you can always come to our house when you need a place to go."

Apparently, Richard had shared some of the punishments I'd told him about. For the first time, I understood what a family should be. The Kontzes were poor, and they weren't perfect, but they loved one another the way Evelyn had loved me. My mood lightened the instant I saw any member of the family, whether at school or on the street.

I continued my sneaky rendezvous in my friend's backyard for several days. Then one afternoon, Mona came home a few minutes early and found I wasn't there. The moment I came in the front door, she said, "I saw you running from the Kontzes' house. You are grounded from seeing them or anyone else. You can't do anything but school and your paper route." She bared her teeth like the mad dogs in Mud Flats. "I will break you."

"Never, ever, ever, ever." I stomped down the hall into my bedroom.

The next morning, I snagged the matches Dad kept next to his Prince Albert pipe tobacco and brought two cherry bombs to school. When I got to science class, Mr. Treba, our teacher, held up a glass tube of mercury and said, "This beautiful silver liquid is valuable and dangerous. Be very careful with it."

No one saw me light the short green fuse and roll the cherry bomb toward Mr. Treba's legs. It stopped at his feet and BOOM! His hand jerked upward, and the tube shot into the air. It smashed on the floor, and liquid mercury marbles rolled across the linoleum. Mr. Treba moaned and fell to his knees, crawling to pick it up, but the mercury ran through his fingers, like water on a sizzling skillet.

"Who did this?" Mr. Treba shouted.

The classroom held a collective breath. He stood and walked over to me. "Empty your pockets."

Mr. Treba tossed the remaining matches and my extra cherry bomb on his desk. "I'm taking you to the principal's office, Mr. Crow," he said, squeezing the back of my neck to steer me out of the room. "Do you have any idea how expensive and toxic mercury is?"

Mona's pinched face and Dad's pulsing vein instantly came to mind. "If you won't turn me in, I'll pick it all up and promise not to do it again."

"It's too late for that, buster!"

In the principal's office, Mr. Lee ordered me to sit down. "I'm calling Mrs. Crow right now, and we're going to get to the bottom of the trouble you've been causing." He seethed at me, looking like he could easily punch me in the face. Mr. Treba folded his arms and stood over me, scowling.

"Mrs. Crow, this is Mr. Lee, the school principal. David caused a major problem at school today. We need to schedule a meeting in my office tomorrow with you and Mr. Crow. What he did today is serious, and I'd rather discuss this in person."

That night, the punishment board stood idle, awaiting consequences after the meeting with Mr. Lee. During dinner, Dad laughed when I mimicked Mr. Treba on his hands and knees, scrambling for the mercury. Mona tossed me one of her menacing stares, but she didn't comment.

The following morning, Mr. Lee sent for me after roll call. When I got to his office, I found Mona sitting on his couch, balancing a notepad on her lap with the Fort Defiance Indian Hospital logo at the top. She wore her official nurse's uniform, a white dress with her lieutenant insignia on the shoulder. Next to Mona sat Miss Brezina holding a manila folder marked "David Crow" in large black letters. She wore a new skirt, crisp and clean, probably purchased with my newspaper money. Mr. Lee directed me to sit in the chair across from the couch.

True to form, Dad didn't attend the meeting, leaving it up to Mona to represent the Crow family.

Miss Brezina handed the folder to Mr. Lee. "Mrs. Crow," he said, "I'd like to go over David's behavioral issues, though we'll only scratch the surface of everything he's done."

Mona's solemn green eyes never blinked, nor did she glance at me.

"David, what happened in science class yesterday?" Mr. Lee said.

"I didn't know Mr. Treba would drop the mercury," I said, hoping for mercy yet again.

"Just what did you think would happen?"

"He would laugh."

"We know about Miss Brezina's skirt, don't we?"

"Yes. I paid for it and said I was sorry."

Miss Brezina fidgeted uncomfortably, straightening her skirt and pulling her knees together.

"Several teachers have reported things placed in their purses, missing supplies and assignment sheets, grades being changed. Mr. Jackson said you pushed

Willie's head into the dirt while he was doing push-ups. Why did you do that?"

"I'd been waiting for a chance to get even with him. He thinks it's cool to put half a tube of Brylcreem in his hair, and I wanted to see his head covered in dirt. Everyone laughed."

"Why did you have to get even?"

"Willie and three other boys held me down on an anthill."

"You should have reported that. I would have talked to Willie and the other boys."

What an idiot. He knew the rules on the reservation. Survival depended on never snitching.

"Mr. Brady said you yell dirty words in Navajo during his class. Who taught you these words?"

"Some of the Navajo boys said it'd be funny if I yelled them in class."

"And you believed them?"

I nodded and laughed.

Mona hunched her shoulders. It was the first indication she wasn't a mannequin.

"Tell me the names of the boys who taught you," Mr. Lee said, his pen poised to write.

"I don't remember."

Henry had worked with me for hours to get the pronunciation just right. My friend Jim laughed hard when we practiced, making it funnier.

Mr. Lee stared at me for a second before returning

to the folder. "You placed glue between each page in Joe's notebook, which had a year's worth of his beautiful drawings. You ruined them."

I never had a prouder moment than getting even with the bastard.

"Joe had it coming. He's one of the boys who held me on the anthill. And he helped beat me up plenty of times on my way home when we lived in Mud Flats."

"You dropped one of your large red firecrackers into the toilet after flushing it, blowing the porcelain top off. Water spewed everywhere. The bathroom filled up with smoke. The toilet top had to be replaced."

My timing had been perfect. I'd laughed until tears ran down my face. Every kid in school loved it.

"You were asked to write a paper apologizing for gluing Mr. Allen's grade book facedown on his desk. Instead you wrote about"—he looked at the file—"hogan and trailer kids, gangs, BB guns, rabid dog packs, Mud Flats, stupid white teachers, and Navajo teachers who aren't fair. You even made fun of drunks."

Mona leaned toward me, glowering. I could almost see steam coming out of her ears. But every word I'd written was true.

"David, your behavior better change—and change fast." Mr. Lee closed the folder. "Mr. Allen thinks you've been acting out because your father recently married Mrs. Crow."

Yeah, well, we all hated her. Sam hadn't laughed since the night he got trash dumped all over him, nor had Sally after her hair had been sheared like a sheep. Lonnie counted down the days like it was a prison sentence. How could Dad have done this to us?

Mona rose from the couch and put her notepad in her purse. "I promise these problems will cease immediately. David's father and I will see to it."

At dinner that night, Mona and Dad ignored me. As we cleared the table, Mona wrote on the punishment board under my name, "Full restriction. No activities allowed."

Except she didn't take away my paper route. I guess she saw it as work. If Mona had known how my route kept my sanity, it would have been the first thing to go. Other than my life, she had nothing else to take from me.

It was time to up the ante.

CHAPTER 34

Our apartment went dark every night by nine o'clock. When Mona came in to check on us, she looked at the bottom bunk to see Sam, but without a step stool, she couldn't see me up top. About a week into my incarceration, I slipped out of the house and rode my bike in the light of a full moon to Mud Flats. My desire to escape was so strong that I didn't care about the danger.

As I neared our old neighborhood, I saw Joe and Willie, the two boys Mr. Lee mentioned during the meeting.

Joe was siphoning gas from a truck parked on Seventh Street while Willie sprayed graffiti on the side of a trailer.

"Looks like fun," I said as I rolled up to them on my Stingray.

"Go home, **Gáagii**," Willie said. "You don't belong here."

Joe coughed and spit. "You could get hurt."

"I want to join you guys. I'll do anything you do."

They laughed and said a few words to each other in Navajo. "Okay, come with us," Willie said.

I left my bike on the corner of Eighth Street, and we walked to the edge of a wash next to a lone hogan surrounded by wine and whiskey bottles.

"Old man Yazza live here," Joe said. "He mean old widower. Nobody like him. You play trick on him."

Willie gathered crab apples that had fallen from a nearby tree into a pile about ten feet from the hogan entrance, a traditional sheepskin. "Throw into door. Don't miss."

The prank seemed simple enough. Winding up like Whitey Ford, I fired ripe, squishy crab apples into the taut sheepskin. Splat noises cracked the still air.

And then I heard a gravelly voice from inside the hogan. "Bad boys. Bad. Go away," Mr. Yazza said, emerging with a shotgun and shaking it in the air. He yelled Navajo words that sounded like a war cry. "Not come back or I shoot you with shotgun!"

All three of us laughed and slunk off out of sight.

"See you tomorrow night, **Gáagii**," Joe said.

My heart pumped a little faster. He'd asked me back. "Okay." I returned to my bike and began the ride home, hoping tomorrow they had something different planned.

The next evening, I sneaked out of the house again. Willie and Joe were waiting. "Let's go back to

Yazza's hogan," Willie said. "You throw more crab apples at Yazza's door."

As we walked, I had a bad feeling. When we got there, Joe piled the crab apples closer to the entrance this time. The moon was still full enough that I could see the outline of the sheepskin door.

"Throw all of 'em," Willie whispered, backing up a couple of steps behind me.

"Mr. Yazza said, 'I shoot you with shotgun,'" I reminded them. "It sounded like he meant it."

"Not worry. He drunk." Joe gave me a crooked smile. "Won't expect it. Can't aim shotgun."

"This last time," added Willie.

Joe handed me a crab apple. "Go, **Gáagii**."

"Yazza can't hit nothin'," Willie said, but he backed up a few more feet.

I should have walked away, but this was my chance to be one of them. The first three fastball crab apples rocketed against the sheepskin: splat, splat, splat. The fourth apple struck Mr. Yazza's chest as he thrust through the door, his double-barrel shotgun aimed directly at me.

I turned to run.

The click of the trigger gave me an instant to jump to the right just before two shots rang out, hitting me on the left side and lifting me into the air. I slammed hard on the ground, gasping for breath. My backside sizzled with a dizzying burn. My butt and thigh throbbed as my jeans, underwear, and skin tore off. A high-pitched "eeeee" filled my ears, worse than after the potpie explosion in the oven.

"Not come back. Never!"

Mr. Yazza didn't need to worry about that unless I couldn't get up. I forced myself to my feet and dragged my left leg like dead weight. Willie and Joe had disappeared.

I hobbled for what seemed like hours, the pain shooting up and down my body, until I reached my bike on Eighth Street. When I got on, I cried out when I tried to sit. I rode home standing up the whole way.

Inside our apartment, I limped to the bathroom and took off what was left of my jeans and underwear. Blood dripped on the linoleum floor. I checked out my wounds in the mirror and let out a loud moan. My left side looked like it had been worked over by a cheese grater.

I filled the tub, hoping to wash away the pain. As soon as my ravaged skin hit the warm water, my body bolted upward like I'd been shocked, and I yelled out. Salt, blood, and pebbly pieces of flesh rose to the surface and floated on the water. Stretching out on my right side, holding on to the edge of the tub,

I stared at my left buttock, hip, and thigh, horrified by the sight.

Dad and Mona stirred in their bedroom. Lonnie and Sally made muffled noises. Sam raced to the bathroom, opened the door, and gasped.

"Goddamn it," Dad said to Mona. "What did the little bastard do this time?" He made his way down the hall and appeared in the doorway in his sleeveless T-shirt and boxer shorts. His trusty belt was wrapped around his hand, the end dangling at his side. He pushed Sam out and closed the door. Staring at me, he was strangely quiet for several moments, and then he plunked himself on the toilet seat and let go of the belt.

"What the hell happened to you? There's blood everywhere. There isn't much left of your jeans—or your ass, for that matter."

In between loud whimpers, I told him what had happened.

"Really stupid," he said. "Didn't you think if he said he'd shoot you, he probably meant it? Dumbass. If that was lead shot, you'd be dead. How did you know he used rock salt?"

"I didn't. I just wanted Willie and Joe to let me join their gang."

"Why do you need that? I never belonged to anyone or anything, and I never missed it."

"I wanted them to like me." Tears rolled down my face, not because of the pain but because of the lengths I'd gone to for acceptance. "I had to do something. You've let Mona take everything from me. I hate my life. I don't care what happens to me."

Dad's chin dropped to his chest and he started mumbling, his eyes losing focus for the longest time. Finally, he raised his head and looked at me, nodding. "I understand," he said. "You'll do whatever it takes to be your own man. I admire that. When I was in the Q and walked into the yard for the first time, a vicious lifer con decided to test me. He wanted to make me his punk. Ugly son of a bitch. He asked me if I was married and where I was from. I was naive—I told him my wife and I were from Texas. In his nastiest voice, he said he'd screwed every woman in Texas and their twats were stretched wider than an ax handle because they were all whores."

He made a fist and punched the palm of his left hand. "I crunched the guy's jaw so hard it knocked him down. Then I jumped on top of him and pounded his head into the concrete. His teeth went flying. I smashed his face into a bloody pulp."

"Did you kill him?" I asked quietly.

"Three more seconds, I would have, but two of his buddies pulled me off. One told me to get up slowly and begin moving. Another handed me a handkerchief. Several small groups formed. The cons pushed me from group to group as we steadily walked away until it was impossible to identify me."

The water had gotten cold, and I pulled the plug with my toe to let the water drain. "Did the guy ever come after you?"

"No. Never. In the code of the cons, I'd been challenged and won. You can't let anyone push you around in the Big House or they'll own you. But one of the con's friends told me that if I ever did something stupid like that again, he'd push me into the center where the armed guards up in the tower would have a clear shot. But I didn't care. I did what I had to do. I passed the test. I could get smokes from anybody, and no one confronted me again."

The sucking noise as the last of the water slipped out of sight startled me, and I turned to see the ugliest bathtub ring in history.

"You're no longer grounded," Dad said, standing up. "You've earned it. You can buy candy bars from the trading post, visit the Kontzes, play sports, go to Gallup with the family on weekends, and eat dinner with us. I'll tell Mona these changes begin at once. I don't care what you do as long as it doesn't come to my attention. She sets the rules inside the house. You set your own rules outside it. You're one tough bastard."

Smiling, he shook his head and looked at me warmly. It had been a long time since that happened.

"What a mess. You really did it this time, boy. Clean up the blood and go to bed. And you have to buy new jeans and underwear."

It took almost a week for me to heal enough to go back to school. Henry greeted me like I was a conquering hero. Everyone knew the story, thanks to Joe and Willie.

Henry gathered a group of our classmates before homeroom. "Let's look at **Gáagii**'s mutilated ass," he said, dragging me to the bathroom to pull down my pants. The kids oohed and aahed.

Of all the dumb pranks I ever pulled, this one had the most value. In Dad's mind, I had somehow passed a test, upheld a code. Impressing him enough to get my life back had been worth it. Mr. Yazza's shotgun did me a world of good, even if it almost killed me.

CHAPTER 35

Late one afternoon the following January, I collected on my paper route and staggered into the kitchen, aching from the cold. Every part of me was frozen: my hands, my nose, my feet—even my eyelashes.

During the winter in Fort Defiance, snow squalls hit us all the time, and the temperature would drop into the teens and stay there for several days. Fires burned in the hogans around the clock, covering the hills under Canyon Bonito with smoke. Horses froze to death standing up, many of them stuck to fences. Even the dog packs hid from sight. When Dad and I drove by the Navajo Inn, we'd see new "Popsicles" lying on the ground, their frightening bluish faces staring back at us.

Mona ordered me to hand over the money and counted it. "You're five dollars short." She narrowed her cruel, beady eyes. "If you're hiding the money, produce it."

"I must have dropped the five-dollar bill," I said. "I didn't know it was missing."

"Well, then you better go find it because you can't come back inside until you do." She walked to the board and wrote, "Lost $5 on paper route." She didn't fill in the punishment execution date.

I held up the weather header on the **Gallup Independent**. "The paper says the temperature will drop to minus seventeen here tonight. I'll freeze to death."

"Nonsense. Out."

Dad stood behind her without speaking, pointing to the door.

How could I possibly find the money in the dark? "But . . ."

Mona pushed me outside.

As I trudged down the street with my head down, trying to stop the wind from hurting my face, I saw lights ahead shining brightly. Fort Defiance Indian Hospital stood like a giant flagstone monument in the swirling snow. I ran to the side entrance. The first two doors were locked, and I started to panic, but the door to the daily clinic opened. They closed at five but had forgotten to lock up.

I spotted a gurney down the well-lit hallway. Finding the light switch, I watched the fluorescent bulbs go dark as I climbed onto the gurney and snuggled under the warm blanket. I finally stopped shivering. It took longer to feel my feet.

There wasn't a sound. Mona worked at the clinic, so I needed to be long gone before it opened at eight. In the meantime, I was safe. Free of Mona and Dad for the night, I fell into a deep sleep, imagining myself escaping from a German concentration camp.

It seemed like only a few minutes had passed when I woke up to the dim light of a new day. My clothes were damp but warm, and I was starving. The large clock said it was seven-thirty. I jumped off the gurney and hurried out into the cold.

When I reached our street, I hid behind a house across from our apartment. Mona strode by a couple of minutes later. Once she passed, I sneaked into our yard and crouched behind our shed. Soon after, Dad walked out the front door. Then I slipped through the back door into the kitchen.

Sam was at the table finishing his cereal. Lonnie and Sally had already driven to school. We had almost twenty minutes before the bus came.

"Where'd you go last night?" he asked.

I poured milk into a bowl of cornflakes and told him about the clinic. On the punishment board, the execution box still didn't have a date. "The money must be repaid" was written in red ink.

"Mona says you have to pay back the money and you can't have any dinner until you do. And every night, you have to wash the dishes and put them away after the family has finished eating."

Lucky for me, my evil stepmother didn't know I was friends with Mr. Ashcroft at the trading post. And she didn't know that he let me leave extra copies of the newspapers for his customers. I usually made enough to pocket some money and still buy candy bars and crackers. Sometimes I stashed away a dollar a day. I'd be able to pay back the five dollars in no time.

Unaware of my plan, Mona hounded me constantly for the money, calling me stupid and irresponsible. On Saturday morning, my anger surged out of control and I cursed at her. Dad hit me with a swift backhand to the face and told me to get into the car.

"Mona has every right to punish you," he said, as we drove off in the sedan to requisition supplies from Uncle Ulysses S. Bia. "My family could have eaten for a week off the money you lost. And you act like it was no big deal."

"Even if it means freezing to death? It was totally unfair."

"Get over it. You would have found somebody to let you in. The Kontzes, for one. Hell, you could have conned half of Fort Defiance into helping you. Unfair? Don't talk to me about unfair. I nearly froze to death plenty of times, and we were always hungry. You ought to try sleeping in a car or under a bridge on a regular basis. Especially in the winter. You have no idea how bad I had it growing up. And you don't know how tough it is in prison. You have it easy."

That was Dad's justification for all his cruel behavior, and he puffed out his chest, winding up to continue. I leaned against the door and prepared myself for a long day of watching out for the police or concerned citizens who might turn us in. During the winter, fewer cars and trucks drove by, so being the lookout was easier except when Dad turned off the car and the temperature dropped inside.

Nothing had changed about our weekend trips since Dad married Mona. As far as I could tell, she never asked any questions about them, even when we got home past dark. Still, Mona had to know what we were doing. Dad brought the BIA tools inside the house in plain sight, though she pretended not to see them.

Dad poked me hard in the arm. "You can't imagine what goes through a man's mind on the bus ride to prison. The diesel tour, they call it." His eyes bugged out, and the vein on his forehead started thumping.

This wasn't good. How stupid of me—I should have kept my mouth shut. I'd gotten him angry, and we might have twelve hours ahead of us today and more tomorrow. As usual, I didn't know what he had planned, but for sure, he'd take his anger out on me.

"That might be the toughest part of all," Dad

said, his voice harsh, "the swelling up of the stark reality that this is it. You're going to wake up in the Big House for untold mornings to come. There's no escape. By that point, you've pushed the fury, or whatever dominated your brain when you committed the crime, so far back so many times that you would swear you didn't do anything wrong. You even use more passive ways of talking, like turning 'when I committed the crime' into 'when the crime was committed.' It doesn't matter—even if what you did was justified."

We drove for a few miles in silence. Then he yelled, "Are you listening, boy? You need to know how to survive in this world. You're the lookout now, but you have to learn to do what I'm teaching you on your own."

"Yes, Dad." I had to calm him down. Otherwise, a slap in the head would come next—or worse. But I also had to keep paying attention to the road to make sure we didn't get caught. Sometimes I wondered if he and I would be cellmates in the Q.

"When the bus unloads at the entrance to the prison, your life as you know it is over," he said. "Before the day has ended, you'll be locked up in a six-by-ten-foot cell. With another inmate. He'll already be there, in the top bunk."

My mind was spinning. How could I trigger him into changing the subject? It was always a gamble—I had to say or ask something without making him feel manipulated, which would make him even madder. But if I could pull it off, it was like hitting the jackpot on a slot machine—stories would come gushing out, and Dad would tell me far more than he ever intended. And he'd forget about being mad at me for a while.

"The odds are fifty-fifty your cellmate did something worse than you. And the odds are equally bad that he has an immutably criminal mind. And he may not be smart either, which is the worst combination."

Here was my chance. Dad had never talked about this before. "Who was in your cell when you got to the Q?" I blurted out, afraid to say anything else until I could gauge his reaction.

He stopped and looked at me. "Buddy. Buddy Figueiredo. He was my first cellmate." He burst out laughing. "Talk about dumb—he was the dumbest con I ever met."

Dad's face lit up and his shoulders relaxed. He reached over and rubbed my head.

Jackpot. I let out a sigh of relief.

Dad unbuttoned the top of his coat, settled down in the seat, and told me about James "Buddy" Figueiredo, who was waiting in the top bunk of cell 1440 in the east block when he arrived. "He had gotten there just hours before," Dad said. "The guy was so stupid he didn't know he was stupid. He had the face of a child and wasn't very tall, but he was extremely muscular. And he had an explosive temper to match."

Buddy's crime was almost comical. In late 1946, he and his three uncles robbed the Sears and Roebuck in Modesto, California, pulling off the most publicized heist in the city's history. On a Saturday evening close to Christmas, Buddy rang the doorbell at the home of the Sears manager. When a teenage boy came to the door, Buddy and two of his uncles pushed their way inside, brandishing handguns, while the third uncle stayed in the car. The gunmen forced the manager, his wife, and his two sons to drive them down to the store and open the safe.

After helping themselves to $23,000, Buddy and his uncles tied up the family, left the store, and drove south a few hundred miles, whooping it up the whole way for getting away with the crime. Buddy sat on his cut of the money for six months before making a down payment on a car upholstery business and a house. Then he became a socialite.

"He was such an idiot," Dad said. "He and his wife attended all the local theater events. He was living large and loving life, bragging that his uncles had given him a lot of money. Nothing like drawing attention to yourself."

It wasn't long before Buddy confessed the crime

to his best friend, who happened to be jealous. Using an FBI wire, his friend got Buddy bragging about the heist, about how he and his uncles masterminded the crime and how much fun it was to be rich. Shortly after the wiretapped confession, the police raided Buddy's house late at night and hauled him to the slammer. Buddy immediately spilled his guts about his uncles' involvement.

"Just an hour after meeting him," Dad said, "I knew Buddy's entire life story. Far more than I ever wanted to know. Then he asked me what he should tell the parole board. He'd be talking to them in no time, he said, because he only had a one-year sentence for breaking and entering. All he had done was go into the house, put a gun to the wife's head, and drive in the car to the store. Buddy didn't understand that he'd also been convicted of kidnapping, which carried a seven-year sentence, along with armed robbery, which carried another seven. I told him he'd have at least eight or nine years to think about what to say to the parole board."

But that wasn't what Buddy wanted to hear. Dad barely got the words out before his cellmate flew into a volcanic rage and tried to choke him. "You're not going to lay a life rap on me!" he screamed at him. A guard had to come in to calm things down, telling them it was the only warning they'd get. A fight in a prison cell was good for sixty days in the hole—no light, bread and water only. And the parole board would lengthen their sentences.

"I told Buddy I was wrong," Dad said. "Hopelessly wrong, schoolboy stupid. Yes, of course, he'd be out in a year. How could I have misunderstood his crime? All he could have been charged with was breaking and entering, and no one even got hurt."

Keeping Buddy on good terms became Dad's top priority. "He was an insane son of a bitch," he said. "Every night I worried he'd jump out of bed while I was sleeping and try to choke me to death. Never again, in my wildest circumstances, have I been around anyone as defensive as he was."

Buddy said to the warden that he needed to get out of prison to take care of his upholstery shop. And he needed the money from the robbery to keep it running.

"I told him to keep talking to the warden, that soon he'd agree, I was sure. It took everything in me not to crack up."

Dad and I both laughed, and the mood in the car remained light for the rest of the day.

Buddy became our secret. When the timing was right, I could just say his name, and Dad would start laughing. In fact, nothing made us laugh harder.

I had found another way to survive.

CHAPTER 36

Early on a Sunday morning in September, someone knocked at the door. We rarely got visitors. I ran to the window, and Dad looked through the peephole.

Mom stood on the porch in a thin blue cotton dress next to a tall woman with a beehive hairdo and bell-bottoms. Two and a half years had passed since we moved from Gallup, but it seemed much longer. I could hardly remember what it was like living with Mom.

"What the hell do you want, Thelma Lou?" Dad yelled through the door. "These kids aren't yours. Get out of here right now."

Mom looked at her friend, and the woman nodded, encouraging her to speak. Mom stared at a paper in her hand. "Thurston, I have a letter from a lawyer. You have to let me see my kids." It sounded like she was reading off the paper.

"That isn't going to happen," Dad said. "Go back to wherever you came from."

Mom's body stiffened, but she didn't leave. In the past, Dad's demand would have sent her away sobbing. Her friend leaned over and said something in Mom's ear.

"They're **our** children, not yours, and I have rights too!" Mom shouted. "You have to let me see them." Her voice trembled, but she acted more like an adult than she ever had.

"I don't have to do a thing. The court gave me full custody, and no one has to see you again—ever."

Sam, Sally, and I gathered behind Dad. Whether they wanted to spend time with Mom wasn't clear, but I wanted to see her. Though she'd brought someone for support, this seemingly brave woman wasn't the mom I remembered. I hoped she'd changed, that she had gotten help for her broken nerves.

"Mr. Crow, you need to read the letter from Thelma Lou's lawyer," Mom's friend said. "She has the legal right of visitation. You can't stop her. You'll be held in contempt."

Dad yanked the door open. Mom's friend was holding up the letter for him to read.

"I don't know who the hell you are, but go bother someone else's kids, like maybe your own." Dad snatched the letter and slammed the door again. His eyes shifted back and forth down the page.

I peeked out the window again to see both women standing with their arms crossed, waiting.

When Dad finished reading, he opened the door. "This is total bullshit, but you can visit once a month for only a few hours. You can't take the kids farther than Gallup. Lonnie doesn't have to go, and she won't."

"I'll see you next Saturday," Mom said with a sad smile. She walked to the passenger side of an oxidized blue '58 Chevy, and her friend got in the driver's seat.

I watched them roll down the street until I couldn't see them anymore.

When she appeared the following weekend, Mom came with a man who had the same big blue eyes, blond crew cut, and toothy smile as the great home run hitter Roger Maris of the New York Yankees, but she called him Ted. It turned out he didn't like baseball and didn't know who Roger Maris was, but when we got to the movies, he bought me all the Cracker Jacks and soda I wanted, placing him firmly on my "good guy" list.

On our way to the theater, Mom twisted around in the passenger seat of Ted's '62 Ford to look at the three of us. She asked Sam and Sally questions to get them to talk, but they either shrugged or gave her one-word answers and then looked away.

"David, tell me what you've been up to." She forced a smile.

"I still like to play baseball and read the newspapers before I deliver them," I said.

Mom's green eyes lit up. "Do the teachers know you have dyslexia? Are they treating you right? If not, you can come live with Ted and me in Albuquerque where the schools are better."

"My grades aren't great and it took me a while to make friends, but now I have a few good ones."

Mom's smile disappeared and her face clouded over. "Your daddy tried to kill me," she said.

My heart sank. I didn't want to talk about Dad.

"When I got home the day you all left me and found that ugly note on the door, I walked to your friend Joey's house. His mother let me stay and said she'd help me find you guys. Every day I went to our house hoping you'd come back. The morning after you and your daddy were there, I wanted to get away from that sad place, so I got in the car and drove very slow because I was crying and hadn't slept. At a stop sign, I hit the brakes and nothing happened. They didn't work. At all. It's a good thing I always took the long way around, or I'd have gone flying down the hill and crashed."

If Mom had taken the shortest way out of town, down Elephant Hill, she wouldn't have survived without brakes. Her car would have hit another vehicle in the intersection a lot harder than the tire Sam and I had launched into the Volkswagen Beetle. Only Mom would have driven an extra four miles to avoid a hill, but it saved her life.

"I walked to the nearest gas station," she continued. "A friendly mechanic took me back to the car and said, 'Lady, I can't fix this without taking it to the shop. Someone cut your brake lines on purpose. They meant to kill you. This wasn't an accident.'"

Dad had disappeared for hours the night we moved to Mud Flats. He must have gone back to Gallup to cut her brakes. When he and I were at the house that awful afternoon, I noticed a small puddle by the rear tire of Mom's car but didn't think anything of it—now I was positive it had been brake fluid.

That was why Dad had been so angry and agitated that day. Maybe he had expected to hear about a fatal accident or read about it in the paper. But as the days passed without any news, he knew his plan hadn't worked. Mom had unknowingly outwitted him.

My head throbbed. The horrible guilt returned, reminding me I had gone along with ditching her.

Mom reached over the back of her seat to grab Sally's arm, but Sally pulled away. "Are you listening?" When Mom tried to do the same with Sam, he crossed his arms over his chest so she couldn't paw him. "Your daddy tried to kill me. I'm not making this up."

Both of them looked out the window. Like children in war zones, they'd become numb to the adults in their lives.

Ted drove into the Chief Theatre parking lot in Gallup. He hadn't said a word the entire trip, as if he'd been hired as our chauffeur. Mom and Ted made us sit right next to them with me closest to Mom. She sniffled throughout the movie and kept reaching for my hand. I let her hold it for a couple of minutes and then pulled away, and she'd try again. Eventually I sat on my hands. As bad as I felt about what happened to her, I wasn't going to let her spoil John Wayne and Richard Widmark starring in **The Alamo**.

But after the movie ended, I thought again about what she'd said. It was obvious Dad saw cutting her brake lines as an easy way to kill her. He would have said she killed herself running a red light and crashing into a truck or a train.

On the car ride home, as if she'd read my mind, she turned in her seat and picked up her story. "I didn't have much money after getting my brakes fixed, adding oil and gas and all, so I drove to Albuquerque, pulled over, and slept in my car. I only had forty dollars left. A policeman stopped by and gave me a blanket. 'God bless you, lady,' he said. 'I hope you have somewhere to go.'"

When Mom tried to get Sally's and Sam's attention again, they continued to ignore her, quietly whispering about the movie. But I looked her in the eye and listened. I wanted to hear the whole story.

"I called your daddy's old boss at Woodmen Accident and Life. In his spare time, he helps people. But he was out every time I called, so I had to live in my car for a while. When I finally reached him, he got me a room, money, and a job as a waitress trainee at the Copper Bull Truck Stop restaurant. Then he got me a lawyer so I could visit you guys."

If a moment existed to rethink the choice of picking Dad over Mom, this was it. But Mom was no choice at all. She was still more of a child than any of us. Whatever was wrong with her hadn't gotten much better.

Besides, I couldn't go without Lonnie, Sam, and Sally. They were all I had in this world. And Dad would kill Mom for sure if any of us were crazy enough to go with her.

I wanted to help her, but nothing could save her, and the mental agony of being around her every day and listening to the broken record of her complaints would have driven me insane.

After our sixth monthly visit, Ted waited in the car as Sam and Sally walked ahead of Mom and me toward the house. She grabbed my wrist with her clammy hand. "I need to tell you something, David."

I stopped and looked at her. As usual, her sad eyes were shiny with tears.

"You have to go with me," she said, her voice rising. "If you tell the lawyer you want me, we can live on welfare in a trailer in Albuquerque. You can help by getting a paper route and doing chores, and you can cut lawns during the summer for extra money. Sam and Sally will mind you. You're the only one who can stop your daddy."

I shook my head and wrenched free from her grasp. "Why don't you just keep visiting us with Ted?"

"I can't. I quit my waitress job, and Ted is moving to Iowa to work as a carpenter. If you won't come with me, I'm going with him." The tears spilled down her face. "You don't love me or you'd live with me. How can you want to be with your dad? I gave birth to you. You owe me—I'm your mother."

"It wouldn't work, Mom," I said softly. "You can't take care of us."

She knew she couldn't change my mind. We hugged each other for a long time, and then she climbed into the car and drove away with Ted.

It would be two years before I saw her again.

PART 4

Washingdoon
1966

Coach Ford (**left**) and me (**right of center**) at a Walter Johnson High School track meet. Bethesda, Maryland. 1970.

CHAPTER 37

After living in Fort Defiance for more than three years, I couldn't imagine living anywhere else. I had grown to love the Navajo people, and the reservation felt like home to me. Every day I tried to outdo myself entertaining my classmates, and they never got tired of it.

I continued playing Little League even after I turned thirteen. Mr. Kontz discovered a rule that allowed an exception if the team was short a player. We had only eight without me. On the nights before our games, he and Mrs. Kontz let our team camp out in their backyard. In the mornings, we crammed into the bed of his old black pickup truck, and he hauled us, sometimes more than fifty miles, to baseball fields. We each brought twenty-five cents to help pay for gas.

Thomas Kontz, Richard's oldest brother, bought us Cokes when we won. After our games, we went to the movies at the Window Rock Civic Center for a dime. Our baseball uniforms got us discounts on candy and hot dogs. Sam and I had a tight group of friends and were as much a part of the team as the Navajo boys. In a place that had once felt so hostile, the Kontz family, Henry, Jim, Tommy, and my other Navajo friends accepted me in a way that seemed impossible when we arrived in Mud Flats.

A month into ninth grade at Window Rock High School, Dad told us to meet in the living room after dinner. Sam, Sally, and I looked at each other with dread. It was just the three of us now that Lonnie had graduated and left for Arizona Western College.

As we piled onto the red couch, I kept thinking that Dad's announcement would have something to do with Mom.

"We're going to Washington, DC, for six months, or Washingdoon, as the Navajos like to call it," Dad told us. "I'm getting advanced training at the BIA national headquarters, a few blocks from the White House."

I felt like I couldn't breathe. Sam and Sally didn't move.

"This is terrible," I said. "I don't want to go anywhere—ever."

Over the summer, I had secured a pitching position on our baseball team and then tried out and made the high school football team. The following spring, I'd be running the one-mile and two-mile races on the track team. On my paper route, people waved instead of shooting me with BB guns, my weirdo customers continued providing much-needed comic relief, and the dog packs ran from me in fear. Mr. Ashcroft and I had long discussions every afternoon before I went to see my second family at the Kontz residence. And on the weekends when I didn't go on stealing trips, Henry and his dad took me everywhere with them. This was my town.

I followed Dad into the kitchen. "Can I stay with the Kontzes while you go to Washingdoon? They have eight kids and won't even notice me."

He poured himself a cup of coffee, not answering, so I continued, "When you come back in the spring, I'll move back home."

"No. Pack up now. Find someone to take your paper route. We're leaving in five days."

"But . . ."

The bulging eyes meant Dad would explode if I pushed him.

On Friday, during classes, at lunch, and after school, I said goodbye to friends, reassuring them I'd be back in the early spring. The Rambler was packed so full the frame groaned under the weight, and we towed the same green plywood trailer from our EPNG days. Friends waved and smiled as we drove off, and I missed them already.

• • •

Dad drove the Rambler for fourteen hours a day with brief stops for gas, food, and a late-night cheap hotel. Mona sat next to him looking straight ahead, going on about how much property she owned in North Carolina and about how glad she was to be getting away from the reservation, hopefully for good.

The brown, rocky terrain turned into fields of wheat and corn. Gradually the flatlands became rolling hills until we finally reached the green East Coast. Walls of trees and shrubs surrounded us on every side. It was hard to believe that this place was in the same country as the Navajo Indian Reservation.

Dad turned off the massive Interstate 495 toward Kensington, Maryland, and drove down a beautiful parkway with a creek running alongside it. The Rambler came to a stop at 3922 Prospect Street, a three-story gray house with a yard full of trees and a beautifully manicured lawn.

It was nicer than any house we'd ever had. Sally got her own bedroom. Sam and I shared a huge room on the third floor that had to be bigger than our whole house in the government compound. The street was lined with cars I had read about but never seen up close: Mercedes Benz, Audi, BMW, and Volvo. Our little suburb had more roads, bridges, libraries, recreation centers, and sidewalks than on the entire reservation. How could the Navajos have so little in a land where there was so much?

After a weekend of moving furniture and unpacking boxes, Sam and I walked down the tree-lined streets to school. Kensington Junior High covered grades seven through nine and looked like a brick fortress on the side of a green hill. A stream flowed out front. Most of the kids were dropped off by their parents in fancy cars like the ones on our street. They dressed in expensive clothes too, better than the ones I'd stared at in the Sears and Roebuck catalog. Several boys waited for their parents to leave, lit a cigarette, and left the school grounds. No one seemed to care.

Inside, I saw more kids crowded around their lockers than in all twelve grades in Fort Defiance. Taking a deep breath, I walked across the hall to the attendance office, Sam beside me. A woman with teased hair assembled our class schedules and handed us a carbon copy, along with a map. We would need it. The building had two large stories with long wings on either side of the center, as well as a basement with the gym and locker rooms.

When I walked into my algebra class, our teacher, Mr. Jones, was writing numbers, parentheses, and letters on the board. He welcomed me, assigned me a seat, and asked everyone to solve the problem. All thirty of the other students got the answer, but I had no idea why letters, numbers and parentheses would be mixed together. Was this some combination of English and math?

My next period was chemistry. The equation on the board looked like hieroglyphics. "You already know about the atomic molecular structure, the periodic table, and the basics of chemical reactions," Mr. Klein said. "We'll spend the next month or two learning to balance chemical equations."

Balancing what? I stared at my desk so no one would notice my tears. My stupidity had finally caught up to me. Kids were laughing and saying the class would be an easy review of what they learned last year. I didn't understand any of it.

At lunch, I carried a tray of food to a table of students I recognized from morning classes. They continued their conversations, ignoring me.

"Hi, I just moved here from the Navajo Indian Reservation," I said to a pretty girl. Surely, she'd be nice to me. "Can I sit with you?"

"You already said that in class this morning. You don't look like an Indian. Where's your loincloth? Are you going to scalp us? Do you live in a tepee?"

Everyone laughed.

Heat rushed to my face. "I'm a Cherokee. Indians don't live like that anymore."

"I wonder how he'll like living in Hanukkah Heights?" the boy next to her asked. "Or is it Kosher Canyon?"

"Huh?" Lunch was as confusing as my classes.

"Did your mother get those clothes at Goodwill

or from a dumpster?" another girl asked. The whole table erupted with laughter again.

I looked down at my clothes and saw them through their eyes: dirty jeans with worn-out knees, a faded flannel shirt, and frayed, stained tennis shoes. A Gilbert Blackgoat pounding would have felt comforting by comparison.

I tried not to make eye contact with anyone for the rest of the day. When I got home that afternoon and said hello to Mona, she offered nothing but stony silence. If she was happier living on the East Coast, she didn't show it.

Apparently, Dad's day hadn't gone so well either. "Headquarters is filled with know-it-all assholes from Harvard. Oh, I mean **Haahvaahd**." He stretched out the word in a snooty accent. "Those guys have their heads shoved so far up their asses, they breathe shit." He brought his fists to his chest. "If they want to take it outside, I'll show them what **Haahvaahd** blood looks like on their fancy shirts and tailored suits."

In this swanky house, my siblings and I got quiet, the way we did when we arrived in Mud Flats and again after Mona first took over our lives. We said nothing at dinner, and later, Sam, Sally, and I sat shell-shocked on the couch in the family room, still reeling from our first day at school.

Sally said, "A few of the kids were nice to me but some made fun of my clothes. Class was really hard."

"I didn't understand my classes either," Sam said. "One of the teachers said I may have to be held back a grade."

"I had no idea what was going on except in PE," I told them both. "The kids my age know so many things I haven't even heard of. I don't even know what questions to ask."

That night, Sam whispered, "Maybe Dad and Mona hate it here too."

"I hope so," I said, but I was afraid we'd never return to Fort Defiance.

Each day felt worse than the day before as it became apparent I was several years behind. Teachers asked why I didn't understand the subjects—every school had to have the same classes. I had no answer. They sure weren't teaching that stuff on the reservation.

I was behind socially too. Every time I approached kids to begin a conversation, they broke it off as quickly as possible. Others walked away as if they hadn't heard me, the way our old neighbors had ignored Mom.

To escape the loneliness and confusion, I turned to running and reading again—as I had in Gallup and Fort Defiance. After school, I ran through the lush neighborhoods along Rock Creek Park just outside our subdivision, often not returning home until dark. Within a couple of weeks, a paper route became available to deliver the **Washington Post** and the **Washington Evening Star**.

Every day, I read the entire **Post**, fascinated with national politics, which was local politics in Washington. I wanted to know all about it. As was my habit, I asked my customers about their days, and they gave me extra change in appreciation for my service. I wanted to be a part of their lives, but fitting in with them didn't seem possible.

In Kensington, there was no Tommy, Henry, Jim, or Richard. The only kids who spent time with me were outcasts themselves—like James and his brother, John. I met them while airing up my bicycle tires at the gas station.

"I bet you never do anything bad," James teased. "You're just a good little paperboy."

"Yeah?" My face stretched into a smile. "Wait here a second."

I checked to make sure the gas station attendant was occupied with the Chevy engine he'd been working on. Then I snatched two valve core removers from an open toolbox behind him, put them in my pocket, and grabbed my bike, telling my new friends to meet me down the street.

In the bank parking lot, I showed them the tools. "We can use these to flatten tires." I demonstrated how they worked, the way Dad did the night of the Window Rock hayride. "The air will escape in just a couple of minutes. We'll take the valve cores, so even if they fill the tires, they'll go flat again. Believe me, no one keeps spare cores."

"How'd you learn to do that?" James asked. "This is really cool. We should flatten every tire in Kensington. Let's start with the PTA meeting tonight."

I laughed. "That will be fun. See you in a couple of hours. We can hit the neighbors you don't like another night."

"Most of them will be at the meeting," he said. "I can't wait."

Shortly after the PTA meeting began that evening, James showed up at the junior high school without his brother. Cars lined both sides of the road for more than half a mile. The working conditions were perfect: a dark sky with just enough brightness from the streetlights and no adults anywhere.

I handed James one of the valve removers. "You take the tires on the passenger side, and I'll take the ones on the driver side. In less time than it takes for the rich bastards to brag about their genius kids, we'll flatten every tire. If we have enough time, we'll get the buses."

Crawling on our hands and knees, we removed every valve core, filling two paper lunch bags. We hit dozens of cars. Then we moved on to two of the buses.

"Let's dump the cores in the creek and come back to watch the parents try to drive home," I said.

We hid behind a tree when the meeting ended. Parents streamed from the building. Taillights glowed red and engines started. A few cars made it to the end of the block, the tire rims grinding on the asphalt. Everyone got out and milled around, chattering up a storm, but I couldn't make out what they were saying. Too bad—it would have been funny.

Tow trucks started appearing, but there weren't enough, so people had to wait in line. Some of them walked away and didn't come back. When the last adult left, we returned to our respective houses, laughing our fool heads off.

The incident made the front page of the **Montgomery County Sentinel**.

I felt powerful and invisible again.

CHAPTER 38

Soon after Christmas, Sam, Sally, and I were washing dishes when Mona summoned us into the living room.

"My father had a heart attack, and I need to help my mother take care of him. Your father has been given leave, and we're all going to my house in Hatteras until my father gets back on his feet. A month, maybe a month and a half. Pack your things, and tell your teachers tomorrow we're leaving at the end of the week."

"I can't miss that much school," I said. "I don't understand my classes as it is. Can't the three of us stay home?"

"No. I can't trust you, and we don't know anyone you can stay with. Get your assignments and do the work while we're gone."

The next morning, I told my math teacher I had to miss school for a while due to a family illness. Mr. Jones sighed and tilted his head. "I know this wasn't your decision," he said, "but you won't be excused for more than a week unless you're the one who's ill."

That night at the dinner table, Dad read the newspaper and Mona gazed at her plate, taking bites of meat loaf as if we weren't there. Sam and Sally glanced over at me with sad eyes.

"The teachers won't accept an excuse unless I'm the one who's sick," I said into the silence as Sam and Sally nodded vigorously.

Dad didn't respond. I took a chance and pulled the paper away from his face. "The teachers won't accept an excuse—"

"I heard you the first time," he said. "Tell the dumb bastards you'll learn a hell of a lot more in Hatteras with me than you will in their uppity-ass classrooms where everyone thinks they're so much better than the rest of us. Who gives a damn what they think? They teach because they can't do." He raised the newspaper to his face again.

"Well, maybe you could help me since you're so smart." I did my best to keep the sarcasm out of my voice.

"I was in and out of school, so I had to teach myself everything. Math explains itself. Biology, geology, science, and literature are part of a natural, logical system. Read it and you'll understand it."

"That doesn't work for me. Maybe I'm stupid like Mom."

"The IQ tests showed you're not too bright, but you can talk your way out of anything, and you're funny."

"I can't talk my way out of anything at this school, and no one thinks I'm funny."

"I'll give you a note to give to your teachers," he said, flipping the page on the newspaper. "You'll be fine."

Justifying my absence was the least of my worries.

Nothing in Kensington was working for me except my paper route. My manager agreed to take care of it until we came back, but I didn't want to come back. I belonged on the Navajo Indian Reservation—that was the only place where my life made sense.

Every minute in Hatteras lasted an eternity. Some local kids caught the school bus in front of Mona's house, and as I watched them board in the morning and get off in the afternoon, I felt as if we had been removed from the world. I had all my assignments with me, but I didn't bother looking at them. I was too far behind for it to matter and couldn't do most of the work anyway.

When we returned to Kensington, we moved to an even bigger rental house with the exalted address of 9715 Kingston Road. For the first time, Sam and I didn't share a room.

On the first day back at school, Mrs. Ralph, my English teacher, walked up and down the aisles, passing out an exam. I gaped at her, wondering why she had given me one when I hadn't been there. She read Dad's note before we left—she knew I would be away for at least a month.

She stood at the front of the room. "As you recall, you are to write a critical essay on the nature of man's struggle against himself. You can use any of the examples we've discussed in class."

All the students started writing frantically. Panicking, I went up to her desk. "Can I take the test another time? It isn't my fault that I was gone."

She leaned toward me, a snarl on her face. "You were taking care of your grandfather? Why? Did the Indians hurt him?"

The class laughed.

I stared at her tiny, mean eyes and beefy jowls, hating her as much as I hated Mona.

"I gave you the assignment. Unless you were ill, your absence is unexcused. I told you that before you left, so it shouldn't come as a surprise. You weren't doing very well anyway."

"What kind of struggle do you mean?" I asked. "Is the man afraid of being eaten by a lion or being shot at in a war, or is he starving?"

"I've explained this many times. Go sit down and write the essay."

Feeling powerless, I slowly walked to my desk. Ten minutes went by, and I still hadn't written a word. The only book I'd read in Hatteras was a silly science fiction novel called **The Shrinking Man** that I'd found at Mona's house in a box of junk. I tried to use the main points to describe the man's struggle, having no knowledge of Mrs. Ralph's lessons:

> **One man, unfairly hit by radioactive fog, that only God understands, begins to shrink, slowly at first, and then rapidly. Until he shrinks down to the size of an atom. No one can see him.**

I paused and looked around the room. All my classmates were still scribbling away. We had nearly forty minutes left, but I had little to add.

When the papers came back, Mrs. Ralph singled out several "brilliant essays," one discussing Michelangelo's personal struggle while he painted the Sistine Chapel and another describing how Helen Keller overcame being deaf, blind, and mute. I knew then what I should have written.

"One student made a mockery of this exam," Mrs. Ralph said, holding up a paper with my name on the front. I wanted to crawl under my desk. She read my essay out loud and everyone roared with laughter.

When she tossed it on my desk, the big red F stood out like a neon sign.

I kept my eyes down, not moving until every student had left the room.

After that, I didn't speak to anyone unless spoken to. Part of me understood how helpless Mom must have felt in the abandoned house in Gallup. Another part related to the shrinking man, becoming smaller and smaller until no one knew I existed.

With each passing day, my classmates seemed happier and more certain of a bright future. They talked about going to college in a few years and taking fancy vacations to Europe. They went on dates and had fun. I fell further behind.

Other than delivering newspapers, reading, and running increasing numbers of miles every day to exhaust myself, I did nothing but dream of returning to Fort Defiance. Dad and Mona talked about staying in the East permanently, but we just couldn't.

In March, we were summoned to the living room once again. Sam, Sally, and I sat on the same red couch we had in Albuquerque, now squeaky and threadbare. Other than the Rambler, this piece of furniture represented the only recognizable part of our old world.

"My training is over," Dad said, "and I put in for a permanent job at the BIA headquarters. My boss said they'd hire me, but first I have to train my replacement in Fort Defiance. We'll get back here in time for you to finish school. Remember to do your assignments so I don't get any more notes saying you're failing. Not that I give a damn."

I jumped to my feet. "You can't mean it. We hate it here. You do too. You hate the know-it-alls at headquarters, the Harvard assholes. We belong in Fort Defiance. That's where our home is, where our friends live."

"Your father can't advance any further in his career in Fort Defiance," Mona said. "And I need to be closer to my mother and father in Hatteras. We have to do what's best for the family."

She meant what was best for **her** family, not ours.

My manager said I had to give up my paper route, but I could apply for a new one when we got back. The drive west seemed to take forever, even though Dad drove his usual fourteen-hour days.

We arrived in Fort Defiance in the middle of the night. Our old apartment was waiting for us. I was too excited to sleep and bounded out of bed early the next morning to get to the bus stop. Friends greeted me with warm smiles. Richard, Henry, and Jim slapped my back and said, "**Gáagii**'s back." My coaches asked me to try out again for baseball and track. Even the teachers were happy to see me.

Every cell in my body wanted to rebel. I belonged in Fort Defiance at Window Rock High School and would never feel that way in Kensington. If I'd stayed, I would have studied hard and looked forward to the future.

But that didn't happen. The five weeks went by in a flash. As my miserable luck would have it, the day I returned, Mrs. Ralph handed out another English exam. Before we left for Fort Defiance, she'd assigned **Silas Marner**, a novel by George Eliot. I never cracked it open. I had no intention of trying to succeed in a world that had nothing to offer me.

"I'd like you to write an analytical review of Silas's personal struggles, his growth, and the lessons one might glean from his life," Mrs. Ralph said, standing before rows of students with bright faces, their sharpened pencils at the ready.

Again, I went up to her desk. Before I could open my mouth, she said, "You were with the Indians this time, right?" She knew the answer, of course, since Dad had written her a note saying we had to leave because of his job.

I nodded. "I was in school at Window Rock High."

The students snickered. A fat kid with thick glasses and zits shouted a mock Indian war cry. Mrs. Ralph giggled, then turned serious. "I gave you the book before you left." She shuffled some papers, dismissing me.

I sat back down and watched my classmates' pencils fly across their papers. I didn't care what they or my teachers thought of me, so it was time to have some fun:

Silas Marner was a conscientious objector living in England during World War II. Hiding from the military, and life itself, he spent long hours in the public library. It was a safe refuge where he could read stacks of anti-war literature and fantasize about the lovely, full-breasted librarian. Her name was Sarah Saddly, and he wanted to bang her like a loose corral gate in a stampede.

Unbeknownst to Silas, German soldiers had killed Sarah's husband on the Western Front. She'd been left with two children and poor prospects for remarriage since most of the men were at war and like her husband would never come home.

When returning an overdue book, Silas finally mustered the courage to ask Sarah on a date. Sarah turned out to be eager for male companionship to fill the hole in her heart and bosom and to provide a father for

her sad, Saddly children. She leapt at the chance for new love.

Silas filled Sarah with endless rounds from his throbbing pistol. Due to his love for her, he joined the war effort and became a hero on Sword Beach at D-Day. After the war, they married, he adopted her children, and she knocked out thirteen more kids, making Mrs. Sarah Marner the happiest and best-serviced woman in all of England. Silas was elected mayor of London and helped rebuild the war-torn city. He was a hero and friend to all, including Prime Minister Winston Churchill.

My essay wasn't returned. Instead Mrs. Ralph handed me a note that read "Tomorrow afternoon at 4:30, you and your father will meet with the county school psychologists and me in Rockville for a conference."

When I got home, Dad and Mona were waiting for me in the kitchen.

"I got a disturbing call from your school principal," Mona said.

"What the hell did you do to warrant a meeting with your teacher and a handful of psychologists?" Dad said. "How did your mouth overload your ass this time? And why the hell does it involve me?"

Mona folded her arms. "You're pure trouble, David. You don't even try to learn or get along. The principal said you wrote an obscene essay that had nothing to do with the test."

"Let me buy a bus ticket for Gallup," I said. "I'll run to Fort Defiance and live with the Kontzes. That'll be best for everyone. Even Sam and Sally agree."

This request, like my previous ones, was met with stony stares and silence.

The following afternoon, Dad and I drove to the Montgomery County Office of Education in Rockville. He mumbled the entire way. I heard "Harvard assholes" three times. As we rolled into the parking lot, he said, "How'd you let this happen?"

"I wanted to have some fun and get even with Mrs. Ralph. Everyone hates me. All the teachers say I need a lot of help with my dyslexia and extensive tutoring to catch up, and they're threatening to fail me for missing so much school."

Dad walked ahead, ignoring me. When we entered the building, a woman at the counter directed us to a conference room where three stern men in suits sat at a big table with Mrs. Ralph. The psychologists stood and introduced themselves, shaking Dad's hand. Mrs. Ralph slowly got to her feet, glancing around the room and then at me.

After everyone was seated, she said, "Mr. Crow, David has missed an unacceptable amount of class. Apparently, you spend a lot of time with a sick grandfather or on an Indian reservation. When he does appear, his lack of understanding regarding assignments is startling."

Dad crossed his legs and scowled. She'd embarrassed him.

"We think something might be wrong with your son. His essay on **Silas Marner** has nothing to do with the book. He made up his own story, inventing several absurd, disturbing sexual references." She handed him my test.

Dad scanned the page. His lips chattered as he tugged at his tie.

Mrs. Ralph directed her attention to me. "Where did you get the material? Certainly not from the book I assigned."

No kidding. "The sex stuff came from cowboy joke books and **Glamour** magazines the girls left on the bus. The war stuff came from books on World War II."

My teacher sat up in her chair. "In other words, you had time to read cowboy joke books and magazines and make up a fantastic story, but you didn't have time to read a book for class."

Dad stood, adjusted his pants, and thrust out his chest. "This little bastard has been putting you on," he said, his voice thundering in the small room. "He knows you don't like him, and he doesn't like you either. He tied up half the PhDs in the whole damn county just to show you he can. He's done this sort of crap all his life, and I haven't been able to beat it out of him."

The horse-faced lead psychologist cleared his throat. "Mr. Crow, please understand that we're concerned about your son. We're here to help him. We don't believe in corporal punishment. David is showing signs of alienating behavior and needs counseling. We would advise you to choose a therapist and attend a series of sessions together. He also needs substantial tutoring and perhaps should repeat a grade."

I stared at my lap. My life was over. Dad would finally be angry enough to kill me, like the other assholes he'd told me about, the ones he said society was better off without.

I glanced up at him, expecting the worst, and did a double take. His face had gone from pinched fury to amusement. Mostly from relief, I burst out laughing. He laughed too.

"**Alienating behavior**," Dad mocked. "Who wouldn't be alienated by the likes of you? David wanted to make you look stupid, and he succeeded beyond his wildest expectations. No one else could have assembled this team of idiots. This goddamn meeting is over."

Dad waved at me to stand up. "Let's get the hell out of here." He smiled and slapped me on the back.

The psychologists had been right about me, but Dad felt disaffected in this world too, especially when confronted by highly educated people. Their diagnosis made us kindred alienated spirits. We walked out of the conference room as Mrs. Ralph and the psychologists stared at us with their mouths open.

In the car, Dad started laughing again. "Jesus H. Christ, what you wrote was funny. 'Bang her like a loose corral gate in a stampede.' How do you come up with these things?"

He turned the key. "Mrs. Ralph is a bigger battle-ax than Miss Brezina. Now I know why you wanted to get even. And those psychologists are like the stupid ones we had in San Quentin. Who cares what they say? The more educated they are, the easier they are to fool."

As we drove back, we mimicked Mrs. Ralph and the psychologists, laughing harder with each new rendition of the meeting. Then Dad went quiet for several minutes.

A couple of blocks from home, he touched my arm. I couldn't believe how gentle he was. "It's time for you to figure out how to get along in the East."

CHAPTER 39

At the end of the summer, close to the start of my sophomore year, I was throwing the football with John, James's brother, in a grassy area along Kensington Parkway. We took turns playing quarterback and receiver to get ready for tryouts. Just before John had to go home, he threw the ball to me, pretending it was the last two minutes of a game.

"Run deep and I'll hit you," he yelled as I raced off. "It'll be high and hard."

Looking up and sprinting at full speed, I tripped over an exposed tree root as the ball sailed past and shattered a bees' nest the size of a large watermelon. Sprawled on my belly, my glasses thrown, I felt a large chunk of the nest twisted in my shirt. Seconds later, my whole torso burned with stings that sent me to my feet screaming. My ears buzzed more intensely than after Mr. Yazza shot me with rock salt.

I ran as fast as I could, but an angry swarm of bees kept up with me, stinging my face, neck, and arms. Hundreds of them. Gulping for air, I swallowed a couple, and my throat seared on the inside, an indescribable, frightening flame. I staggered back to our house and collapsed on my bed. By then, my eyes had swelled shut, and I fought to breathe. Sam and Sally ran into my room after me.

"There are bees flying everywhere in front of the house!" Sally shrieked. "Some are still on you!"

"You look like a cactus," Sam said. "You have stingers all over your head."

"Let's call Mona." Sally headed for the door. "He could die. Look at him. He isn't breathing right."

Sam came back a few minutes later. "Mona said to never call her at the hospital again. She'll be home in a few hours. She said to put some ice on the stings and turn off the lights."

The stings settled into throbbing pain, different from the buckle end of a belt or a shotgun blast or an explosion from an oven. A sort of numbness came with the intense ache, deadening every cell in my body, and I gasped for air as if I'd run uphill for miles.

I lay there for what seemed like days. It was dusk by the time I heard Mona's quick steps as she entered my room. Sitting on the bed, she held my hand. It was the first time she had ever touched me.

"Are you having trouble breathing?" she asked, making it sound as if breathing were akin to taking a bath.

"For a while I couldn't breathe right, but it's better now."

"Good." She got up from the bed. "If the stings were going to kill you, you'd already be dead. I'll be back shortly. Let me change clothes first."

When Mona came back, she helped me arch my back to lift my torso from the mattress and then pulled off my T-shirt. Dozens of stingers fell onto the sheet, and I heard popping noises like someone was stomping on Bubble Wrap.

"I'll poke your stings to drain them and clean them with alcohol. It might hurt a little, but it's necessary." She gently stuck me with her needle, over and over, which didn't hurt nearly as much as the scorching alcohol. "My, look at all the stingers that came out of you. You're very fortunate. Now get some rest."

The next morning, I heard her rapid footsteps enter my room. "Here's some toast and warm milk," she said in her normal monotone. "Stay put and I'll bring you soup tonight."

Other than eating twice a day, I didn't move. Sam and Sally came to visit, but I barely heard them. On the fourth day, I could see and hear again and had the strength to get out of bed.

When I walked into the kitchen, Mona looked at me with her thin, tight smile. "You have bad eyesight, you can't hear well, you're scrawny, you're dyslexic and not terribly bright, but you're one tough little fellow. You'll be okay." Those were the kindest words she ever spoke to me.

I enrolled at Walter Johnson High School, named for baseball's greatest right-handed pitcher, the "Big Train." The building was a larger, fancier version of the junior high. But just before classes started, Mona's dad suffered another heart attack, this one worse than before, and we had yet another family meeting in the living room. Mona said all of us would be leaving for Hatteras in two days.

"Not much happens the first month of school anyway," she said.

"What are you talking about?" I said, my voice rising. "I'll probably flunk out even if I work extra hard from day one. Being a month late will make it impossible. And I just started football tryouts. I can make the team, but not if we're gone. It's not fair."

"You're too skinny to make the team, and even if you do, you'll sit on the bench, so it doesn't matter."

"It doesn't matter to you, but it matters to me. It's my chance to be one of the guys. You can't yank us out of school for a month or more again."

Mona ignored me, and Dad said it was up to her to decide what was best for us.

I stared at both of them, hot anger shooting

through me. I wanted to run as fast as I could out the door, get a bus ticket, and go back to Fort Defiance. The Kontz family or Henry would have taken me in. But Dad would have hunted me down and beaten me. There was no escape from him.

When we returned to Kensington, I walked into Walter Johnson clueless about what the students had been doing for the past month, though I was getting used to that. The halls were filled with happy, well-dressed kids moving with purpose, like the ones in junior high, but there were a whole lot more of them. Oh, how I wished to be liked by them, to understand school and life the way they did.

The secretary in the main office told me to report to the guidance counselor.

"We don't have a complete transcript for you from last year," the counselor said, looking at my file. "Where's the rest of it?"

"We spent part of the year in Fort Defiance, but you should have all my grades from there." That was a lie. I never told Window Rock High School where to send my records. "Maybe they didn't get entered properly."

She flipped through my file again. "We don't have anything from Fort Defiance. You can't go to school here with an incomplete transcript."

"We traveled so often, neither school could keep up with me. But I'm a sophomore. Honest. I finished ninth grade at Kensington Junior High."

"School started almost five weeks ago. Where have you been?"

"We had to go to North Carolina. My stepmother's father had a heart attack about the time school started, and my parents made me go with them to help. We were there for a month last winter when he had his first heart attack. They don't seem to think it's important for me to be in school. I have a note from my stepmother if that will help."

She didn't reach for the note. It wasn't clear whether she accepted my explanation or simply didn't know what to do with me, but she ended up sending me to class with a full schedule.

It was no surprise I couldn't do the work. And my struggles with dyslexia and ever-worsening eyesight made things even harder. D minuses filled every grading slot. None of the teachers wanted to fail me.

I did become better at not drawing attention to myself, the opposite of what I'd wanted to do in Gallup and Fort Defiance. But as I learned from Mrs. Ralph and the other teachers and students in Kensington, no one thought I was funny or endearing.

I shuffled from class to class without doing anything while my fellow students matured and worked hard to get good grades. The only kids doing as poorly were the heavy drug users. No one cared about them either. The parents and schools seemed lax to the point of letting the kids raise themselves. Students had access to smoking rooms and could get passes to drive away from school during the day—almost any excuse worked. Many of my peers freely used marijuana. I slid by unnoticed.

CHAPTER 40

On a Saturday morning in October, Sam and I went with Dad to run errands. On our way home, we stopped off at the post office, and Dad hurried in and came out with two brown packages that he tossed into the trunk. Messages and supplies from his new compadres.

It hadn't taken him long to resume his stealing operations. When Sam wasn't in the car, Dad would let things slip about the criminal connections he'd found in West Virginia. He didn't ask me to be his lookout, but I knew about the PO boxes and could easily guess what he was doing when he disappeared for stretches at a time.

As he pulled our new Ford Country Squire station wagon into the driveway, we saw Sally crying in the front yard. She had a bruise under her eye and a swollen lower lip. The card table she used to sell lemonade was upside down, and paper cups littered the grass. "What the hell happened here?" Dad asked.

"A boy from across the street rode his bike by our house and smashed my lemonade stand," she said, sobbing. "Then he threw my bike into the creek and hit me when I tried to stop him."

Sam fished out her bike while I righted the card table, gathered the cups, and picked up the empty plastic pitcher. Dad put some ice in a washcloth for her lip. How could this boy hit a defenseless girl? Sam and I had done a lot of bad things, but we would never have done something like that.

Dad, Sam, and I walked over to the neighbor's house. A fat man wearing rimless glasses and a coat and tie answered the door. His clothes seemed too formal for a weekend. "I'm John Sturdivant," he said. "Who might you be?"

"I might be Thurston Crow, the neighbor across the street who wants to know what you're going to do about your dumbass son. He smashed my daughter's lemonade stand, threw her bicycle into the creek, and hit her."

"I think you're mistaken, sir," the man said. "Please stay here a moment while I query my son."

Who the hell says "query"? I'd never heard the word before but understood that the pretentious fool planned to ask his son for his version of what happened. Dad kept saying "query" over and over again, his face creasing deeper with each pronouncement.

When the man finally returned, he said, "I'm sorry for your trouble, sir, but you are mistaken. My son says he rode by your house this morning and might have knocked over a cup of lemonade. I regret that, but boys will be boys, as you know. He didn't smash your daughter's lemonade stand or throw her bike into the creek, and he certainly didn't strike her. He would never do such a thing. Good day." He closed the door in our faces.

Dad marched back toward the house, and Sam and I trotted to keep up with him. The Y vein on his forehead pulsed. His eyes bulged. His chest poked out like he was trying to stretch his shirt to the breaking point. His lips chattered like a machine gun. For once, he was angry at someone besides us.

Twitching his arms, he stopped and looked at us. "David and Sam, I think you boys know what to do."

Hell yes, we knew what to do. We'd trained for this moment all our lives. Query Man deserved the full Crow treatment. It was the first time Sam and I had plotted together since our days in Gallup. Soon we were laughing and coming up with all kinds of ideas for ruining Query Man's life. Too bad we didn't have any of Mr. Pino's cherry bombs.

Dad went to his bedroom, leaving us to divide up our duties. Riffling through the Yellow Pages, I looked for products and services that could be delivered on short notice. We started with the florists. Sam read off the phone numbers of every place within a ten-mile range.

"We're having a surprise birthday celebration today," I told each one. "Please send a rush order of flowers with balloons." They promised delivery by midafternoon, and none asked for payment in advance.

Then we hit pizza parlors. "I'm having a large party. Can you deliver ten pizzas, five with cheese only and the other five with pepperoni?"

"We'll have them to you in an hour," the first one said. Once I realized how quickly they'd arrive, I staggered the deliveries over several hours.

Sears and Roebuck came next. "We're surprising our mom," I said to the salesman. "My dad asked me to make this call. Can you bring us a new washer and dryer today? Our old machines are worn out." The guy was happy to help when I told him, "My dad will be waiting with his Sears credit card. He's downstairs right now unhooking the washer."

The sucker on the phone at Hechinger's lumber store said they'd deliver four-by-four posts for the nice garden we told him Dad was building for our mom, who'd just gotten out of the hospital. Sam showed me a flyer he found on our front porch advertising a ton of fill dirt for a hundred dollars. When I called, the voice on the other end promised to drop it on Query Man's driveway before the end of the day.

Cab companies were the easiest to schedule. The dispatchers spoke broken English, though, and I had to repeat myself several times.

"I need a ride to the airport," I told each one. "I'm leaving tonight at eleven on a trip to Europe with my family. Honk the horn loud—I'm hard of hearing." A fleet of cabs would appear all at once.

Who knew the Yellow Pages could be so much fun? When Sam and I ran out of things to order over the phone, we hid in the bushes to watch deliveries to our neighbor's house, one after another. We laughed until our stomachs ached as Query Man and his pudgy wife got angrier with each arrival.

It was disappointing to see that Query Man was able to stop the washer and dryer delivery, along with the lumber. But the florists and pizza guys wouldn't take back their orders and insisted on being paid. Query Man had to open his wallet a few times. When the truck brought the dirt, he stood in the street shouting at the driver that he didn't order any damn dirt. Sadly, the man drove away.

At dusk, we prepared for our physical assault. Sam and I gathered eggs, water balloons, a potato, five pounds of sugar, honey, toilet paper, a screwdriver, a valve core remover, and a flashlight—the essential tools in our line of work. Using Dad's socks as gloves, we filled a paper bag with dog shit from nearby yards. That was my brother's idea.

As soon as it got dark, we crept to the house and saw that the curtains and shades were closed. Query Man must have thought we'd had enough fun for one day. Sam sneaked to the porch and unscrewed the two front light bulbs without making a sound. No one came out to check.

We began by removing all four valve cores from the guy's station wagon, replacing the caps on the stems, and then I emptied the five-pound bag of sugar into the gas tank. Sam inserted a potato inside the tailpipe, carefully wiping away the residue and peels. I unscrewed the front and back license plates and threw them in the bushes behind the creek near where his son had thrown Sally's bike. He'd never know where to find them. Still no one in the house stirred.

Query Man had left his car unlocked. Big mistake. Using a pair of Dad's boxer shorts as gloves this time, Sam smeared dog shit on the inside of the windshield and globbed the rest of it on the outside of the glass, followed by a mixture of honey and mashed toilet paper. A lovely concoction. We had just enough of everything to do the job. Sam left the shorts on the driver's seat.

Next, we rolled down the passenger side window a couple of inches and inserted a nearby garden hose, gently rolling the window up to make it snug. We wanted to ensure proper interior hydration. In the dim glow of the streetlight, the hose looked like a snake trying to crawl into the car. Sam turned the water on at a low level so no one would hear it.

Now, we needed to let him know that revenge had been served Thurston Crow–style. We lined up eggs and water balloons on his front lawn where it sloped down to the street and started firing our weapons at his house.

When Query Man opened the door, we could see his silhouette in the hallway light. My left-handed, flame-thrower brother nailed him in the head with a perfectly timed egg, and I ripped two water balloons into his chest. Query Man waddled out into the yard, wiping his face and yelling, as we dashed off laughing.

"We hit him hard, Dad," I said when we entered the house. "And we ordered about a million dollars' worth of stuff. Best of all, he won't be using his car anytime soon, that's for sure."

It wasn't long before a loud knock came at our door. Dad waited awhile before answering. Mona was nowhere in sight, knowing to stay away during a Crow revenge session.

"Mr. Crow," he said, "your boys attacked me and my house with eggs and water balloons tonight.

And this afternoon, we received deliveries of all kinds of things we didn't order. Flowers. Pizza. Fill dirt. A washer and dryer. Lumber. Your boys are responsible for that too."

From the hallway, Sam, Sally, and I watched Dad's eyes go wide and his jaw drop as if he couldn't believe his ears. I had to put my hand over Sam's mouth to keep him quiet.

"I can't imagine my boys doing anything like that. Let me **query** them."

Dad flashed the world's fakest smile and gently closed the door. He loved getting to use the word "query" on Query Man. We took turns peering through the peephole to watch the guy squirm on the porch. A few minutes later, Dad winked at us and opened the door.

"My sons said they walked by your house and may have thrown an egg or two, but boys will be boys, as we know." Dad puffed out his chest. "But they certainly didn't do anything else, so get your fat ass off my porch and don't come back."

Dad slammed the door hard enough to send a gust of air through the entryway. A moment later, Query Man knocked again. When Dad opened the door, the guy made the incredible mistake of moving toward him and bumping into his chest. With the same swing that flattened the Mexican man at the Black Bear Gas Station, Dad drilled our neighbor in the nose. His glasses flew off as he landed hard on the concrete steps. Blood streamed down his jowly face and onto his white shirt.

Query Man sat up, panting, his breaths gurgled. "What kind of man strikes another in what should be a neighborly discussion about the behavior of our boys? You'll be hearing from the county police, mister." He started feeling around for his glasses.

"Good luck with getting the cops to help you, asshole. You got what was coming to you."

About an hour later, a Montgomery County police officer knocked on the door. A tall, thin, pimply-faced man, he had a gun in his holster and a walkie-talkie on his belt. He seemed too young to be a cop. Query Man stood behind him, and a police car sat in our driveway. The officer asked politely if he could come inside, and Query Man, his eyes and nose swollen, followed him into the foyer. Dad brushed Sam and me away.

"Mr. Crow, your neighbor says you struck him in the face after he complained that your sons vandalized his house. Apparently, they also placed orders for a variety of goods and services that he did not authorize."

It bothered me that every time someone gave an account of our misdeeds, the description never captured their beauty. Unauthorized goods and services were the least of his worries.

Dad walked into the hallway, snagged Sally's upper arm, and dragged her to the door. "Tell this nice officer what happened to you."

She looked up at the young guy with her big brown eyes and bruised face. "The boy across the street smashed my lemonade stand and poured the lemonade on the ground," she said, crying. "And then he threw my bike into the creek and hit me in the face."

Her lip had turned purple and was so swollen she lisped. The officer looked at her, then at Query Man, then at Dad.

"This man assaulted me in my home," Dad said, pushing Sally behind him as if to protect her. He lowered his head to appear meek and whispered for maximum dramatic effect. "He forced me to defend myself and my family after his son beat up my poor daughter and destroyed her property. I feared my neighbor would slug me again since he refused to acknowledge the great wrong that had been done. My sons repaired their sister's bike and broken lemonade stand, and I iced her lip and black eye. She may still need to go to a doctor if the swelling near her brain doesn't subside." Dad lowered his head even further. "What would you have done, officer, if you were attacked in your home by a vicious neighbor after his son attacked your daughter?"

The officer's eyebrows pinched in disgust as he looked from one man to the other. Sam laughed, and I shoved him into the living room.

"I'm going to drop the entire matter," the officer said, shaking his head. "Both of you need to control your sons and yourselves. You should be embarrassed for having a physical confrontation over something your sons did. I don't want to hear from either of you unless you want to spend time at Montgomery County Police Headquarters. And I would advise against that."

Sam peeked into the hallway. The policeman smiled at my brother, who had the face of an angel. He had no idea what that blond boy was capable of.

Query Man's face sagged in defeat, and he shuffled across the street without realizing the extent of his losses, particularly his car. And he still had three cabs coming to take him to the airport for his phantom trip to Europe.

Presumably, he was too embarrassed to file charges since we never heard from him or the police again.

I swelled with pride, feeling powerful and invisible again.

While waiting for the school bus on Monday, I walked over to my next-door neighbor, Mary, the prettiest girl I'd seen since Violet back in Gallup. I wanted her to be my girlfriend. She usually waited for me to start the conversation, but that day, she talked to me first.

"Did you and your brother really rub dog poop all over the inside of the Sturdivant's car and then put a running hose in it?"

"His son smashed my sister's lemonade stand, threw her bike in the creek, and hit her. He deserved it. I hope we ruined his car." I burst out laughing.

"They had to tow it to the shop to get it fixed. My mother is Mrs. Sturdivant's best friend, and she told us all about it. She said your dad punched Mr. Sturdivant in the face, and you ordered all kinds of things for their house without their permission. And then you threw eggs and balloons at him. You're a disgusting pig. Don't ever talk to me again."

I was devastated. The other kids at the bus stop heard her. Some nodded their heads. An older boy said, "No one wants your family in our neighborhood." The students turned their backs on me as I moved as far away from them as possible. When I got on the bus, no one looked at me. I walked to the back row and sat by myself. Why didn't they think it was funny? After all, the Sturdivant kid started it.

When I collected for my paper route, a woman who'd always been friendly to me said, "What you did to the Sturdivants was mean and wrong. Your father should go to jail for hitting Mr. Sturdivant.

And he should have to pay for all the terrible damage you caused. You should be ashamed of yourself, young man."

Why were we so wrong? The kid really hurt Sally and ruined her stand. Dad trained us to not just get even but "to get one up." Justice meant revenge, he said. It was the law of the world. I'm surprised he didn't tell us to kill their dog and put its head on a stick in their yard.

Dad sure as hell wasn't sorry for what we had done. He told Sam and me again and again how proud he was of us.

Getting revenge was the only thing I excelled in.

I woke up that night with a knot in my stomach, thinking about what Mary and my paper route customer had said and how angry they were. For the first time, I saw my behavior from someone else's point of view.

We'd have gotten away with what we did in Fort Defiance, but we were playing in a new league with a new set of rules. I realized how far off Dad's sense of right and wrong was from the civilized world.

The feeling of shame stayed with me for a while. Though it was different from the way I'd felt when I hurt Mom, it was bad just the same. I wanted to change but had no idea where to start.

And I wanted Mary to talk to me again.

CHAPTER 41

In early February, I came home from indoor track practice to find Dad talking loudly with Mona in the living room. As soon as he saw me, he yelled, "Sam and Sally, get in here—right now!"

My brother and sister raced into the room. Sally whispered to me that Dad had been yelling for over an hour.

Pacing in front of the couch, Dad waved a piece of paper in the air. "Your mother's coming for a visit," he said. "Her lawyer got in touch with me, complaining that we left Fort Defiance without leaving a phone number or forwarding address. She's mad, but I don't give a shit. She married a truck driver—a guy named Wally—and they adopted a baby boy. You'd think that would keep the crazy bitch occupied, but she has the legal right to see all of you. She'll be here on Saturday, and I'm not too goddamn happy about it."

Dad reached for a cigarette, though he usually smoked a pipe. His hand shook when he lit it. Taking two long drags, he said, "Her lawyer is threatening to sue for permanent custody of all three of you. Now that she has a husband, a baby, and a stable household, she's trying to force me back into court. I didn't tell her we were leaving for the East Coast because I wanted to protect you. Her lawyer calls it kidnapping. That's total bullshit, of course, but she thinks I'll pay her and let you go live in Albuquerque with her fat-ass truck-driver husband. Since we don't have a published number or address, her lawyer went to a lot of trouble to track us down. The dumb bitch couldn't have pulled this off without a lot of help."

"What do you want us to do, Dad?" I asked.

"I'll do whatever David does," Sam said.

Sally looked at Sam and me and then at Dad, nodding.

Mona gave her usual tight smile and put her hand on Dad's shoulder. "You're so lucky to having a loving mother and father to stop you from leaving for Albuquerque where you'd live in a trailer park surrounded by poor Mexicans."

I almost gagged.

"Tell the bitch not to come back again," Dad said. "Tell Wally to stop encouraging her. Make her cry and regret she came to visit. Make this whole trip a disaster. You know what to do."

I thought our days of hurting Mom were over. No way would I upset her on purpose again. We could promise to visit in the summer, but probably nothing would come of that since plane tickets for three kids would be expensive. And if Mom hadn't changed, seeing her would just open old wounds. I just wanted the whole thing to go away.

That Saturday, after delivering papers, I rode my bike to a nearby track and ran laps until my legs felt like rubber. When I came home, Sam and Sally were waiting for me.

"Where were you, David?" Sally asked, her large eyes full of worry. "We thought you'd left for good."

"I wouldn't do that to you and Sam," I said. "This will be okay. Mom will leave in a few days, and things will go back to normal."

"What if her lawyer wins and we have to go back to Albuquerque?" Sam asked.

"I'm fifteen, you're thirteen, and Sally is ten. They can't make us go since we haven't been with Mom for five years."

"It's not like you're a lawyer. How do you know?"

"I just do, Sam, so stop worrying."

The three of us watched from the living room, where we had a view of the street. It was ten-thirty now, and they were a half hour late. Only a couple of cars passed, and finally, a truck with a camper top pulled into our driveway.

Wally walked around to help Mom. He was short and about as fat as he was tall, with a close-cropped crew cut and thin mustache. Holding the baby, Mom got out of the truck slowly and took her usual fidgety steps, moving like a flighty bird.

They seemed to take forever to get to the door and ring the bell. Mona invited them inside. "Thurston," she said, "please come and greet Thelma Lou, Wally, and their baby."

"Sit down and let's talk," Dad said, walking toward the door. His voice was almost reasonable, and I let out a sigh of relief. I figured Dad might deck him.

Mom handed the baby to Wally and lunged at Sally and Sam. They both pulled back. She turned to me. "How's my oldest boy? Are you being treated well, honey?"

"All of us are fine, Mom. Why don't we go get something to eat?"

I nodded to Wally, but he didn't move. "We have business to discuss with your father and Mona," he said. "We need to clear up some things, like why he took you kids three thousand miles away without permission and without telling us how to find you."

Dad glared at Wally and curled his hands into a fist. Wally didn't seem to realize he was only one comment away from getting his head bashed in.

Mona jumped in. "You kids go with Wally and

Thelma Lou now," she said. "We don't need to talk about this in front of you."

I pulled Sam and Sally out the front door, and we walked to Wally's truck without looking back. A moment later Wally came down the stairs with the baby and Mom soon followed. He unlocked the doors, and the three of us squeezed into the back cab, already cramped with tools, dirty rags, and chewing tobacco.

Wally inched his way out of the driveway. "We'll go eat and catch up on what's been going on in your lives," he said.

Mom started crying, reminding me of all the times she cried when she lived with us.

Wally patted her hand and said, "There, there, Thelma Lou. We'll get your kids back."

I tensed up and looked over at Sam and Sally. "Don't worry," I whispered. "They aren't taking us anywhere."

Wally and Mom acted like they didn't hear me. Several miles later, we took the turnoff to the neighboring city of Rockville, so they weren't driving us back to Albuquerque yet.

We pulled into the parking lot of the diner, but before we could get out, Mom turned around to face us. "Your daddy tried to kill me, and he kidnapped you guys. Wally and I have a lawyer. You can leave with us to go to Albuquerque. Thurston can't stop you."

I couldn't believe it. This was practically the same line she used with us in Fort Defiance, but it was Ted then instead of Wally. Mom and Wally had hired a lawyer who clearly worried Dad. Not that he gave a damn about us, but he'd never let Mom win at anything. The thought of him paying child support was complete bullshit—as he said many times. I scooted forward and rested my arms on the back of her seat. We had people fighting over us like we were property, but none of them had our best interests in mind.

"Mom, we live in Maryland now," I said. "We can't go with you. Please don't get your lawyer to fight Dad. You know how that'll turn out."

We ate in silence, except for Mom's whimpering, and then they took us to their small hotel room. Sam, Sally, and I sat on one of the twin beds, and after putting down the baby, Mom sat next to me and grabbed my hand. Wally locked the door, dragged a chair over in front of it, and sat down, making it clear we would have to go through him to get out. The walls began to close in, and I jumped up to push him away from the door.

"No one locks us in," I said.

His eyes were fierce behind his thick glasses. "You children are going to listen to what your mother has to say. You don't know her side of the story."

But we did know. I leaned against the wall and motioned for Sam and Sally to sit.

"Your daddy tried to kill me many times, and he took you away. He turned you against me. If you'll come with Wally and me now, you can live with us in Albuquerque and be away from him for good."

All three of us shook our heads.

"I gave birth to you. You owe me." Mom looked over at me, hoping for support, but telling us we owed her made me grit my teeth. "Wally has forms from our lawyer for you to sign," she said. "We'll tell your daddy you're coming with us, okay? There's nothing he can do about it."

"We aren't going with you." I pushed away from the wall and squared my shoulders. "Take us home. Right now."

Sam and Sally got up from the bed and joined me at the door.

Wally's eyes looked sad. He'd driven thousands of miles to help Mom make her case, and it wasn't working out the way they had planned.

But she wasn't saying anything I hadn't heard before. And even with an adoring husband and a beautiful baby boy, Mom didn't seem happy. She blamed her misery on Dad's cruelty and on missing us, but I'd never seen her content for more than a few infrequent moments.

She didn't ask us about school or about anything

going on in our lives. Her singular focus seemed to be getting even with Dad and dragging us away because of a debt we owed her rather than providing a satisfying family life. Every conversation had always been about her and how life cheated her, and I couldn't take another minute of it. Life hadn't done me any favors either, and she bore some of that responsibility.

The next day, Sam, Sally, and I had to endure another visit and more of the same badgering to get us to go with them to Albuquerque. We couldn't wait for Mom to leave town. When we drove up to our driveway for the last time, Sam and Sally said goodbye and ran for the door. I stood next to Mom's side of the truck to talk to her.

"I love you, Mom, but we can't go with you—we can't take another change. I'm sorry. It won't work. I promise to come to Albuquerque to visit. You have Wally and your new son now. Don't ask us to leave."

Mom sobbed almost as hard as she had in the Gallup courthouse. She held my hand for the longest time, and I didn't pull away even when it became wet and clammy.

"Let's go, Thelma Lou," Wally said. "That no-account Crow has brainwashed these damn kids and they're not worth getting upset about. We need to get out of here."

I pulled my hand back as Wally reached over to

roll up the window. Standing at the end of the drive-way, I watched the truck slowly make its way down Kingston Road, then right on Kensington Parkway and out of sight.

I wondered when I'd see Mom again, but I knew whenever it was, it wouldn't go well. It never had. I wanted to find peace with her, but it eluded me again. All I ever seemed to do was disappoint her.

CHAPTER 42

My track coach, Chauncey Ford, paid close attention to everything I did. No one was tougher on me. During one of our first meets in March, he told me to wait until the eighth and final lap to sprint to the finish. But I got excited and took off during the seventh, and then died on the eighth and was caught by four runners. When the meet was over, we loaded onto the bus, along with the cheerleaders.

Coach Ford got on last and stood at the front. "Crow, get up here. You need to learn a lesson. You and I are going back to the track while everyone waits for us. I want you to run three laps, each under sixty seconds or you can't ride home with us."

One of the shot-putters called me an asshole as I climbed off the bus.

I ran the first lap in seventy-two seconds, the second in eighty, and the third one slower than that.

"You can run the five miles back to school," the

coach said. "I'll be waiting for you. After all, you love to run."

He climbed on the bus and it drove away. I was stunned. He hadn't yelled or cursed, but his fierce brown eyes told me he was serious. When I got back to school it was dark. He was waiting, just as he said.

"No one on the team has more potential or tries harder. But you think you have all the answers. Well, you don't. Life is going to get tougher and tougher unless you listen. Go home. Next time maybe you'll pay more attention." He gently touched my arm and smiled. "You can do better, and I expect it from you."

I walked home in the dark. It turned out that Coach Ford had called the house and told Mona that I would be late but that everything was fine. When I got home, I ate dinner, took a shower, and collapsed into bed. Dad left me alone. I heard him say that it looked like I'd picked cotton for sixteen hours. Falling into a deep sleep, I dreamed about the track meet and Coach Ford.

The next day at practice, he acted like nothing had happened. From then on, I wanted to please him more than anyone else in my life. My teammates made several sarcastic remarks, and my new nickname was "Birdbrain, the Crow That Couldn't Fly Right," but I didn't mind. I'd been called worse.

• • •

Coach Ford announced that we would compete against Woodrow Wilson High School in Washington, DC, on Thursday, April 4. My teammates weren't happy with the news. Our team was all white, and our opponents would be all black. The guys told me that black athletes ran faster than lightning and loved to fight. As the days passed, everyone grew more nervous, making racial comments I didn't understand. Coach Ford was the only black person in our all-white school, and he was popular, so why wouldn't the black athletes at Woodrow Wilson be the same?

It was cool and windy when we got on the bus and left for the meet. No one spoke. Usually we joked around and bragged about how we'd beat the other team, but not that day.

As we crossed the Montgomery County line into the District of Columbia, we stared out at the black faces. Some looked sickly and angry. The neighborhood was badly run-down—broken windows, barbed-wire fences, weeds my height. The men looked almost as poor as the Navajos huddled around the bars in Gallup. It was such a stark difference from where we lived in Kensington, which surprised me. I'd thought everyone in the East was rich. Even so, the area was high class compared to the reservation, where many Navajos didn't have electricity or running water.

When our bus pulled up to Woodrow Wilson High School, no one smiled or welcomed us, not the coach, students, or spectators. Since they had a white coach, I figured his team would get along with us. But as we warmed up on the track, the Wilson athletes told us we sucked. We taunted back.

One of their sprinters shoved one of ours at the starting blocks, and trash talk erupted through the crowd. The spectators booed our athletes in every event. They threw cups of ice at us, and we yelled back at them.

"Which one of you thieves took my running spikes?" one of our sprinters shouted, pointing to a group of Wilson athletes standing near the high-jump pit. The accusation brought them to our side of the field. One punch led to another and it turned into a brawl.

The coaches blew their whistles and separated us and then spoke quietly with each other. I thought the meet would be suspended, but Coach Ford signaled for us to get ready for the next events. The pushing and shoving continued.

When I took my place for the two-mile run, the final event, I had to wait for Wilson's only competitor, a fat kid who'd thrown the shot put earlier.

"I don't want to run the two mile," I heard him tell his coach.

"If you don't, we'll have to scratch," the coach said. "We just need one point, which we'll get if you finish."

For a quarter mile, the fat kid stayed with me, so I picked up speed and pulled away from him. Behind me, I heard a loud groan and glanced over my shoulder. My opponent had fallen onto the infield. Running alone for the next mile and three-quarters felt like an easy workout.

The instant I finished, Coach Ford hurried our team to the bus, and we drove off.

"Listen carefully to what I have to say," he said in his calm, fatherly way. "Thefts can happen anywhere. It's up to you to keep track of your equipment. Black or white, it doesn't matter. I'm disappointed that you taunted their team and got into fights. That's not good sportsmanship, and it's not what I've taught you. I don't care what they said to you first. You should never respond to unkindness with more of the same. It makes you lesser. Let's go home and do better."

I loved Coach Ford. He always took the high road, and I was proud to be on his team.

It was after dark when I got home. Dad wasn't there. He should have arrived hours earlier. Mona, Sam, and Sally sat in the living room, watching Walter Cronkite announce that Dr. Martin Luther King Jr. had been assassinated.

The news footage showed burning cars and buildings near where our bus had traveled a couple of hours before. People were caught on camera carrying clothes and appliances out of stores through broken windows. Murders were reported blocks from where Dad worked. Mona called his office repeatedly but got no answer.

At ten o'clock, we went to bed, but I couldn't sleep. I listened to reports on the radio of how the burning and looting were worsening, and the death toll was climbing. Dad might have gotten into trouble that even he couldn't get out of.

Around midnight, his car pulled into the driveway, and I jumped out of bed. Mona ran outside, and I followed behind her. The light above the garage lit up the inside of Dad's Country Squire, and I could see a large console-style stereo system in the back. Dad looked up at me and smiled.

"Where have you been?" Mona said. "Are you okay? I've been worried sick."

"I had a beer with one of the guys from work. Then on my way home, I drove past a stereo equipment store, and four black men stuck guns in my facc. They dragged me from the car, held me facedown for hours, and threatened to blow my brains out."

Mona gasped. "Oh my God."

"When they let me up, they told me to take this fucking stereo and get my honky ass out of there."

"It's a miracle you're all right. Those men could've

killed you," she said, touching his arm. "You had no choice but to take the stereo to save yourself."

There's no way she believed that story. Much like how Mom got on Dad's good side by asking for his help to punish us, Mona kept on Dad's good side by playing along with him no matter what he said. How the hell did he find two women who would put up with his bullshit?

Several days went by without any more details from Dad about what had happened. But the news continued to report the seriousness of the rioting, burning, and looting in DC, so the events of that terrible night stayed on my mind. When he and I were alone, I asked him if he had been afraid.

"Afraid of what?"

"Afraid you'd be murdered."

"Of course not. They knew I was one of them."

My jaw dropped. But why was I surprised? "You mean a looter. What if they had tried to kill you?"

"Oh, come on. We understood each other. We've all been screwed by the white man for too long. We're tired of being exploited. I met some guys on the street, and we hid in the store until the fuzz moved along. We cleaned out the joint. Got a couple of watches and radios out of it too. Two guys helped carry the stereo to the station wagon. Anyone would have done the same thing if they'd had the chance."

No one else would have done that, and no one else could have convinced those rioters that he was one of them. How had he managed to get away with so much in his life?

For the millionth time, I wished he wasn't my father.

CHAPTER 43

In eleventh grade, I liked my world affairs class, though I was barely passing. One day in the fall, the teacher announced a special trip to the Soviet Union organized by the school. It would cost each student $600.

As we left for our next class, James said, "This is going to be so cool."

"Yeah, but there's no way my dad will let me go."

"Sure he will."

I shook my head.

"At least ask him."

I knew Dad and Mona could afford it. Between their good government jobs and Dad's criminal operations, they had a comfortable income—but they shared very little of it with us kids. They went on expensive vacations and never took us. Just recently, the two of them had gone to Hawaii.

Since our move to DC, Mona had allowed us to keep whatever we earned but made us pay for everything other than basic food, clothing, and shelter. Every fall, she took us to Sears and bought each of us a pair of jeans, a pair of shoes, a couple of shirts, and a coat. Everything else I needed or wanted—socks, glasses, track shoes, school pictures—was my responsibility.

Luckily, I had started caddying the year before. A kid at school told me how I could make extra money on the weekends at Burning Tree Country Club. “Show up on Saturday morning at seven,” he’d said.

I was there at six. Soon I was caddying up to four rounds a weekend. Adding in the tips, I could earn $150. Mona never knew how much I made.

Encouraged by James, I decided to bring up the school trip the next morning at breakfast, when Dad was rested. “I’d be gone ten days,” I said. “We’ll go to Moscow, see the Kremlin and Red Square.” I got excited talking about it. “I might never get another chance like this. I’d really like—”

Dad exploded from his chair. “People in hell would like ice water too!” he yelled. “I’m not going to waste a goddamn penny on you.”

“But, Dad, I can pay you back—with interest.”

He leaned toward me, his eyes bulging. “Who do you think you are? I had nothing when I was a kid. You act so privileged. Let me tell you—you’re nothing special, boy.” He stormed out of the room.

Mona scoffed. “How dare you ask such a thing,”

• • •

The morning after school let out the following summer, I delivered my papers as usual. I'd grown to love the beauty of Maryland and its large trees, plush grass lawns, and well-tended houses.

But I wanted to live with the Kontz family for my last year of high school. I had few friends and was getting D minuses in all my classes except PE. I belonged on the reservation, where it felt like home. I'd written Richard once more about staying with his family. He wrote back that his parents would need ten dollars a week for room and board. I'd been saving money from my paper route and from caddying. I felt certain I could get my old paper route back and work for Mr. Ashcroft on the weekends at the Fort Defiance Trading Post.

During dinner that night, I showed Dad Richard's letter and begged him to let me leave. I'd already asked Sam and Sally. They didn't want me to go, but I told them in one year I'd be gone anyway and it would mean everything to me to go back. They said it was okay with them.

Dad's face turned red, and he slammed his fist on the table, shaking the glasses of milk. "I'm so damn sick of you. You don't know this yet, but I got you a job at a sod farm for the summer, you ungrateful little bastard."

If he was so sick of me, why wouldn't he let me go? "I already have a job caddying on weekends, and I deliver newspapers in the mornings," I said, my voice flat with disappointment. "Isn't that enough?"

"I want you busier than a one-legged man in a butt-kicking contest—it's the only way to shut you up. Don't ever mention the Kontzes or Fort Defiance again. **Comprendo**?"

Mona gave me her usual sneer. "You have no respect for the sacrifices we've made to give you a fine education in the East, **Mr. Brezhnev.**" She never missed a chance to bring up the Soviet trip from so many months before.

I ignored her and got up from the table.

After delivering newspapers the next day, I rode my bike twelve miles to the J. T. Patton Turf Farm. I reported to the supervisor, a fat, sour-looking man with a weathered face and crew cut, who pointed to a pickup and told me to join the other workers. Some were close to my age, but several had gray hair and bald spots. None of them said anything. We drove to an enormous field of beautiful grass. I followed the men to a sod-harvesting tractor that cut swaths of grass approximately six feet long.

We got on our knees, rolled the sod like a sleeping bag, and lifted the large, heavy bundles onto a truck until it was filled. And then we started all over again with a new truck. By midmorning my arms ached, my head was dizzy from the blazing sun, and my legs felt like mush. It was the toughest work I had ever known.

Dad talked about picking cotton day after day in the Texas and Oklahoma heat as a boy. This work had to have been every bit as hard.

On a muggy morning in the middle of July, our supervisor lined us up and told us we were driving a truck full of sod to a new housing development. I welcomed the break from rolling and loading. Unloading the sod and making brand-new lawns had to be easier, and I asked an older worker if that was the case.

He lit an unfiltered cigarette and said, "We have all day to empty this truck, and then the next day, we'll fill it back up. Don't make no difference to me. The days just run into each other until winter."

Though the man looked at least forty, he was probably in his thirties and acted like this was all he'd ever do for the rest of his life. It worried me that I might wind up the same way.

The new housing development was about sixty miles away, the supervisor said, and we'd have to drive slowly on the interstate because of the heavy load. It would take a couple of hours. The men walked over to the pickups parked ahead of the large sod truck, and as I turned to join them, the supervisor motioned me back.

"I want you to stay on top of the truck and make sure the sod doesn't roll off," he said. "If you see it slipping, bang on the top of the cab, and we'll stop. You have to catch it early because the sod is locked together, so if one piece comes off, it'll take the rest with it, like a stack of falling dominoes."

Nodding absentmindedly, I crawled on top of the turf. All I had to do was stare at sod. How hard could that be? This was my lucky day, getting to rest for two hours on soft grass. As the truck rolled down the interstate, I jostled along on what felt like a turf waterbed, and my eyelids grew heavy.

When the truck jolted to a stop, my eyes flew open, and it took a second for me to remember where I was. My body had melted into the soft sod. Two Maryland State Police cars were parked behind us, their lights flashing. Troopers stood at the side of the road talking to our supervisor.

Layers of sod covered the highway for what appeared to be miles. A trooper's face appeared above the sod that was left. He pointed a thick finger at me. "Get down from there. How old are you, anyway?"

"Sixteen," I said. Close enough.

He looked below him at my supervisor. "You're going to get a hell of a fine for littering the highway," he said, stepping down the ladder. "And not only does your guy look like he just woke up, he says he's sixteen. You have to be at least eighteen to ride in an open truck."

"You're fired," the supervisor yelled as I climbed off the truck. "How hard could it be to stay awake?"

"Sorry. I didn't mean to fall asleep, but the sod was so soft." In my exhausted state, I could have fallen asleep standing up.

"Mr. Patton is a friend of your dad's. That's the only reason you got this job. They're not going to be happy about this."

One of the workers slapped me on the back. "You're the first guy who ever sodded an interstate," he said. "We'll be laughing about this forever."

The men made me go to the housing development and lay the sod on the dirt yards. There wasn't enough, of course, so we quit early. I climbed into one of the pickups, and the men looked at me and laughed for most of the ride. They didn't care. My mistake had made their day a little shorter.

Back at the main office, the supervisor said the company was fined a thousand dollars and the driver was issued a large ticket for what I had done. "I'm really sorry," I said, but he had already walked away and didn't hear me.

I took my time riding my bike, in no hurry to get home. It was a lead-pipe cinch, as Dad would say, that Mr. Patton had called him. I parked my bike and walked up the stairs. He was waiting on the porch, his Y vein pulsing, his eyes bugged out. His belt was wrapped around his hand, the buckle dangling.

But I was done with that.

When he swung, I pushed his chest and blocked him from hitting me. I stood face-to-face with him, clenching my teeth, raising my hands into fists. He stepped closer, but I stood my ground without flinching.

"You're never hitting me again without me fighting back. It doesn't matter how hard you hit, I will stand up to you. If you kick me out, I'll take a bus to Gallup. No more belt buckles or fists."

I expected him to swing hard and not let up. But he didn't. He had the same expression on his face he'd had when I was in the bathtub full of salt and blood the night Mr. Yazza shot me. I remembered what he said about me being willing to do anything to be my own man, and he admired that.

Still, he could have smashed me to the ground as he'd done to countless men, but he didn't. He lowered his hand with the belt and stared at me.

Something passed through his eyes. He had a vacant look as if his mind were far away. Maybe he was thinking about the first time he stood up to his own father after years of being beaten with a wet rope until he collapsed. Maybe he'd been expecting this for a long time.

He dropped his head for a moment and then looked up and poked me in the chest. "I'm not finished with you. I've lined up a job where you'll pump gas, change flats, and drive a tow truck seventy hours a week. Even you can't screw this up."

"Falling asleep wasn't my fault. You have me working twelve-hour days after delivering newspapers. I'm exhausted all the time."

"You still have plenty of energy to flap your gums about Fort Defiance, though, don't you? You haven't done a thing to succeed here. My father couldn't read or write a single word. My mother made me work in the fields and didn't let me go to school. And I've done well for myself. If you're too dumb or dyslexic or nearsighted or deaf to figure out how to learn, that's not my problem. You've had it a lot easier than I did."

I started the gas station job the next day, but Dad didn't speak to me for weeks. When we passed each other in the house, he shook his head and scrunched his face in disgust. At dinner, he wouldn't eat with the rest of us, and I asked Mona why. "He doesn't want to have to talk to you," she said.

Toward the end of summer, I got home from the gas station after eleven o'clock, my shirt, pants, and underwear soaked in sweat. My eyes burned with fatigue. I smelled like gasoline, and my fingernails were caked with grease. My knees ached after running in the early morning, delivering newspapers, and then working twelve hours.

Dad sat in the living room watching the evening news in his boxer shorts. "Come in here," he said. "I want to talk to you." The TV blared so loud, I could barely hear him.

"My entire body hurts. I just want to go to sleep."

He sat erect and squinted at me, mumbling something to himself. Pages of the newspaper lay scattered at his feet, and an empty whiskey glass sat on the TV tray in front of him.

"Get used to being tired and dirty," he slurred. "Someday you'll be toothless, bald, and old. But the worst part is that at work you'll be reporting to a kid about your age now. You're bad in school, you don't have any mechanical skills, and you never go along with the program. You're completely worthless. It makes my ass hurt to look at you."

He dismissed me with a wave of his hand. Of all the mean things he'd ever said to me, nothing seemed truer. Other than manual labor, sports, and reading things teachers didn't assign in school, I had little going for me, and time was running out.

High school came to a merciful end on June 18, 1970. Initially, Walter Johnson was going to fail me.

I needed a D average or better to graduate, but even with the B from Coach Ford in economics, my grades were too low. The coach visited all my teachers and the principal, telling them I was close to passing and it didn't make sense to hold me back. Somehow, his magic worked, and they agreed to let me go.

"You're the worst student I've ever known who doesn't have a drug problem," the counselor told me two days before graduation. An attractive woman in her thirties, she kept pushing her glasses up on her nose as she talked. "You have painfully few academic credentials. Giving you a high school diploma is a sin."

I sat in front of her desk, glancing around her office. What was the point in unleashing this lecture when high school was over?

She tapped a pencil on an empty notepad and glared at me, waiting for my response.

"At least you're getting rid of me. Isn't that all you care about?"

"What did you get out of high school besides running track?"

"The whole thing felt like a giant fart joke." If she wanted to be nasty, I'd throw it right back at her.

"You should consider going into auto mechanics," she said, as if all idiots should provide tune-ups for brilliant college-educated guidance counselors who were too important to get their hands dirty.

"You're a real inspiration. I'd dedicate my first

tune-up to you, except no male is less mechanical than me. I can damage a car in short order, though." I burst out laughing, thinking about Query Man. "But I have no idea how to fix one."

Sighing, she leaned her elbows on the desk. "So what are you going to do?"

"Come back to Walter Johnson in twenty years and show you my pay stub. It will be bigger than the combined salaries of everyone in this dump."

She sat back in her chair and pursed her lips. My bravado hadn't sounded convincing to me either.

"You didn't get above a D minus in any of your academic subjects except economics. And you flunked math. If I'm not mistaken, Mr. Ford is your economics teacher as well as your coach. Without him, you wouldn't have graduated." She shuffled my file back together. "If you ever decide to take yourself seriously, the only school that will accept you is Montgomery Junior College. They're required to take anyone with a diploma from a Montgomery County high school."

"You're kidding. They have to take me?" I stood and walked to the door. "I'm on my way to big-time success. Montgomery College, here I come!"

After dinner that night, I overheard Mona telling Dad that I needed to find a new place to live before the end of the month. She didn't have to worry. I was just as eager to leave.

Dad walked into my room while I was reading the **Washington Post** on my bed. "Mona thinks you won't graduate. You failed math and didn't exactly light the school up in any of your other subjects."

"I'm getting my diploma. I found out today. Coach Ford vouched for me. I should be scared about going into the world, but I'm not. Being your son gives me an edge."

He raised his brows. "An edge on what? You have fast feet and a fast mouth, but not much else. You're on your own the way I was at age twelve when my father died. I've been hard on you, but you deserved it. Jesus, you're a destructive son of a bitch."

"You taught me well." I threw my legs over the side of the bed and stood to stretch. "If I can survive you, Mom, and Mona, I can survive anything."

Dad smiled. He'd taken that as a compliment. "You're the best bullshit artist I know, and I've known some good ones. Hell, I'm a good one. I've seen your smarts in action. You can get people to do anything for you. That's priceless. You would've had an easier time of talking yourself out of San Quentin than I did, and I did it with relative ease."

"I'm not sure what to do next." Though long before, I'd decided whatever I did wouldn't land me in prison. I couldn't think of a career that required the art of bullshit besides politics, but that was a useless profession. My thorough reading of the **Washington Post** each day convinced me of that.

"Life skills are more important than a formal education." Dad put his hands on my shoulders and looked down at me with a soft smile. "A formal education will earn you a salary. Self-education will make you a fortune. You aren't doing well on the formal education side of the ledger. You don't seem to like working for other people, but you like to work. Read the great books, learn from the geniuses of the ages, and run your mouth right. It's time for you to figure it out on your own."

Dad meant well, at least as well as he could, given his warped sense of fatherhood. But what would I do in the world alone? My poor hearing, bad vision, and dyslexia presented more impediments than I admitted, even to myself. And academically, I was light years behind my peers.

Still, I somehow knew that despite my physical limitations and all the shit I'd been through—or maybe because of it—I could do better. I wouldn't lay sod, pump gas, and deliver papers the rest my life.

And I had no desire to find out if I could talk my way out of San Quentin.

CHAPTER 44

After graduation, I bought a rusted, badly faded purple '65 Rambler for a hundred dollars and still felt ripped off. It leaked transmission fluid and belched oil worse than the Ford station wagon Dad gave Mom when we ditched her.

James's mom offered me a room at their house for twenty-five dollars a week, including meals. With nowhere else to go, I took it. The summer crept by as I worked construction, laying the foundation of an apartment complex. In the intense heat and humidity, I pushed wheelbarrows of concrete and unloaded tons of brick and cinder blocks off trucks. It was nearly as hard as the work on the sod farm.

Many of the laborers staggered out of their cars just before the whistle blew at 7 a.m., looking haggard and hungover. Dad's words haunted me—someday I'd be a bald, toothless old man reporting to kids half my age, performing manual labor that deadened the mind and used up the body.

When James took off for college at the beginning of August, his mother asked me to leave. She was tired of my filthy clothes and the grime in the bathtub. While driving back from my construction job, I saw a run-down brick building that had an apartment for $150 a month. After paying for the first month, I had enough money left to buy an air mattress, my only piece of furniture.

Every morning on the way to work, I stopped at a diner for breakfast. For eighty-nine cents, I'd get two eggs, toast with Smuckers strawberry jam, coffee, and water. That would often have to last me until late in the day. Food trucks came to the construction site at noon, and I'd sometimes have enough for a hot dog and drink. Caddying on the weekends, I'd get a free hot dog after every eighteen holes, so I worked two rounds whenever I could.

At breakfast one morning near the end of summer, I picked up a copy of the **Montgomery County Sentinel** and read that the fall semester at the junior college would begin in three days. According to the nasty guidance counselor, they'd have to accept me. And if I didn't go to college then, I probably never would.

I quit my construction job that afternoon, caddied on Saturday and Sunday, and got up early Monday morning to purchase a money order from a 7-Eleven for tuition, thinking that's all I'd need to enroll.

• • •

Arriving at the Montgomery College parking lot at about eight o'clock, I watched students hurrying to class carrying books and backpacks. I found the campus directory on the edge of the parking lot and decided to start at the top, in true Thurston Crow fashion. As Dad said, PhDs, doctors, and psychiatrists were easy to bullshit. Based on his record, it had to be true. If he could talk his way out of the Q, I could at least talk my way into a college that had to take me. He would have loved it.

I burst into Dr. Herm Davis's office in the main administrative building, thinking he was the president, but it turned out he was the director of financial aid. At the desk inside the door sat a middle-aged woman wearing a red blouse, thick red lipstick, and too much mascara. She tilted her head down and stared at me over her glasses.

"I'm Gladys, Dr. Davis's secretary," she said. "State your business."

"Is Dr. Davis in?" I asked.

"Do you have an appointment?"

"No, but he'll want to meet me."

"Are you a student here?"

"Not yet, but I will be."

She shook her head. "Generally, you can't just stroll in here and expect Dr. Davis to see you. But you're fortunate that he had an appointment cancel this morning, so he has a few free minutes now. Wait here."

As she rose from her desk, Dr. Davis came bounding out of his office. The door was open, and he must have heard us. Dressed in a well-made tweed suit, he had a bushy mustache and a big, warm smile. "I'm Herm." He clasped my hand. "How can I help you, young man?"

"I'm David Crow." I held up my Walter Johnson High School diploma and a small mirror. I breathed on the glass. "The steam on the mirror proves I'm alive," I said. "And the diploma proves I'm a Montgomery County high school graduate. You have to accept me."

"Is that right?" Dr. Davis let out a big laugh. "You're a real character, aren't you?" He put his hand on my back and led me into his office. "Come on in," he said. "Have you filled out an application?"

"No. I thought you could do that when you showed up for class."

"Gladys," he called out, "please bring in an application. We're going to launch this earnest young man's academic career."

He told me to have a seat, and I plopped down on his couch as he sat behind his large mahogany desk. Gladys came in and tossed an application on my lap.

I scanned the form. "Should I fill this out now?"

"What do you think?" she said. "Am I supposed to write what you want to get out of Montgomery College, or do you think you can handle that?"

Dr. Davis took a phone call but motioned for me to stay. Gladys went back to her desk, and I stared at the blank space where I was supposed to write a short essay. What should I say?

I took a pen off Dr. Davis's desk and began writing. "Thank you, Montgomery College. Without you, I would probably be doing manual labor for the rest of my life." I scratched that out. "I wish to go to Montgomery College to further my education." I scratched that out too. "I wish to go to Montgomery College to obtain a higher education in the hope that this will be the start of a big career." I couldn't think of anything else.

When I handed Gladys my messy application, she wrinkled her nose in disgust and handed it back to me. "Would you be good enough to fill in your full name, address, and telephone number? Or is that too much trouble?"

After I scribbled down the information, she waited until Dr. Davis got off the phone and then told him the application was complete.

"Please stamp 'admitted' on it, Gladys, and let's sign him up for some classes. Tell the instructors I'd appreciate it if they would add him to their rosters. And, David, come back in here before you leave."

She pushed her glasses up and frowned at me. "Have you selected the classes you'd like to take? Obviously not. You are totally unprepared. You haven't even read through the course book, have you?"

"No, but I have a money order for tuition."

"That's the only thing you've done right. If Dr. Davis didn't have such a big heart, you'd be out on the street trying to figure out how to get in."

She narrowed her eyes at me like I was a lazy bullshitter unworthy of her help, and she was right. A few phone calls later, she gruffly handed me my list of classes. "No one has ever come to this office without applying to the school and left with their entire schedule filled out."

"Thanks." I smiled. "You've made me feel right at home."

She waved me away, not appreciating my sarcasm. I ducked back into Dr. Davis's office, and he pointed to a chair in front of his desk. "So, David, tell me a little bit about yourself."

I studied his kind face. How much could I say? Would he even believe me? "Dad is an ex-con from San Quentin," I said, and Dr. Davis's eyebrows shot up. Then I told him about George and hiding on the Indian reservation. "No one cares what you've done wrong if you're willing to work there. Along the way, Mom went crazy—or maybe she always was. Dad lost his job in the life insurance business, and we went broke and ditched Mom, and I nearly got my butt shot off by a mean Navajo drunk . . ." I ticked off on my fingers. "It's been a wild ride, and I won't even be eighteen until Sunday."

"How'd you get to Walter Johnson?"

"Actually, that was never supposed to happen. Dad was going to work for the BIA in Washington for only six months, but most of high school, we went back and forth between here, Fort Defiance, and North Carolina, where my stepmother's parents live. I missed nearly a year of classes. Thanks to my track coach, Chauncey Ford, Walter Johnson gave me a diploma. But I didn't pass anything. I'd be pumping gas, caddying, and working construction the rest of my life without his help and yours. You're giving me a chance—thank you."

"I'm not sure I understood most of what you said, but you're welcome to come to my office anytime. You certainly know how to find me." He got up and walked around his desk to shake my hand again. "Based on what I've seen, you'll be just fine. Welcome to Montgomery College, David Crow."

Over the next two years, I lived in several apartments and rarely saw anyone in my family. I worked hard to get my grades up and earn money at caddying and other part-time jobs. Some days I was down to less than a dollar for food, I barely made the rent, and the Rambler practically ran on fumes.

Plus, my eyes continued to get worse. The optician told me that the only way to correct my severe myopia and astigmatism was to buy special Zeiss glasses from Germany. But each lens cost five hundred dollars, an impossible amount. I asked him to make cheap glasses for reading while I wore hard contact lenses out in public. The glasses were so thick I might as well have been looking through a telescope, and the contacts felt like sandpaper. My eyes ached from the moment I got up until I could finally close them to sleep.

Even so, I passed all my classes, and with the training I'd gotten from Coach Ford, I made the cross-country and track team. Then in the spring of my second year, I earned an associate of arts degree.

I was convinced it would now be easy to get into the University of Maryland, but they turned me down three times. On a whim, I wrote to Northern Arizona University in Flagstaff, about two hundred miles from Fort Defiance. They said my times were fast enough to try out for the cross-country and track team, but I'd have to pay out-of-state tuition and room and board and enter on probation. The total cost would amount to about the same as two pairs of Zeiss glasses.

All of it was out of the question.

One afternoon, I drove to the University of Maryland, found the track coach, and handed him a letter of recommendation from Jim Davis, my Montgomery College coach. Maryland's coach was impressed and wrote a letter to the dean of students at the university. I was accepted as a sophomore, again on probation, and made the team.

No matter how much I struggled, I had to make this work.

I got an afternoon job at the Maryland Student Union, along with a night job at a local 7-Eleven, and caddied on weekends around practice and meets. Due to a shortage of campus housing, the coach let me live in a locker room in the old coliseum for free, along with several other runners and wrestlers. It was damp, dark, and chilly, but I had a cot to sleep on.

Early in my junior year, I joined the Sigma Chi fraternity and moved into the frat house, an enormous, three-story brick colonial. I felt an immediate kinship with more than sixty guys, who became in many cases like real brothers. The day I arrived, Mike, my short, skinny roommate and our talented chef, asked me if I wanted a job as a busboy.

"Will I get meals?" I asked.

Mike nodded, and I started working that night, eating better than I had in years.

When I called Dad to tell him how well things were going, he said, "I never got to go to school.

There's nothing to brag about, boy. You've had it easy. Is that all you called about?"

He hung up.

Sam joined the army the day he graduated from high school, right after Dad gave him the same speech about being on his own at twelve. I drove Sam to the bus station, and we hugged for a long time, not knowing when we would see each other again. He was still fearless and reckless. As I watched him board for Fort Dix, I couldn't imagine how he'd survive in the military.

Lonnie had transferred to the University of Maryland to complete her undergraduate degree in education, and she was now working on her doctorate at night and teaching elementary school during the day. Sally moved in with her to finish high school.

I was grateful none of the Crow children were stuck in the house with Mona and Dad.

The frat house pulsed with energy and excitement. It was new and strange and wonderful. Surrounded by good friends and laughter, I felt safe for the first time in my life.

In late September, one of my frat brothers told me a woman named Mona was on the phone. She'd never called before. Even more shocking, when I spoke to her, she asked me to come to their house that Saturday. I dreaded seeing her. Time hadn't lessened my hatred for her.

As I stood on the front porch, my knuckles froze an inch from the door. This wouldn't be good. I took a big breath and knocked anyway.

Mona opened the door only a crack. "You've received an unmarked brown envelope," she said. "It has an Albuquerque postmark but no return address. Wait here." She closed the door. When she returned, she shoved the package at me and said, "This is for you. Take it and go."

Nothing had changed since I'd seen her the previous Christmas—the same stony behavior, more like a mail clerk than my stepmother of eight years. She didn't say goodbye. She hadn't said hello. Why did she marry a guy with kids she despised? Did Dad make her happy? How could he? He was as restless as a tomcat. And I was certain she couldn't make anyone happy, much less him.

I went to my car and stared at the large envelope on my lap. With an Albuquerque postmark, it had to be from Mom. Probably bad news. I drove back to the frat house, and thankfully, the parking lot was empty.

My hands shook as I ripped open the package. Inside were pictures of me and a note in Mom's unmistakable, childlike handwriting: "I'm no longer your mother. These are yours."

I flipped through one photo after another—from the EPNG days, a few from Albuquerque, and two from my tenth birthday party in Gallup. One had Violet hugging me as I blew out the candles. How I faked that smile I'll never know. Each picture brought back a worse memory until I couldn't look anymore.

It was as though I'd witnessed my own funeral and no one had come to say goodbye. I couldn't stop crying. My childhood replayed in my mind—along with a voice telling me that every horrible thing that happened had been my fault.

I hadn't hurt this much since the day in Gallup when Mom begged me not to leave her in that cold, empty house. I deserved this for not going with her. Since her awful visit in Kensington, I hadn't been in touch. Comforting her seemed impossible, so I'd given up.

I sat alone in the parking lot, feeling lost. I had begun to lower my guard to let in a few of my fraternity brothers, but if they really got to know me, they'd want nothing to do with me. Choking on guilt, struggling to inhale, I vowed never to let anyone get close enough to hurt me again.

CHAPTER 45

Lonnie called every Saturday that fall to see how I was doing, though there was little to say. Sometimes she invited me to her apartment for a meal and a place to study. But the air was always heavy with unspoken words about our childhood, and I seldom stayed long.

I'd written several letters to Sam, now stationed in Korea. He wrote back to tell me he chewed on opium beans to soothe his nerves while he patrolled the North Korean border. If his letters were accurate—and Sam never lied—his dependency on opium and alcohol was growing.

One Friday morning in late October, a fraternity brother knocked on my door. "Your dad's on the phone. He really needs to talk to you."

Every scary thought ran through my mind. Had Sam been hurt? What about Lonnie and Sally? Something had to be wrong.

"Dad, is everything all right?"

"No, damn it, it's not," he said, as if I should have known. "Go to the house tomorrow and start a huge fight with Mona." He acted like this was a routine request.

"Why?"

"What do you mean 'why'?" he yelled. "I'm leaving her for a woman I met on the Blackfeet Indian Reservation. She's eighteen but seems much older." He lowered his voice. "It's something that just happened."

Something that just happened. What the hell did that mean? Like spilling coffee on your shirt or taking the wrong turn? I was furious. He was using me again to do something sleazy and cruel.

"Tell Mona you're leaving her. Why do I have to start a fight with her? She's going to figure it out pretty soon anyway when you move out."

"Because right after your fight, she'll tell me all about it, and I'll say, 'If you can't even get along with David, then I have to leave you.'"

"That's crazy, Dad. There's no connection between how Mona feels about me and whether you want to stay with her. Don't you see that? Besides, she and I have never gotten along."

"Think of something. What's wrong with you? The day you can't think of a reason to hate that frigid bitch will be a cold day in hell."

"We haven't talked since she handed me the envelope from Mom two months ago."

"What envelope? I have no idea what you're talking about or why it matters."

"Mona and I don't see each other except when you ask me to come home for a few hours on Thanksgiving and Christmas. She acts like she wants me to leave as soon as possible every time. I don't even see you that often. I wouldn't know what to say to her on a good day."

"Get your ass over there and do it!" Dad yelled again. Then he hung up.

On Saturday, I woke up thinking about the time Mona sent me into the brutal cold to find the lost five-dollar bill. And the garbage she and Dad put in Sam's bed. I didn't care whether Dad stayed or left. Either way, they were both pathetic, and nothing would change that.

Still, I did what Dad ordered me to do and drove to their house on Burning Tree Road in Bethesda, where we had moved my junior year of high school. Going as slowly as possible, I tried to think of what to say. Oddly, I had seldom yelled back at Mona for any of the mean things she'd done—I'd hated her silently. I pulled into the driveway without remembering the final miles of the ride. Her white Chevy Nova was in the carport and Dad's was gone, as he had planned it.

I sat there for a long time, staring at the front door of the split-level. My left hand trembled, the way it had the last few years when I was nervous. Sweat beaded on my forehead. I could carry on a conversation with the light bulb inside a refrigerator, but words escaped me now. Mona peered out from the curtain. Once I realized she saw me, I hurried to the door.

Before I could knock, she opened it. "Why did you come? If you want money, you aren't getting any. If you want to stay here, you can't. Your father and I agree that you should make your own way."

Her nasty greeting inflamed every nerve. What a bitch. I couldn't help but remember how she had stuffed all my things into a box after high school graduation and tossed it out on the front porch. I didn't need to stage an argument. She was far more likely to pick a fight than the other way around. She just had. How could she have thought I came to her for help?

"I don't want anything," I said. "I just thought it'd be nice to pay you a visit." It would have been impossible to sound less sincere.

"This is about your father, isn't it? Something's going on with him. Do you know what it is?"

"No," I lied.

"He comes and goes at all hours. He's anxious. He won't talk to me. He makes trips to West Virginia. He has post office boxes he thinks I don't know about.

He's buried all kinds of things in the yard. And some guys are after him. Did he kill someone? He's in real trouble, isn't he?" She paused, glaring at me. "You **do** know something, don't you?"

Yes, I knew about the boxes of stolen weapons and coins Dad had buried in the yard. He told me about them when he gave me the combination to a safe that would have detailed instructions for getting revenge if anything ever happened to him. And he was always talking about killing people.

But no matter what I said to Mona, I'd only make things worse. This was a fool's errand, just as I expected.

"I've got to get back to school." I turned and walked to my car. "Sorry I bothered you."

Stopping at a pay phone, I called Dad. He picked up on the first ring.

"Did you make her cry?" he asked.

"I don't think that's possible. I didn't have to start a fight. She yelled at me right off, thinking I wanted money or a place to stay. She knew it didn't make sense for me to visit. I left without saying much."

"You're as useless as tits on a boar hog." He slammed down the phone.

In early November, Dad called to say that he had left Mona, but it sure wasn't because I'd helped him. He and Caroline had moved into a condominium in College Park, a few short miles from campus. Whenever I went outside, I looked for Dad's Ford Capri, afraid I'd run into them.

The week of Thanksgiving, the fraternity house and college campus were empty. I felt empty too. Even the noisy furnace had been turned off to save money. I usually went to Dad and Mona's for a few hours on Thursday, but that wouldn't be happening this year.

Wednesday afternoon, I jumped when the frat house phone on the second floor interrupted the quiet.

"Hello, David." It was Mona. "Your father is gone. Lonnie and Sally are celebrating the holiday together, and since Sam is out of the country, would you like to have Thanksgiving dinner with me?"

"Uh . . ." I didn't know what to say. Not only was I her last choice, but she probably invited me just to find out what I knew about Dad.

"Come over at one o'clock and stay for at least an hour or so."

Was that fear I heard in her voice? I couldn't help it—I felt sorry for her. "Okay, sure. See you tomorrow."

Minutes after the call, I wanted to cancel. Over the next twenty-four hours, my emotions changed by the minute—from yes to no to hell no. And then back to yes.

A girl from one of my classes invited me to her

family celebration, but I told her I'd get into trouble if I missed a holiday at home. That was a lie, of course. But I didn't want her family to ask where my family was and what they were doing. No one needed to know.

When I arrived, Mona greeted me at the door with a stiff, formal handshake, but her eyes held deep sadness. Opera music blared from the same stereo system that Dad and I unloaded from his car the night of the Martin Luther King assassination. Bloody Marys and turkey sat on the table, along with dressing and cranberry sauce. She bustled around like she was expecting the entire family. She raised her glass and toasted to my good health. After we ate for a few moments, the conversation turned to Dad.

"Have you heard from your father?"

"No, I guess he's been busy." We both pretended he hadn't run off with another woman.

"Your father is trying to find himself," she said. "It's hard to be a Cherokee in the East. In Fort Defiance, he had Indians around him every day. He had a true purpose. Now he feels lost without his circle of Navajo and Cherokee friends."

"Ah, really?" I tried to sound sympathetic, but what bullshit! Dad's true purpose was breaking the law and carrying on with young women. Did she really feel sorry for him, or was this how she rationalized what he had done?

"His work for the BIA in Washington has made him long for his Cherokee roots. Many of the workers at headquarters are Anglos, and he feels abandoned. Once he works through this, he'll return."

She had always accepted whatever Dad told her. Surely, if he wanted to reconcile, her reasoning would allow him back without having to admit what he'd done. After all, how long could he stay with his teen-age Indian mistress?

Mona had tears in her eyes. Under the thick makeup, her face was puffy, the way Mom's looked much of the time, and I realized Mona must have been crying before I got there. I felt genuine sorrow for her, which I hadn't thought possible.

CHAPTER 46

In January, I received my grades for the fall semester. All of them had dropped to Cs. I wasn't surprised.

Since the call from Dad about moving in with Caroline, I had stopped caring about the future. It didn't seem possible I could ever be successful or happy, no matter what I did. Maybe even more than that, it didn't seem possible I could ever be free of Dad's control.

And I was tired all the time. When track season started, I underperformed at workouts and stopped caring about that too. That's when I knew something was very wrong.

The nurse at health services said I had mono. Other than instructing me to rest, she had nothing to offer. My track coach told me to try out again in the fall, after I got well. I was crushed. Running was my life.

My heart wasn't into continuing at school. When spring break started, I withdrew from my classes, even though making it through college had been my singular goal since the fateful day with Gladys and Dr. Herm Davis. I left a note for Mike, saying I needed time off to figure out some things, but I would be back. I had no real plan, so I didn't know what else to say.

I drove to Gallup, hardly stopping to eat or rest, pushing my Rambler to the limit. I wanted to go to a place where I felt normal, where I belonged. On the edge of Route 66, I rented a cockroach-infested room at a dive motel for a month. The heater groaned and shook, but for two dollars a night, I couldn't complain. Besides, the drunks out front seemed familiar.

The next morning, I drove to the end of the strip on Route 66, a few blocks from Pino's Curios. The thought of seeing Ray Pino again made me smile. Gallup looked dirtier than I remembered, or maybe the fancy, rich East made me feel that way. Near where our condemned duplex used to be on South Second Street, I saw a sign at a construction site: "Day Laborers Wanted, $10/Day." I pulled over.

When I asked for the foreman, a flabby, overweight man stirring concrete and smoking a cigarette pointed at a taller guy with a huge gut.

"Do you need a laborer?" I asked the man with "BUCK, FOREMAN" stenciled on his shirt.

"Yeah, we need a college-educated genius to swing a hammer and carry cinder blocks and mortar," he said. The half-dozen Mexican workers in earshot laughed. "Show up tomorrow at seven o'clock, Professor Dumb Fuck."

I glanced down at my University of Maryland sweatshirt and swore under my breath. "I dropped out of college and came back home." It was the only heavy piece of clothing I had, so I ripped it off and turned it inside out. Wearing a shirt with a college name on it was a dumb thing to do. It might as well have read, "I'm from Harvard and you're stupid."

Buck cracked a surly smile. "You found yourself working with a bunch of fucking ex-cons. This is philosophy class without the tits."

Over the next several weeks, I asked each of them why they'd gone to prison and if the experience had changed them. Was it true what Dad said—that no one could be rehabilitated, beginning with himself?

"Stop trying to figure us out," said one beefy worker with tobacco-stained teeth. "All any of us wants is some ass, lots of whiskey, and money."

I focused on my job every day, not thinking about the future. I'd go see Mr. Pino as often as I could, and we'd laugh about the crazy stunts Sam and I had pulled. Soon I felt stronger. Early one morning in June, I ran the twenty-five miles from Gallup to Fort Defiance and hitchhiked back.

On weekends, I drove all over the reservation to fill my time, always ending up at the postmaster's house in Fort Defiance to see the Kontzes, the only real family I'd ever known. None of my close friends were around anymore. Henry, Richard, and Jim had gone off to college, and Tommy had been killed in a gang fight. When I found out Evelyn had passed away, I was heartbroken. I'd never had a chance to thank her for all she had done for me.

Mrs. Kontz and I visited as she sorted mail, delivered a steady stream of local news to her customers, and kept her kids quiet in the back room. She asked me questions about living back east, and in the middle of my answers, she would stop sorting packages to look at me, but she wouldn't tell me what was on her mind.

When I stopped by in the late afternoon, Mr. Kontz was usually there, and we reminisced about 4-H and Little League. I'd tell him he was more like a father to me than my own father, but he didn't respond, sometimes cutting off the conversation. One day near the end of August, Mrs. Kontz told me her husband wanted to talk to me alone when he got home.

I was happy he wanted to spend time with me. I'd read recently that not only had he fought in the Pacific during World War II, but he was one of the Navajo code talkers who developed the only unbreakable code of the war. Without them, we wouldn't have defeated the Japanese. I couldn't wait to ask him about it.

But when he walked through the door, Mr. Kontz barely said hello before telling me to follow him outside. In their small backyard, he pulled up two plastic chairs in the dirt. "Sit down and listen," he said, his dark eyes fierce.

My chest tightened as I sat across from him.

"What you doing here?" he said. "It okay for you to visit. Work the summer. But you still here. Why? You don't belong here. What you do without education?"

"This is home for me."

"No, is not. Never was."

"Sure it is."

"You want to be laborer rest of your life like kids who stay on reservation? They Navajo. They live the way of their fathers, near where umbilical cords are buried. That not for you."

"Mr. Kontz, I—"

He waved a hand in my face. "Go back to your people. You not Navajo."

"But we're Cherokee."

He scoffed. "That is lie. You not Cherokee."

"What?"

"Your father not Cherokee. He lies. You know he lies."

I shook my head. What was he saying? "We **are** Cherokee, and this is my home."

"No, David, you Anglo."

I turned away, my head spinning.

"Fort Defiance not your home. Gallup not your home either. I never understand why you try come back in high school."

You not Cherokee.

"You afraid of your father, afraid of who you are. Face your fear."

I stared at the tumbleweeds wedged into the fence, unable to speak.

Mr. Kontz had to be telling the truth. Honesty meant everything to him. He was brutal to anyone he caught in a lie.

If I wasn't a Cherokee, what the hell was I? And if I didn't belong on the reservation, where did I belong? I thought that Mr. Kontz loved me like a son, that I'd be a part of his family forever.

Your father not Cherokee. Dad had been lying all this time, and Mr. Kontz knew it. Everyone knew it—but us. I flashed back to Gilbert when he forced me to say I wasn't an Indian.

He was right. I was a liar.

I felt sick.

Mr. Kontz stood and reached out his hand. The conversation was over.

I grabbed his hand and got to my feet without looking into his eyes, not wanting him to see my tears. Keeping my head down, I left the yard through the gate and hurried to my car.

I slowly drove back to Gallup, dizzy with embarrassment and shame.

This wasn't the first time I'd found out that Dad had lied about his past. Among his many fairy tales was the one about being a war hero. The numbers simply didn't add up. He enlisted in the navy in May of 1945 at age eighteen, completed basic training, and then spent three months stationed in New Orleans. The Japanese had surrendered by then.

But this news from Mr. Kontz hurt a lot more. Mostly because I wanted to believe the lie so much.

The millions of stories Dad had told us about suffering at the hands of the white man—all bullshit. And his insistence that we were the pale kind of Cherokees—more bullshit. And training me to be a brave warrior—bullshit, bullshit, bullshit!

It was all one BIG LIE.

The sun was going down as I turned onto Route 66 in Gallup. Unable to face my lonely motel room, I stopped at the American Bar on Coal Avenue and ordered a beer. I was about to take a sip when an old

Navajo man teetered over to the bar and leaned into me. “Buy me a beer, you son of a bitch.”

His bloodshot eyes and boozy fumes told me he’d been drinking all day. I nodded to the bartender, and as he placed the beer on the counter, the Navajo slurred, “What is rich bastard like you doing here?”

I was dressed in jeans, tennis shoes, and a well-worn shirt, but to him, I must have looked rich. I felt nothing but pity and sadness for him, as I did for the other drunk Navajos there. No doubt they had arrived in the morning and would remain all night.

It suddenly occurred to me that these were the same men Sam and I tormented with cherry bombs and firecrackers. We also knocked off their hats and pulled down their pants. These were the guys whose wives came looking for them on Sunday mornings. How the hell did I ever think it was funny to hurt them? How could we have been so cruel?

I didn’t think I could feel any worse than I did when I first walked in, but I was wrong.

The Navajo man beside me was still waiting for an answer. “I’m so sorry,” I mumbled.

I couldn’t get out of there fast enough.

As I hurried to my car, Mr. Kontz’s words swirled around in my head. **What you do without education? . . . You want to be laborer rest of your life? . . . You Anglo . . . Not Cherokee . . . You don’t belong here**.

At that moment, I was sure of two things: I couldn't stay there. And Mr. Kontz loved me enough to be totally honest.

First thing Monday morning, I dropped some coins into the pay phone outside the motel and called the University of Maryland Admissions Office.

"There's good news and bad news," said the male voice on the line. "You officially withdrew, rather than failing out or you would not be allowed to come back to the University of Maryland. Period." He repeated the word "period" as though he needed to discipline a bad child.

"We accepted you because Montgomery College has a relationship with our university, but if you don't return this fall, you'll have to reapply for admission. Unfortunately, your grade point average, combined with your abysmal high school record, is too low for readmittance. You have a week to return to campus, fill out your class schedule, and begin classes, or you're out."

"What if I decided to wait and transfer to another college later?"

"Believe me, no other college will accept you. If I were you, Mr. Crow, I'd get back here, fast."

I felt a jolt of panic. "Thank you," I said and hung up.

If I drove hard, I could get back to Maryland in time and pretend this Gallup interlude had never happened. I hoped my fraternity would let me come back and the coach would allow me to run with the cross-country and track team again. Burning Tree had seen me come and go, and they always seemed happy to give me caddying jobs.

I threw my few clothes into the back of the Rambler, gassed up, and headed east.

CHAPTER 47

As I drove down Route 66 past all the stores and restaurants, nothing seemed the same. For years, whenever I thought of home, Gallup and Fort Defiance came to mind, but that day, all I felt was a deep sense of guilt and loss.

It was pointless to confront Dad about the lies. He would just explode into a rage. No, it was up to me to find my own truth. But how would I begin? The Crow children had been lied to since birth—the myths had become our identity. Being a Cherokee was the only point of family pride. I had no good truths to replace the lie.

Were we nothing more than Okie white trash?

Approaching Albuquerque, I saw the turnoff that led to Mom's part of town. On an impulse, I took the road and made my way to her house. We hadn't been in contact since she sent the package of pictures and the note. Surely she felt upset about that. And I wanted to apologize for being a bad son.

When I arrived, Wally's car was gone. As I knocked on the door, my stomach knotted, all visions of a happy reunion fading. Was this another big mistake?

Mom answered the door, and her face torqued into a snarl. "What do you want?"

My mouth opened and closed.

"You're not the only one who bleeds when they're cut, mister. Don't you want to know why your daddy tried to kill Cleo? And why George wanted to kill your daddy?"

"Do we have to talk about Dad?"

"I loved him and waited for him to get out of prison."

Mom's adopted son, John, now almost seven, appeared next to her and smiled at me.

"Do we have to talk about every bad thing that happened to you?" I returned the young boy's smile. "It's all we ever talk about."

"They should've given him the electric chair. He just missed it. No one knows how Cleo lived through that beating. Thurston wanted him dead. The warden told me not to take him back because he was a cold-blooded killer. But I did. And what did it get me? Nothing but trouble."

"Why did you mail me those pictures? That hurt."

"Not as much as you hurt me. You had it coming. You don't want me. You only want your daddy."

"At least every conversation with him isn't about the past, things I have no control over."

"You chose him over me." She crossed her arms and pouted, like she was upset I didn't pick her to be on my kickball team on the play-ground.

"I'm not living with him anymore. I'm struggling to make my own way in life."

"I'll forgive you if you move to Albuquerque. Wally can get you a job driving a truck. We can see each other almost every day."

"Mom, I can't. I'm headed back to college."

"You don't love me or you'd stay here."

Her definition of love was obligation and guilt. It was the only love the Crow family had to offer.

"Can't you forgive me? Dad treated you wrong—we all did—but we were scared kids. Can we have a relationship that isn't based on the past?"

"Yes." Then she blurted a verbatim repetition of her previous complaints, as if her mind were stuck on an endless loop.

"I don't think you love me at all," I said, wanting her to deny it.

"You have a lot to answer for." She closed the door in my face.

Mom had no intention of ever forgiving a Crow. I

went to my car and got back on the road for school, cursing myself for stopping.

Five days later, I arrived in College Park, drove to a 7-Eleven, and bought two money orders—one for room and board at Sigma Chi and one for tuition. My heart hammered against my chest as I stepped into the fraternity house. If my frat brothers didn't want me back, I didn't know what I'd do.

BA, our Sigma Chi comedian, a stocky, red-faced Irishman, saw me first. "David?" He jumped up from the threadbare couch. "Oh man, is that you? Hey, guys! It's Half-Breed!" He shouted pseudo Indian war cries and threw his arms around me for a quick hug. "Where the hell have you been? We thought you might've been scalped."

My roommate, Mike, came into the common room from the kitchen. "Well, if it isn't the aimless wanderer." He smiled.

"Is my bed available?" I asked.

"Savin' it for you," he said.

"Hopefully nothing died in it while you were gone," BA said.

Marty and Billy tumbled into the room from the stairwell, along with Tom, Tony, and Doug.

"He lives!" Marty said, shaking my hand and throwing his other arm around my shoulder.

"You going back on the track team?" Billy asked.

"That's my plan."

"Good to have you back, man," Tom said, giving me a pat on the back.

I swallowed hard, amazed at how excited everyone was to see me.

Cher's hit "Half-Breed" was popular then, and for days, BA, Tom, and Billy would break out into the song whenever they saw me. BA whooped his war cry and did a celebration dance as we all sang the chorus. We laughed ourselves silly.

Of course, now I knew that the Crows didn't have a drop of Indian blood in them. But this didn't seem like the time to set the record straight. And they probably wouldn't have believed me anyway.

Within a week, it seemed like I'd never left. My cross-country coach let me compete for my spot on the team, and I made varsity again—barely. Mike rehired me as a busboy to help me pay for meals, and I went back to caddying at Burning Tree Country Club on the weekends.

Mr. Kontz had been right—I'd needed to get my butt back to school. The biggest difference when I returned, though, was I realized how much I mattered to my fraternity brothers. I didn't belong on the reservation—I belonged there, with them.

• • •

On Parents' Day, about a month after classes started, my fraternity brothers' parents and siblings arrived for food, drinks, and a football game, making it one of the best days in the fall. I was on my bed, reading a book, when Mike came into our room. "Uh . . . David . . . your dad's looking for you."

I instantly broke into a cold sweat. "How did he find out it was Parents' Day? I sure as hell didn't tell him."

"I think all the parents got a letter. Your dad's in dirty work clothes with grease on his face. It doesn't look good, man—you better get down there."

Dashing through the house, I found him on the first floor landing next to the trophy case. He was talking at a group of my brothers and their parents. It wasn't a conversation—he was holding court.

"Well, hot damn, look at these fancy digs, with fancy light fixtures, real carpet, indoor plumbing, fine food, and all sorts of goodies." Dad's ridiculous fake country accent made me boil with anger and embarrassment. "Ahhh, shit. Is this how AWWs live? You know, AWW? 'Ain't We Wonderful'!"

My brothers laughed, but their parents went stiff and stepped away from him.

I grabbed his wrist to get his attention. "Dad, please stop it."

"Your so-called brothers have their heads up their asses, thinking they're better than Okies like me.

They have all this fancy crap, including indoor shit-houses. We never had one of those. I didn't go to school. We didn't have electricity, running water, or books. I always wondered how the AWWs live," he yelled. "Now I find that my son is one of them. Ain't that the goddamn petunias?"

I tugged his arm to make him leave. He pulled out of my grasp and stood silent, glancing around the now empty room. The composite picture of the fraternity members on the living room wall caught his eye. He walked over, found my photo, and poked it with his grimy finger.

"These fancy assholes pretend to be your brother. What a load of crap. Do you think they give a damn about you? You don't really believe that shit, do you, boy?"

"I believe you wanted to humiliate me in front of everyone and you succeeded."

"You've humiliated yourself. This fraternity and your so-called brothers are complete phonies. No wonder you fit right in." He turned and walked out the front door to his car.

For months after Dad's visit, my fraternity brothers mimicked his fake country accent, making fun of him for being a jerk to them and to me. But they stuck by me in ways Dad could never imagine.

• • •

That semester, I met a girl named Molly in our government relations class. We had many things in common until we discussed our families and our futures. It was against my better judgment, but I accepted an invitation to have dinner with her parents, and it went well.

A few days later, we went to get coffee after class and sat at a table in the cafeteria. "When do I get to meet your dad?" she asked, her brown eyes hopeful.

"Never." I sipped my coffee and burned my tongue.

"I'm not good enough to meet your father after you've met my family?"

"You're plenty good enough. You're amazing. But you can't meet Dad. He'll act horribly, like he did on Parents' Day. I can't let anyone meet him." I blew on my coffee and took another sip. "Besides, he's living with an eighteen-year-old girl he met on the Blackfeet Indian Reservation. I guess she's nineteen by now, about three years younger than you. How will that work if they meet your parents?"

"If I like you, they'll accept your family."

I put down my cup and stared at her. "You've got to be kidding. No one will accept my family. If they did, they'd be just as crazy. Your family is nice and normal." I slumped back in my chair and sighed. "This won't work. Forget about me."

But she didn't.

To push her away, I drank too much at parties, acted silly, and pretended to be a full-blooded Cherokee warrior making loud whooping noises after too many beers. My fraternity brothers had grown used to this new drunken behavior and all the wild stories about my past, whether they believed them or not. But Molly wanted no part of it. The inappropriate stories about my childhood, always out of context and embarrassing, upset her, but she wouldn't break up with me. At a particularly rowdy party, I threw up in the parking lot and fell asleep in the front yard. She made her way back to her dorm alone that night.

The next day, Molly called me. "I know what you're doing," she said in a scolding but forgiving tone. "You want to drive me away because you've been hurt so badly. You think you don't deserve to be loved. I feel sorry for you. You're giving up on yourself."

"But I'm **not** lovable." My voice caught, and I choked back tears. "At some point, you'll stop loving me. Everyone else has."

"Not me. I'll always love you. And if you love me, you'll let me meet your dad. I'll learn to love your family."

Even though I kept getting drunk at parties, Molly was persistent. "This is just a phase," she'd say. "You'll outgrow it."

Fat chance.

CHAPTER 48

I was studying in my room when a shout came down from the second floor. "Half-Breed, phone call." It was BA. "Sounds like your next date. She must be really hard up."

I knew it couldn't be Molly. She said she wouldn't call me until I promised to behave better and agreed to introduce her to Dad. It would have been so much easier if she'd just given up on me.

I reached the pay phone just as a coed stumbled out of the bathroom in a towel, hoping I wouldn't notice her.

"Hello," I said. "This is David Crow."

"Do you know where Thurston is?" It was Caroline, her smoky voice tight with tension.

I flashed back to the first and last time I had seen her. She and Dad picked me up the previous Christmas on the way to Mona's house for what was the most miserable dinner ever. Caroline sat at a drugstore lunch counter and waited for us.

She looked like the kind of cheap hooker you'd find in a Gallup strip bar—I couldn't help but gape at her. She wore a white blouse stretched tight over numerous rolls and a pink miniskirt hiked up, exposing her underwear. Her thick eyeliner could have been applied with a charcoal briquette, and her full lips looked slathered in pink frosting. The putrid smell of her cheap perfume made my eyes water.

"He's been gone six days this time," Caroline said. "I'm worried."

"What do you mean, 'this time'?"

"He travels to West Virginia a lot. He and some guys hide stuff in a warehouse and then sell it to some other guys. I heard him on the phone threatening to kill somebody for double-crossing him. He's never been gone this long before."

Mona had told me similar stories the year before, including the part about murder. "I don't know where he is, but if I hear anything, I'll call you."

"Something else I need to tell you. Someone's been calling, breathing heavily, and hanging up."

Dad had never gone missing for that long, and no one had ever called his house to scare him—at least not that I knew of.

What do you tell a nineteen-year-old stupid enough to be with a dangerous forty-seven-year-old man who brags about killing people and getting away with it? "Give it until the middle of the week," I said.

"If you don't hear from him by then, call me. He'll be fine."

Two days later, Caroline called to let me know he'd shown up, and I called Dad. "Caroline's been worried," I said. "Where were you?"

"It's none of your business. I want a sackful of revenge for all I've been through. Life has cheated me. My mother killed my father. I didn't get to eat right, go to school, or have a normal life. They worked me to death. People hate me because I'm Cherokee. Nothing about my life has been fair. What the hell do you care? And why is this any of your business?"

There it was. The BIG LIE. "Has it occurred to you that you might go back to prison or even get killed?"

"Nothing's going to happen to me. The next time Caroline calls, tell her you don't know anything. You never seem very interested in my life anyway. All I hear about is your track team, your fancy fraternity, and your classes."

The phone went dead.

A month later, I'd just gotten back from caddying when Caroline called again.

"Your f-father needs your help!" came her hysterical voice through the phone. She sobbed and stuttered. "You h-have to drive to Wheeling, West Virginia. Men are after him. Something . . . something happened to one of them, and it's bad. You need to leave right now! He said you could get there in five hours."

"What am I supposed to do when I get there?"

"There's a truck stop on the main highway just outside of town. He says you can't miss it. It's the only one for miles. Go to the pay phone and call this number." She rattled off the number as I scrambled to write it down on a 7-Eleven receipt I found in my pocket.

"Hurry!" She hung up.

I grabbed my jacket and sped down the highway in my old Rambler, my thoughts racing just as fast. If ever there was a time to get out of Dad's grasp, this was it. But I couldn't seem to let go of him, even though he might very well destroy me—and soon. Maybe I wasn't any different from Mom or Mona—or Caroline, for that matter. Certainly, I wasn't any braver.

Since we first started going on the stealing trips, I had looked out for him. Hell, before that, when I used to listen at the door, I'd fantasize about talking him out of his craziness. I could have been done with him and all of the stress right now, yet I continued to hurry down the road.

I gassed up on Route 1 leading out of College

Park. I was terrible at reading maps while driving, so I bought one and wrote out directions. My hands shook worse than ever, and I had to start over several times. It took me almost twenty minutes, but at least I wouldn't get lost.

As the afternoon light faded, I turned onto I-70 West, telling myself that Dad needed me. I was important to him—at least for now. Maybe his life was worth saving. But he was violent and evil. He hadn't changed since getting out of the Q. All I was really doing was helping him commit more crimes and perhaps more murders. My insides twisted in agony. I felt like that scared little kid spinning wildly in the snow, hearing that we had to get rid of Mom.

It took forever before I saw the "Welcome to Wheeling" sign. The truck stop stood out like a beacon in the night. Eighteen-wheelers were moving in and out as cars gassed up on the opposite side. A bank of pay phones stood outside the station—all empty. I pulled out the scrap of paper with the phone number and then worried I might have written it down wrong. When I was nervous and had to work with numbers, my dyslexia got worse.

But Dad answered immediately and told me he was about a mile away. He had me drive past the gas station and turn onto a two-lane highway, then follow it to a dirt road and turn again. It seemed a lot farther than a mile from the truck stop.

I had to maneuver around broken-down cars and barrels of trash, finally pulling into the driveway of a shack with a missing window and a sagging porch. Dad flew out of the house and waved his arms in front of my car. Before I could stop, he jumped in and threw a duffel bag into the back seat. It landed with a thump. He told me to back out and follow the guys in the Chevy waiting in the street.

"Don't get too close to them," he said. "Go very slowly and look around for anything that doesn't make sense, like a car following us or any noise at all. You know what to do."

I backed out into the road and stopped. "What the hell have you done?" I turned on my interior light and took a good look at Dad. He had blood on his face, his sleeves, and his khaki pants. I glanced in the back seat. "And what's in the bag?" It was covered in blood too.

He stared at me for a moment, his eyes bulging and lips chattering, like he was trying to decide what to do. "Shut up and go open the damn trunk. We don't have time for this nonsense."

As I watched him grab the bag and toss it into the trunk, my skin went hot and cold at the same time. Sweat poured off my brow. Soon my underwear was soaked.

"What have you dragged me into?" I said, closing the trunk.

"You don't want to know, so don't ask. You don't want to know what I'm about to do, so don't ask about that either. Just do what I tell you and we can be on our way home soon."

Dad walked over to the driver of the car in front of us. I saw another man in the passenger seat but couldn't get a good look at either one of them. I had never been so grateful for darkness in my life.

When Dad got back in the car, the Chevy took off and bumped up and down in front of us on the rugged dirt road. I kept checking the rearview mirror for headlights, my heart thundering in my ears. We didn't go far before turning right onto another dirt road lined with trees so close the branches scratched against the doors.

Dad fidgeted in his seat, talking to himself. I could smell his sweat. Raising his head, he rubbed his forehead like he was trying to remove a stain and then squeezed his hands tight.

"No one can ever know what's in the trunk of that car," he said. "That no-good son of a bitch."

If the police pulled us over, they'd take one look at Dad and we'd be arrested at once. My life would end. How many years in prison for this?

Half a mile later, the trees thinned, replaced by bushes. The Chevy stopped in front of what appeared to be an abandoned building. All I could see in the dark was a boxy outline.

"Listen carefully," Dad said. "If anything seems wrong, like a car coming or someone approaching on foot, or anything unusual, flash your lights three times. You know the drill. It will take us only about fifteen minutes to do what we need to do."

The two men got out of the Chevy and opened the trunk. Dad held the flashlight as they removed what had to have been a body wrapped in black plastic. It was about six feet long and lumpy, and they had a hard time holding on to it as they moved into thick brush. Dad pulled out two shovels from the trunk and followed close behind.

My stomach heaved. I threw open the Rambler door and vomited just like I did when I saw the decapitated man near the Navajo Inn. Shaking uncontrollably, I turned around every few seconds to make certain no one was coming. What would happen if someone did? We were sitting ducks.

Less than a hundred feet away, one of the three men pointed the flashlight at the ground while the other two started digging. I couldn't tell which one was Dad. The men traded off, always two of them digging and one holding the light.

When they came out of the brush, the two men tossed the shovels into the trunk and climbed into the Chevy while Dad hurried back to my car. "Go, but not too fast!" he yelled.

The road was so narrow I had to do a three-point

turn and bounced the car into a gully, nearly getting us stuck. The men followed behind us until we reached the end of the road. Dad told me to turn right and make my way back to the main highway. Luckily the men turned left at the next opportunity. After a few moments, their lights disappeared into the night.

We drove for a long time without speaking. I kept shaking and sweating until even my arms and hands were slick and chilled with perspiration. Dad suddenly pointed at a hamburger shop just off the highway. "Hey, drive through that fast food joint over there."

The girl at the window didn't seem to notice either of us as she took our order and handed me our bag of food and drinks. Dad pulled out his burger and fries and ate hungrily, as if burying a body was no big deal. I couldn't eat.

Back on the highway, I asked, "Did you kill someone?" The answer was obvious, but I wanted to hear him say it.

"What the hell difference does it make to you?"

"Lots, because if you did, I have knowledge of a murder, making me as guilty as you. And I helped you hide the body and get away."

"Did you learn that in one of those smart-ass college courses you're taking? You say it like you know what you're talking about. You don't understand anything about real life, boy."

"You don't need to go to college to understand murder—or what it means to be an accessory to one." My hands ached from gripping the steering wheel, and my head buzzed as if I'd been hit.

He never answered questions honestly without unleashing a vicious attack to keep me on the defensive. And it had always worked. Until now. "Did you kill someone or not?"

"I told you long ago, there's no justice in this world. The real murderers are in the police departments and government."

"What the hell are you talking about? Murder is murder."

"Cut the pretentious crap! The worst murderers are found in the institutions you revere. Every man in the Q was vastly superior to the screws guarding them. The legal killers are far more lethal than the illegal ones. And just so you know, no one does the right thing unless they get something back for it. And no one feels loved either. Welcome to the real world. People fake love for lots of reasons—sex, money, and financial security. Love, like religion, is make-believe for idiots."

"Your world isn't really that grim, is it?"

"Yes, and so is yours."

No, my world wasn't like that at all. "What about

when someone does something nice and expects nothing in return?"

"You're stupid if you think they don't expect something in return. No one gives something for nothing."

"Yeah? So what does someone get for covering up a murder?"

We drove the rest of the way in silence, arriving at Dad's condo after midnight. I opened the trunk, and he retrieved the bloody duffel bag. How would Caroline react when he came through the door?

Mustering all my courage, and trying not to shake, I stared him in the face under the streetlight. "Dad, I will never do anything illegal or immoral for you again. You would have ruined my life if I'd been caught with you tonight."

"I'll call when I need you and you'll answer like always."

"No, I won't."

"Goddamn right you will."

Watching him walk away, I made a solemn promise that my life's work would be proving him wrong about me. I would become his exact opposite.

PART 5

Capitol Hill
1975

My dad on the day he was released from San Quentin State Prison. 1951.

CHAPTER 49

Throughout my years caddying at Burning Tree Country Club, I rubbed shoulders with presidents, senators, ambassadors, and generals and followed every word they said. As graduation approached, I became convinced I could get a job working for one of them.

Listening to the politically powerful offered me a window into the world that had nothing to do with my personal circumstances. Without giving it much thought, I'd started reading about Congress. Soon the Gallup poll had replaced Gallup, New Mexico, and I signed up for more political science classes. During my last year in college, I found myself poring over everything on the syllabuses and most of the additional reading lists. I devoured the **Washington Post**, **New York Times**, **Wall Street Journal**, and other publications that offered insight into politics.

What I once thought was a useless profession now fascinated me. It occurred to me that the Navajo people were victims of the worst of the political system, and even those who wanted to help them didn't have a clue what they were about. These misguided civil servants reminded me of the easterners who came to the reservation to experience the pure Native American spirit, to touch Mother Earth and Father Sky, only to find that Navajos lived in third-world poverty with little hope of better lives. They left as soon as possible, never to return.

I grew up hating the BIA. Bureaucrats controlled every aspect of Navajo life, taking away most of their freedom under the guise of knowing what was best for them. It hadn't worked. Surely there had to be a better way.

No one influenced me more than Mr. Ashcroft. During our many afternoon conversations at the trading post, he'd tell me about the Navajos, how they were butchered like animals during the Long Walk, similar to what Evelyn had told us. He said that when the Navajos were allowed to go back to their sacred lands, the government rounded up their sheep, their greatest source of pride and income, and burned them in pits while they stood and wept.

The BIA claimed that they got rid of the sheep to prevent erosion, but all they needed to do was return the land to the rightful owners—the Navajos—and they would have solved the problem.

The Anglo government took away the Navajos'

livelihood and dignity, giving them welfare and unemployment instead.

"Be careful whenever everything is given to you," Mr. Ashcroft said. "Because then you'll be totally beholden to your masters."

What he said was true. His stories made me understand the unhappy faces I saw. Nothing about the rules helped the Navajo people.

An even more blatant example of the government's hypocrisy was their role in regulating alcohol. The politicians and bureaucrats pretended to care about alcoholism but allowed minors to drink with adults all day and all night. They just opened more jail cells and operated additional paddy wagons, letting the drunks back out in time for Sam and me to fire cherry bombs at them. As Dad said, "Half the PhDs in the country study Indian alcoholism, but nothing changes. No one in the government really gives a shit. They just want the tax revenue."

Things always seemed to get worse when the government took on too big a role. I wanted to work to change that.

In May of 1975, at the age of twenty-two, I graduated from the University of Maryland. I purposely didn't invite anyone for fear Dad would make a huge scene, maybe even with Caroline in tow. Lonnie showed up, even though I hadn't told her when the ceremony would take place. She gave me a big hug and then handed me a brand-new Cross pen set. "I'm proud of you, David," she said. I turned down her invitation for dinner, telling her I needed to get to my caddy job.

After Lonnie left, I stood alone for a long while on the lawn outside Cole Field House, near the football field. Watching my classmates clad in caps and gowns and surrounded by family members made my heart heavy. Molly spotted me through the crowd and ran over. She graduated that day too. Rising on her toes, she kissed me, and for a moment, I felt happy.

Since Dad's body dump months before, I'd been cutting our conversations short or avoiding her altogether. But she hadn't given up and now held my hand as her parents joined us on the lawn and I met her brother and sister. Her mother invited me to dinner that night, being careful not to make it seem like I had nowhere else to go.

"Uh . . . thanks," I said. "But I can't." I pulled away abruptly and walked into the throng of people. Molly followed me until her family was out of earshot.

"I feel sorry for you, David," she said, her tender eyes filled with disappointment. "I love you, but you won't let anyone get close. If you would show me who you really are, you might be surprised that I'd still love you."

"There's no way. I don't deserve your love, even though I love you. I'm sure you can do much better than me." I walked away from Molly one last time. I had nothing to offer her.

In the parking lot at the fraternity house, I stared at the large brick building that had been my home for three years. Then I climbed into my Rambler with my clothes and few belongings stowed in the back seat and trunk. I could come back and sleep in the empty house during the summer if I needed to, but all my brothers would be gone.

Driving straight to the country club in time to caddy that Friday afternoon, I caught an eighteen-hole round for four golfers. My face must have looked as lost as I felt because after the last hole, a silver-haired golfer said, "Young man, what's going on in your life?"

"I graduated from the University of Maryland a few hours ago." I tried to sound confident, but I could barely form the words.

"Why aren't you celebrating this wonderful accomplishment with your family?"

My eyes dropped to my feet. "They couldn't come."

"I'm so sorry." He handed me a twenty-dollar bill.

Within a few days of graduation, I had rented a small, cheap apartment and returned to working construction. Every morning I ran up to ten miles to stay in top shape. As soon as I saved enough money to buy a suit and dress shoes, I started applying for entry-level jobs on Capitol Hill. My plan was to work for a member of Congress, but the competition was stiff—most of the applicants had Ivy League educations, fancy internships, and family connections that opened doors. No one wanted to hire me.

Then one morning in late September, Dad called me. "If you drive to the Library of Congress this minute, you can get a GS-3 clerk job in the mail room."

In a strange twist, Dad had befriended the son of New Mexico Senator Joe Montoya the year before and spent time at the senator's house. When Dad discovered that Senator Montoya was disturbed by his son's ongoing, embarrassing antics, he exploited the situation, as he always did. Dad offered to keep the son's name out of the headlines in exchange for a job on the senator's Environment and Public Works Committee. Only my dad could have gone from a maximum-security prison to a prestigious position in the Senate. He proudly told anyone who'd listen that the senator had hired his first full-blooded Cherokee.

Thanks to Dad's connections, I dashed off to the Library of Congress and started working the next day. Though I did little more than carry books to congressional offices and had to continue caddying on weekends to pay bills, I was now just across the street from the Capitol with a job that gave me plenty of time to read, plot, and strategize. Better yet, I had access to the Congressional Reading Room and every newspaper in the country.

I had my own national paper route, with clerks bringing me papers upon request.

The House of Representatives and Senate offices are located on one large Capitol Hill campus, and Dad called regularly to have lunch with me. His demeanor had changed, just as it had in Albuquerque when he started working for Woodmen Accident and Life. Swollen with a new swagger, he bragged about his powerful role in writing legislation for clean water and how he exchanged regular greetings with Senator Joe Biden and Vice President Nelson Rockefeller. Dad's wardrobe changed too. He now wore suits with bolo ties and turquoise rings, telling his fellow staffers about his Cherokee heritage.

One day at lunch in the Dirksen Senate cafeteria, Dad blurted out, "I've been running with Cassius Clay."

"You mean Muhammad Ali? How are you doing that?" This sounded like another one of his ridiculous exaggerations.

He took a huge bite of his BLT. "I don't call him

by his Muslim name. Clay and his entourage run through the woods near my condo each morning. His training site is at a nearby hotel. He's defending his heavyweight boxing title next month in Landover, Maryland, and I'm going to teach the asshole a lesson."

"What lesson is that?" I asked, thinking he was kidding. He couldn't possibly believe he was a threat to Muhammad Ali.

"Every morning, I wait for the punk and his fat thug bodyguards to jog past me. Then I run by them in the woods and yell for Clay to catch me. He jogs with his head down, ignoring me, and I run past him easily. I swing my fist in the air and yell, 'I'll make you fight me. What are you afraid of, chicken shit?'"

How delusional could Dad be? "Are you really hoping he'll fight you?"

"If he's such a great champion, why won't he run with me and box me?"

"Because he's loosening up with an early morning jog before he spars and hits the punching bag. Why would he try to catch a stranger or fight him? He keeps bodyguards around to stop nut jobs from harassing him."

I tossed the last french fry into my mouth, expecting Dad to laugh, but he glared at me with bugged-out eyes and twitching lips.

Dad kept up his routine for the next month, hiding in different parts of the wooded trail, hoping to ambush Ali. Each time, Ali's bodyguards expertly intervened. Somehow, the Greatest defeated Jimmy Young and retained his world heavyweight title, blissfully unaware that Thurston Crow had been targeting him.

CHAPTER 50

Joe Montoya, Dad's boss, had been a congressman or senator most of my life. I remembered reading about him on my paper route when he was considered a bright star. But in the early 1970s, questions started circulating about his financial matters, and there were whiffs of corruption and scandal. As his bid for reelection approached in 1976, the leading newspapers in New Mexico called him ripe for defeat.

Dad was unfazed by the reports and volunteered to work on the senator's campaign the final two weeks. I took time off to help. I felt sorry for Dad, knowing that his political career would end if the senator lost, which in my mind was a certainty. Sitting alongside Dad in one of the dingy campaign offices in Santa Fe, I worked the phones, asking voters to come out for the senator.

On Election Day, Montoya was clobbered by his little-known Republican opponent, a former NASA astronaut. The staff cried, drank, and hugged one another until late at night. Dad told them not to worry, that lots of Democratic members of Congress would want to hire them. As we drove back to Washington together, Dad veered from being angry because the goddamn Republican Party was full of lying sons of bitches to being wildly optimistic that his future was bright because of his popularity with powerful members of the Senate, not to mention the deep connection he was certain he shared with incoming President Jimmy Carter, whom he'd met briefly at a fundraiser.

But no one returned his calls. No hotshot Democratic senator or lobbying firm would hire him. Senators, staffers, and lobbyists avoided him. He learned the hardest lesson in politics: No one stays friends with anyone associated with a loser. Dad filed for unemployment and rarely left his condo. When he called me, he was often drunk, slurring his words and cursing the Republican Party. Several times I asked him about his plans, but he'd immediately return to his rant about Montoya's loss.

As new members of Congress looked to fill staff positions, I ramped up my job search. I scoured the openings and spent the evening before an interview reading everything I could. I was turned down again and again, and then I got a chance to talk with Congressman Tom Coleman of Missouri.

"Only my campaign manager and my wife know as much about me as you do," he said. "You're hired."

His predecessor had died in a plane crash during the summer, so Congressman Coleman was seated immediately after the election, and I began working for him in early December. I'd be answering constituent mail—the lowest position in politics—but it was a start.

Dad called to tell me he had spoken to Montoya. "I told him I had stayed loyal to him, worked hard for him, and campaigned for him," he said. "Now he needed to call in a favor and get me a good job."

The former senator's health had rapidly declined, his new irrelevance taking a bitter toll. After getting reelected for forty years, he'd become a lonely, ignored figure and the butt of jokes all over Capitol Hill.

"Thurston, I have no favors to call in," Montoya said. "I can't help anybody, including myself. Remember, I gave you a big break by putting you on the committee staff. We lost. You need to help yourself."

I could hear Dad pounding the table. "Such a weak, sniveling asshole," he said.

"What are you going to do?" I asked.

"What the hell do you think I'm going to do? I'm going to kill the little bastard and you're going to help me."

He hung up.

I flashed to West Virginia and immediately broke

out in a sweat. Leaning back in my chair, I took a couple of deep breaths to calm down. As angry as he was, Dad was liable to do anything. But he probably wouldn't attempt to pull off such a dangerous murder plot without an accomplice and alibi—meaning me—so I decided not to do anything unless he mentioned it again.

One late afternoon, a few days later, I came back to work after running an errand, and the phone rang.

"Where the hell have you been?" Dad barked. "Do you ever work?"

Ignoring him, I asked, "What's wrong?"

"We need to meet on Saturday morning at seven at the IHOP on Riverdale Road. Do you know the one I mean?"

"Yes," I said.

Dad slammed the phone down.

I groaned. I knew this was about Montoya.

When I arrived at the restaurant, Dad was sitting in a booth in the back, digging into his scrambled eggs. "Why are you late?" A huge gob of egg, toast, and jelly filled his mouth.

"It's a quarter to seven. I'm fifteen minutes early."

"Listen to me carefully. I'm going to kill that fucking little Mexican prick. And you're going to help me." He thrust his fork toward me.

"Would you please keep your voice down?" I looked around the restaurant. Luckily no one was nearby.

"The senator is too busy to make a few calls for me, but he wasn't too busy to come up with a scheme to steal millions of dollars and not pay taxes on it. He got what he richly deserved. You and I are going to finish off the bastard."

"Dad, the senator lost. It happens all the time. He can't help you, so leave him alone."

"You have a political job with the party that took my job. So now you know everything, pontificating like a self-righteous son of a bitch."

"No, I'm not going to help you. Never. Forget it. I meant what I said when we came back from West Virginia."

"Oh, hell, boy, I didn't pay any attention to that. My plan will work, but you'll have to do your part. The way you always have. I'll call the senator and tell him I'm sorry for yelling at him. I'll pretend my car is in the shop and ask him to pick me up. No one will know we got together that day. You'll follow us in your car without him noticing. The senator and I will go to lunch in his car. Afterward, we'll drive into the country, have a talk, and clear the air. And then, I'll kill him and stick him in the trunk of his car. I'll hide his car out of sight in the woods. You'll pick me up at a rendezvous point. When the police find him dead in his trunk, no one will know who did it. You'll be my alibi."

I pulled a few dollars out of my pocket and tossed them on the table. "I'm not having anything do with this. In fact, I'll call the senator's wife and let her know what you're planning. If anything happens to him, I'll go to the police." I stood and walked away.

Dad yelled, "Come back here, damn you."

A week or two went by before I heard from him again.

"I have to see you tonight," he said over the phone. "I need someone to talk to, and you're the only one I can trust." He would disown me as a traitor one minute and take me back as a loyalist the next if he needed something.

"What's wrong now?" I asked. Had he gone ahead and killed Montoya?

"Plenty. Meet me at the same IHOP at eight."

The restaurant was nearly empty. Dad was in the same booth, and he'd already finished eating when I sat across from him. He looked at me and gave a tight smile.

"What's going on?" I asked.

"I dropped Caroline off at Montgomery Mall in Bethesda yesterday at about five. We were supposed to meet at seven-thirty. After an hour of waiting in the parking lot, I walked through the mall looking for her, but she was nowhere to be found."

I relaxed in my seat, relieved it wasn't about Montoya. Still, this sounded serious. Caroline hardly knew anyone in Bethesda, or even anyone in the entire DC area.

"I finally gave up and went home. I wasn't in the door five minutes when the Montgomery County Police Department called to tell me to come get her. They'd been calling for over an hour. Caroline was being held for shoplifting more than five thousand dollars' worth of jewelry."

"Oh my God. So what happened at the police station?"

"Nothing really. They made it easy. They agreed to drop all charges if she returned to the Blackfeet Indian Reservation."

"Why do you think she did it?"

"She's been acting funny lately, like she missed home. And I've been gone a lot. She got upset when I talked on the phone about the things I needed to do. I guess she was listening in."

"Are you glad she's gone?"

"Sort of," he said. "I called Mona and told her I'd be back on Saturday."

My breath caught, wondering how that conversation had gone. "What did she say?"

"I told her there would be no discussion about the

past three years, that I'd come and go as I goddamn well pleased, and that she needed to be ready at ten in the morning to help me unload. And she said fine."

His return to Mona was that simple.

As Dad settled back in with Mona, I sabotaged yet another relationship. Nothing had changed since I'd been with Molly. If anyone got too close, I would purposely break dates, act distracted, or come up with an excuse to get away as fast as possible. But the second I was alone, I regretted my behavior, though not enough to change it. Just beneath the surface, I was afraid that they would find out the truth—my dad was a violent criminal, I had been his accomplice, and, as if that weren't enough, my own mother didn't love me. How could I ever be honest with them and introduce my family?

One of my few female friends and several of my frat brothers urged me to make one more attempt to reconcile with Mom, thinking that all my troubles with women stemmed from my lousy relationship with her. If I really listened to her side of the story, they said, and asked for her forgiveness in a gentle, sincere way, maybe she and I could get past our history and start over. "Besides, every mom loves her children, right? And wants what's best for them. It's a rule."

Though they knew only cursory details about my family history, I felt lifted by their optimism as I took a week off in May, just before Mother's Day, and drove to Albuquerque. Surely Mom would see me as a grown man now and treat me differently, no longer holding my childhood against me. Surely she'd want to help me.

When I arrived at her house, Wally's car was gone again. Mom came to the door and gave me a thin smile that sagged into a frown.

I told myself not to let it bother me. "Can we move beyond what has happened to you and to us?" I asked.

"If you'll listen to my side of the story for once."

"I promise to listen. I won't interrupt."

Mom sighed and waved me inside. I followed her down a short hallway into the kitchen. John was home from school watching television in the living room.

"My mother didn't love me, and my daddy didn't protect me from my cruel older brothers," she said, sitting at her wooden kitchen table. "I loved your daddy and waited for him to get out of prison, but he was different when he got home. He got meaner and meaner and beat me, and after we had four kids together, he abandoned me. You all did!"

I sat at the table opposite her, grateful for the space between us. Nothing had changed. When I tried agreeing with everything she said to soften her, it didn't work. She went on and on, complaining about every member of her family back to her earliest memory.

I used a different tack. "What about Wally and your son? They love you. It's obvious. I hope to be as lucky someday."

"Wally's not much to look at, though, is he?"

My eyes widened before I could catch myself. "Why does that matter? He really loves you. Isn't that the most important thing? You must love Wally for reasons other than his looks."

We sat in silence before she started up again. "Your daddy took the best years of my life. He got me when I was young and beautiful. He gave back nothing." She tossed up a hand. "And then he had to take you guys away from me too."

"Mom, if he hadn't left, you wouldn't be with Wally and your son now. You lucked out and don't even know it. Dad certainly would have killed you. He nearly did."

"Why didn't you stay with me?"

"I've always felt awful for not staying, for not standing up to Dad, and for not being a better son. All that happened to you haunts me. But you act like you were my child and I was a bad parent. That's not fair either."

Her lips quivered. "I loved your daddy. I needed him to take care of me, to take care of you kids, to make everything right, but you all used me up and dumped me like a stray dog. Even you, my oldest boy!"

Her words hurt almost worse than the belt buckle. "Dad was terrible to you. He's terrible to everyone. The best thing was for you to be away from him. Every time I try to make it up to you, you blame me for what he did—and for what I did as a child. How can we ever start over?"

She stared at me, not answering.

I'd come to apologize, but anger swelled inside me. "Did it ever occur to you that you let us down too?"

She slapped her hand on the table. "Don't you ever talk that way to me again! You're the one who testified I was unfit. You told the judge about the knife. How could you? The knife accidentally flew out of my hand. You did me dirty. You're just like your daddy. You could have changed his mind, but you didn't even try. Too bad if you feel guilty, because you should."

Mom rose from her chair. "You need to go—and don't come back. Wally will be mad at you for upsetting me."

There was nothing left to say. Our conversation was over, and we had no basis to begin another one.

By the following spring, I had sabotaged two more relationships.

CHAPTER 51

In early 1978, over a year after I started working for Congressman Coleman, I became a lobbyist for an agricultural trade association. Not only did I get my own office, but I also got help with graduate school. I couldn't have afforded George Washington University otherwise. And as much as my eyes hurt to read for endless hours, I knew having an advanced degree would make up for my academic weakness, even if I had been admitted on probation.

Three and sometimes four nights a week, I went to class to learn more about the political process. My classmates were congressional staffers from all over the country, and my professors were staff directors and counsels for senior members of Congress. I made it a point to get to know everyone.

Dad had eventually given up on his plot to murder Senator Montoya and managed to get a midlevel job with the forestry service. After I became a lobbyist, he'd puff up his chest whenever he saw me and say,

"You've had bottom-feeder jobs no one cares about, while I was a top Senate staffer rubbing shoulders with giants. Just how prestigious is it to work for farmers? Not very."

No matter how hard I tried to ignore his comments, they gnawed at me. Nothing I did would ever make me as smart as Dad, but I was proud of the work I did on behalf of the agricultural community. Farmers fed the world, and that counted for plenty in my mind.

Then on November 4, 1980, Ronald Reagan won the presidency, and two months later, I received a call that would change my life.

Since my niche was agriculture, I wanted to work on the legislative staff of the new secretary of agriculture, John Block. I had a powerful ally on the White House legislative staff who gave me an inside track on an open position, and I feverishly collected letters of support from members of the House Committee on Agriculture. But the competition was fierce.

By New Year's, I still hadn't heard anything and assumed applicants with better political connections and academic credentials had beaten me out. Early the next week, I was writing a strategy memo explaining how to influence Congress when the phone rang.

"Mr. Crow," a woman's soft voice said, "I'm pleased to inform you that the Secretary of Agriculture and the White House Office of Personnel have selected you to join the administration at the US Department of Agriculture."

I almost asked her to repeat what she said, not sure I'd heard her correctly. But she went on about the next steps, about where I needed to go for interviews and paperwork, so I knew I wasn't mistaken.

After hanging up, I jumped from my chair and flew out the door, oblivious to the bitter cold. I walked for miles around the mall leading to the Capitol and thought about Evelyn, Rex Kontz, Chauncey Ford, Herm Davis, and Tom Coleman. I'd worked hard, but there was no way I could have done it without them.

This meant that after more than a decade, I could stop caddying. I had learned so much from the country club's members and made enough money to survive, but I could finally let it go.

What would that nasty high school counselor say to me now?

By then, all my siblings had successful careers too. Lonnie had finished her doctorate in early childhood development and was an associate professor. After Sam completed his tour with the army, he received a two-year degree as a medical technician and worked at hospitals and clinics in Montgomery County. Sally earned her bachelor's degree in education, like Lonnie, and taught in Buxton, North Carolina, not far from Mona's house in Hatteras.

When I called to tell Dad about my new job for

Secretary Block, he sputtered and yelled, "Jesus Christ, how the hell did that happen? You were a peon in Coleman's office, and he was practically a nobody. After that, you bought lunch for people and gave them money that wasn't yours. That was real hard. Surely, there are legions of assholes who have more going for them than you. Did you bribe somebody or do you have something on them?"

My mind filled with rage. But what had I expected? For him to congratulate me? How absurd.

"With your dipshit party in power, I'm reduced to being a bureaucrat. I'm not in charge of a goddamn thing, and now I'll be reporting to a bunch of smart-ass, know-it-all kids like you. All you are is a glorified caddy and bullshit artist."

He far overestimated my authority. Still, my new position was an important stepping-stone for my career, and I hated wanting his approval. "Dad, why can't you be happy for me?"

"Because you failed as a son and you're not much of a man. How could someone as incompetent as you be in charge of anyone, much less me?"

The next evening, Mona called. "You've greatly disappointed your father," she said, spitting her venom into the phone. "You're working for his enemies. How dare you? He has many more years before retirement, and now he's forced to report to his ungrateful son. I'd watch my back if I were you." She hung up.

• • •

I had to fill out what seemed like a million pieces of paperwork, and the White House ran a background check. I kept thinking about Dad's lies and crimes. Would they all catch up to me? The sins of the father. A few of my colleagues had to drop out of the process because of exaggerations they'd made. My stomach stayed in a knot until I found out I'd passed.

My official duties began in February. My goals were simply to fit in, jump into the work—and steer clear of Dad. He and I were both employed by the USDA now, but so were thousands of people and only a few had political jobs, so it seemed we could easily avoid each other.

One afternoon, when I returned from a congressional hearing, Ann, our secretary, took me aside so no one would overhear us. Though my new position was a step-up in status and salary, I no longer had my own office. My desk now sat in a giant, open bull pen, along with a dozen others.

A short, older woman, Ann had kind eyes and a warm smile. "Your father came by today to see you," she said, her voice low. "When I told him you wouldn't be back for hours, he bowed several times before the pictures of President Reagan and Secretary Block and then cursed really loud and left. He slammed the door so hard the wall shook. I thought you should know."

Seething inside, I did my best to shrug it off. "He was probably trying to be funny. I'm sorry. I'll make sure it doesn't happen again."

Later that week, I sat at my desk returning phone calls about the upcoming farm bill when his voice blasted across the room, loud enough to make it hard for me to hear the person on the other end of the line. My left hand started shaking immediately.

"He's in, Mr. Crow, but on the phone," Ann said in a soothing tone. "Please have a seat in the waiting area. I'm sure he'll love seeing you."

"I realize the great man has enormous public responsibilities. I'll just sit here and wait for an audience. Or am I disturbing him as he performs his duties for the almighty Reagan?"

I hung up as quickly as I could and ran to Ann's desk. My colleagues and I had access to two vacant offices near the reception area if we needed to have a private conversation. I motioned for Dad to follow me into one of them and pulled the door tight behind us. He sat in a plush leather chair facing an empty desk, squeezing his fists and tapping his feet. I stayed standing.

"What do you want, Dad?" I asked.

He got up and bowed. "Mr. Crow, sir, may I have

a brief word? I am but a humble bureaucrat honored to have an audience with a man of your supreme intelligence and influence."

"Keep it down. People are trying to work out there. Please go."

His eyes narrowed with hatred. "Oh, are you ashamed of your Okie father? The uneducated, uncouth, monkey who raised you and made it possible for you to become a fucking elitist Republican? Is that too much for you? You ungrateful son of a bitch."

"I'm not ashamed. I'm proud of you," I said, trying to sound sincere. I needed to placate him enough to get him to leave, but if I went too far, he'd see through it and make things worse. "No one could have come as far as you have. You were born with nothing and did great things. And my new job wouldn't have been possible without you. I'm very grateful."

"You're saying I'm responsible for you?" He was yelling so loud, I wanted to cover my ears. "I'm disgusted and sickened at the sight of you. You're a sellout. You stand for nothing but ass-kissing. I'm exposing you for what you are. You are a complete fraud. Your office needs to know that."

He opened the door and stomped into the reception area. I followed close behind as several sets of eyes watched. Everyone would have heard what he said.

Dad turned to face the bull pen. "Look at this

group of ass-kissing know-it-alls," he said, and then poked my chest with his finger. "You're the greatest disappointment of my life. A complete waste of time." He disappeared into the hallway.

I stood quietly for a few moments, listening to his fading footsteps, burning with shame. On the way back to my desk, I looked at everyone and said, "I apologize for my father's behavior."

When all of them started laughing, I wanted to sink into the floor and disappear. I learned quickly that these people were not my friends—they would use Dad's performance to their advantage. Someone would hurry to tell Secretary Block, and he had far more important things to deal with.

How could I explain away Dad's sickeningly inappropriate behavior? How could I keep my position if he continued?

At the end of February, Dad took an official forestry trip to Alaska. I was relieved he wasn't around to bother me, but I knew it wouldn't last. Almost a week after he returned, Mona called. "Your father took a severe fall on a slippery dirt road during his trip. He's in the hospital now and heavily sedated. He may never walk or work again. They're sending him home in a few days, and he'll be confined to bed. You've been acting like you're too important to talk to him at work, but I think you should call when he gets better and apologize for embarrassing him."

"Embarrassing **him**?" I yelled into the phone. "You've got to be kidding!"

Mona's voice didn't sound right. Could he really be that injured?

After Dad got home from the hospital, I called every day, but Mona always answered. "He's reduced to sitting in his easy chair, hunched over, unable to walk, and he doesn't want to talk to you."

On a Saturday in mid-March, my curiosity got the best of me. If Dad was as hurt as Mona said, I wanted to know. I drove to their house and opened the door. They never locked it. Dad was watching TV and drinking a beer. He was dressed normally and looked fine. "Why the hell are you here?" he barked. "You don't give a shit about me. Get the fuck out of my house."

"I do care, Dad. I'm happy your injuries aren't as severe as we thought."

"I'm crippled. My back is broken. I had polio as a child, and my bones are curved. I can walk and do most things I need to do. I'm stronger than wild onions—Cherokees are. But I'm all used up. I began work at four years old in the cotton patch while my mother and father beat me. The government owes me disability."

Polio? Another lie. Dad continued rambling, making no sense. He'd fallen on purpose, I was sure. It made me sick to my stomach. Deciding that he was fine after all, I excused myself and drove home.

In the early afternoon on March 30, President Reagan was shot. All of us stayed glued to the television, worried he wouldn't pull through. The entire city went quiet. As I was wrapping up to go home after an extremely tense couple of hours, Ann said, "Your dad is on the phone. He's anxious to talk to you."

"Screw Reagan!" he shouted into the phone. "I hope the B-movie-star son of a bitch dies and they fire your ass. Reagan got exactly what he deserved. Someone ought to kill every fucking one of you Republicans."

"You bastard. Leave me alone." I hung up.

A week later, Mona called. "Your father has officially retired. The government tried to make him go back to work because he can walk, but they don't understand the stress of his life. At least he won't be exposed to you anymore."

But I knew Dad wasn't finished with me.

CHAPTER 52

The following Wednesday, dusk had fallen when I returned to the office after several hours of listening to congressional complaints. One congressman yelled at me again for not getting his son appointed to the Federal Farm Credit Board, demanding that Block rectify this slight by the next morning. I loved my new job, even though it often seemed that no one was pleased with our work.

Ann's furrowed brow told me something was up. My shoulders sagged. I was too tired to deal with Dad.

"Is everything okay, Ann?"

"Your sister Sally has been waiting on hold for over twenty minutes. She cried so loud, I could barely make out what she said—something about you being the only one who could save her."

What had Dad done? "It'll be all right. You can go now. And thank you for everything." I forced my face to relax for Ann's sake, the sweat already beading on my forehead.

All my colleagues had gone home, and the large room was eerily dark and quiet. Sitting at my desk, I stared at the blinking yellow light on my phone. My hand trembled as I punched the button and picked up the receiver. "Hey, Sally, what's wrong?"

"David, thank God!" she shrieked. "Help me!"

"Okay, okay. Try to calm down."

She sucked in a ragged breath. "Dad just called. He told me I have to take him and Mona to the deserted, swampy part of her property early Saturday morning. He's going to tell her it's time to clear the brush and he wants me to help, same as always. When Mona's back is turned, he's going to hit her over the head with a shovel and chop her up with an ax—'deep-six her into pieces,' he said. David, I can't believe this is happening!" Her voice pitched higher. "He wants me to help bury her, and then he'll hide in the back seat of my car and I'm supposed to drive him to my trailer . . . say we were together all day . . . say we never saw Mona." She became more hysterical as sobs came in spurts. "If I don't help him . . . he might kill me too!"

A wave of hot anger swept through me. I could handle whatever came my way, but forcing my little sister to help murder our stepmother was beyond anything I thought he was capable of.

"We have two days," I said, keeping my voice steady. "Do you know if he's in Hatteras or Bethesda?"

"No. He and Mona drive back and forth all the time. I'm not sure where he was when he called. He might already be in Hatteras. He told me to pick the two of them up at seven at Mona's house."

"Go stay with a friend, and don't go home until I say it's okay."

"I can stay with Ellie, another teacher at my school. She lives in a trailer a few miles from me." Sally gave me her number.

"Does Dad know Ellie or where she lives?"

"No, she's new. I just met her this year."

"Good. I'll check in with you tomorrow after I figure out what to do."

"He made me swear not to tell anyone. He said he'd kill me if I did. But I didn't know what else to do. Please, David. Stop him!"

"I will, but get the hell out of your trailer. Immediately." I twisted the phone cord around my finger and swiveled back and forth in my chair. "I'll have a plan soon."

"You better." The fear in her voice made my heart ache.

"We'll talk tomorrow."

Sally had always been more fragile and emotional than the rest of us, but anyone would have been shaken by what she was going through.

My plan would have to be bulletproof. But what could I do? How could I stop him?

Slumping in my chair, I knew in that moment that it had all come down to this—all the anger, the beatings, the lies.

How did I possibly think I could live a normal, happy life? I was lucky to have lasted twenty-eight years. It should never have gone this far—I should have done more to stop him. Whether it was about Mom or the stealing trips or the body in West Virginia, I had been too weak, cowering to his demands.

Not this time.

Dad's logic was simple: He knew that if he involved Sally in a murder plot to kill Mona, she would ask for my help, even when she swore to keep silent. And he knew that I wouldn't let anything happen to Sally. Once again, he was trying to manipulate me into helping him.

But wait—what if he was actually using Sally to draw me into a trap? Mona might simply be the bait, though he wouldn't hesitate to kill her. His plots hinged on accomplices—George, the men in West Virginia, me, and now Sally. He reveled in the dilemma he created.

Dad probably hated me more than he hated Mona because of my supposed position of power. Maybe he hoped he could kill us both, keep Mona's property and money, and own Sally.

Mona's disappearance wouldn't be easily explained or ignored. Her family was one of the oldest and best known in Hatteras. In spite of his intelligence, when he was angry enough, Dad didn't worry about the consequences—or he figured he could talk or bully his way out of trouble, as he had done his whole life.

And he was quick to justify murder if he thought there was something to gain. Oh my God. Instead of owning Sally, he might kill her too. No witnesses. The perfect crime. How many times had he told me?

To think that as a kid, I'd felt sorry for him when I found out he had been sent to prison. He deserved a far harsher sentence. If I had been his judge, I would have kept him in the Q for decades, if not forever.

What would my impeccably pedigreed political colleagues think if they knew my dad was planning to murder his family?

I burst into nervous laughter, remembering how afraid I was that a hint of scandal would ruin my political career. What career? What life, for that matter? My only concern was to save my stepmother, my sister—and myself.

Driving home that night, I felt a panic unlike any I'd ever known. I had no idea where Dad was. If I was the immediate target, he would be watching me.

Was he tailing me? I looked in the rearview mirror as sweat soaked my palms, making the steering wheel slippery. I wiped my hands on my pants, but they were instantly wet again.

My head felt like it was being squeezed, as though locked in a vise. I became dizzy and disoriented, my mind spinning with thoughts that Dad might kill me before Saturday.

Could I outthink him? Scare him? Set my own trap? Understanding his mind had been my mission since the first time he told me we had to get rid of Mom. But how could I scare a man who thought life in San Quentin had been a cakewalk? A man who enjoyed killing sons of bitches who richly deserved it? Not me. He understood my frailties, insecurities, and fears. He'd created them.

Warning Mona wouldn't work. She'd defend him until the moment he chopped her up and tossed her body parts into the swamp. Going to the police would be a waste of time. The police chief in Hatteras was Dad's best friend. He believed Dad's stories about being a full-blooded Cherokee orphan, a war hero, a prizefighter, and a man who saved his four children from an insane mother. Hatteras was one big safe house for Dad.

As I approached my neighborhood, it occurred to me he might ambush me outside my house. Why hadn't I thought of that earlier? Or was I being paranoid? No. He was capable of anything when he fell into a rage.

I slowed the car and parked about a mile away. My street was well lit, and he'd spot me if he drove by. Before getting out, I ripped off my jacket, tie, and shirt—I could run much faster in my undershirt. Cautiously, I walked through the yards in the shadows, looking over my shoulder and turning around in case he sneaked up on me, which would have been easy to do in my frightened state of mind.

After running from pursuers a good part of my life, I was used to hiding in the shadows. But now, I was trying to save myself from the ultimate bully, my murderous father.

When I reached my block, I slipped into the neighbor's yard across the street from my house and fell prone onto the grass, looking for signs of Dad. The temperature was dropping, but it had been sunny all day, so the ground was still warm. Half an hour went by before I rose and crept to the house. Standing on my tiptoes, I peered through the living room window. It was still and dark inside, no sign of anyone, but if he was lying in wait, that's exactly what he would want me to think.

I crouched down and made my way around to the back door leading into the kitchen. My hand shook as I fumbled to fit the key into the lock, cursing myself for making enough noise to alert Dad if he was inside. Fear gripped my throat as I opened the door and turned on the light.

A stack of cans shaped in a pyramid sat on the kitchen table. Nothing had been there when I left for work that morning.

A message from Dad.

I jumped back, knocking the screen door open, and stumbled on the landing. Afraid he'd leap out and shoot or stab me, I scrambled to my feet and bolted down the street to my car.

My hands trembled so badly it took several attempts to open the door. Inside my Mustang, I felt strangely comforted behind locked doors. I hit the gas pedal and the car shot forward, the wheels squealing as I weaved recklessly down the street, nearly hitting several parked cars. After driving a few miles, I pulled into an unfamiliar neighborhood and parked in the dark, far away from a streetlight.

What had I been thinking, going inside the house? Big mistake—it could have been fatal. And then driving like a maniac? No more. I needed to calm down and think clearly.

Reclining the seat, I leaned back, closed my eyes, and crossed my arms against my chest to stop shaking. I flashed back to the bullies in Mud Flats—the red ants, Coke bottles, BB guns—child's play compared to this—and then I thought of Gilbert, how I had trained with Dad and took the fight to him.

I shot upright. Dad probably thought I'd drive straight to Hatteras to wait for him there. He'd think I was too scared to stay after he broke into my house. My instincts told me he was in Bethesda and wouldn't go to Hatteras until Friday.

Within thirty minutes, I had made it to Bethesda and parked about a half mile from Dad's house, the split-level where I lived at the end of high school. I was on familiar turf. I knew all about the other houses in the cul-de-sac, the streetlight at the end of Dad's driveway, and, most importantly, the escape routes through the woods.

I ran the short distance to the next-door neighbor's yard and cut across their driveway. Shrouded in large oaks and pines, I dropped to my stomach and crept toward the edge of their property until I had a clear view of Dad's carport.

I'd been right. His red Ford Capri was there. Mona's car was missing, which meant she was probably in Hatteras—she never went anywhere else.

It was just past midnight, and Dad planned to murder Mona on Saturday, so I needed to attack him within the next twenty-four hours. The thought made me vomit the way I had after seeing the decapitated man on the reservation—and the body in West Virginia.

He would never expect me to make the first move.

CHAPTER 53

After leaving Dad's house, I was exhausted and needed a safe place to sleep. An hour later, I checked into the Harrington in DC, a cheap tourist hotel where Dad would never think to look for me. I used their underground parking to keep my car off the street.

Sleep came only in snatches, my dreams more vivid than usual—panting, gasping, sprinting away from an invisible pursuer I somehow knew was my father. I ran into blocked escape routes, ambushes in blind alleys, and dead ends. I couldn't breathe. And there was always the sweat. The sheets were soaked.

Jolting awake for the fourth or fifth time, I wondered if all sons of murderers faced being murdered for not following their fathers' codes. What an awful thought. But had I ever really stood a chance? No. It was the Crow legacy, the stench from birth.

You've betrayed me after all I've done for you, Dad boomed, standing over me with a wrench in one hand and a gun in the other. **I taught you, molded you, and formed you into my image, but you failed me. For that, you must die**.

My eyes snapped open and my heart banged against my chest. I glanced at my watch: four-thirty.

When the light seeped in under the curtains, I got up and called in sick, claiming a migraine, and then grabbed a quick breakfast at the buffet. The room was full of noisy kids visiting the capital over Easter vacation, a distraction I didn't need. After buying underwear and running clothes at a local Hecht's department store, I went on a five-mile run to clear my mind and formulate a plan. By the time I got back to the hotel, I knew what to do.

The night before, as I was about to leave work, I'd stuffed several legal notepads into my briefcase, along with a handful of the ubiquitous government pens. I pulled out one of each, sat at the desk in my room, and started writing.

My first letters were to my bosses, saying I planned to resign because of a family issue that would create embarrassment for the department.

Then I wrote a letter to the Hatteras police chief, describing Dad's plot—the location of the swamp, the tools to be used in the murder, and Sally, his getaway and alibi. I made it clear that she was Dad's hostage, not an accomplice. I wrote similar letters to the **Coastland Times**, the North Carolina State Police chief, and three nosy Hatteras residents, including a local minister Dad hated.

I wrote the final two letters to Sigma Chi alums, one who worked for the FBI, and another who was an undercover narcotics cop. Dad would be pissed off because he despised Sigma Chi and the FBI, but more than that, my fraternity brothers would see that he was brought to justice if I was found dead.

After checking for errors, I gathered all the letters and walked to a nearby copy store. For the next half hour, I used their Xerox machine to make multiple copies. Before leaving, I bought a red marker and an assortment of large and small envelopes. On the way back, I stopped at the post office for stamps.

In my room, I laid everything out on the bed and started assembling four packets of the copies I'd made. The first would go to my friend Fran at work. I inserted a note, asking him to mail the letters, and then wrote on the outside of the packet to open it if I didn't show up on Monday. Since we saw each other every day, it wouldn't take him long to notice I had disappeared.

The next packet was for Dad and the other two were backups. I called information for the correct addresses and made sure everything was neat and legible. And I put extra postage on all the envelopes just in case.

It took me most of the afternoon to finish. I had

to be thorough. The letters were my insurance policy against Dad getting away with his horrific plans if he did kill me or Mona or Sally—or all three of us.

It was close to four when I dropped the packet off at work with the guard and asked him to deliver it to Fran. As I drove away, I took a deep breath for the first time since Sally had called, knowing now that Dad would be punished if his plan succeeded. But there was still plenty for me to do. I stopped at a grocery store and a hardware store to pick up the supplies I'd need that night and filled up at a gas station.

Back at the hotel, I had one more letter to write.

I forged a confession from Dad for the murder of Mona Tully Crow, his wife of Hatteras, North Carolina. He explained that he forced his daughter Sally to help him under the threat of death. The next paragraphs detailed how he tried to kill Mom by cutting her brake lines in Gallup, how he bludgeoned Cleo's skull, the way he betrayed George, how he beat the guy to death in New Orleans when he was in the navy, the body dump in Wheeling, West Virginia, and the plan to kill the senator.

The letter ended with "I'm a pathetic human being, hell-bent on destroying the lives of my children and all who inadvertently threaten me because of my profound inferiority complex."

I wrote it with the red marker, adding a dramatic flair. I had a special place in mind for that letter.

Finished with my preparations, I called Sally.

"Ellie says I can stay as long as I need to," she said through muffled tears. I could hear dogs barking in the background. "Do you have a plan yet?"

"Yes, he'll be stopped in his tracks." I pressed a pen hard on the notepad next to the phone, tearing a hole in it.

"You can't scare him." Her voice broke. "He's smarter and stronger than any of us, even you."

"My plan will work. After tonight, he won't bother you or Mona again."

Hanging up, I closed my eyes and rested before my next move. I shook all over, no doubt the same way Dad's victims did when he had them cornered. As the minutes passed, I got worried that I'd chicken out and run away. But if I did that, I might as well be dead along with Sally and Mona.

A sudden surge of strength came over me, and I knew to act on it at once. After all, it was a miracle I was still alive.

The assault began shortly after midnight. I came armed with the essentials in my line of work: a crescent wrench, a valve core remover, a pocketknife, a screwdriver, a potato, a funnel, tape, glue, and rags—all in a brown paper bag—along with a five-pound bag of sugar and Dad's packet of letters. The weather was on my side. There was a slight breeze and no rain.

I staked out an area in the woods where I'd been the night before to stash my gear and watch the house. Dad's Capri was still the only car there, pointed toward the street, the way he always parked. Fortunately, he had turned off all the outdoor lights. The streetlight at the bottom of his driveway made it easy for him to see any motion, but if I was careful, I could perform most of my work in the shadows.

Leaving everything in the woods, I crawled to the carport, hid behind the Capri, and studied the wall of windows across the front of the house. Dad's bedroom was in the back. There were no curtains—they had fallen apart years ago and hadn't been replaced—so if he turned on any lights, I'd see them. The front door was warped so badly it was difficult to open and made a loud, scraping noise. Still, if he was waiting in the front of the house with a loaded gun, it wouldn't take him long to yank open the door and fire a shot.

But I had a much bigger concern. The back of the house wasn't visible from the carport. If Dad raced out the back door, he could cover the ten yards to the carport in mere seconds and fire an unobstructed shot. I'd be a dead man.

He wouldn't hesitate to use a gun on me. Many years earlier, when we lived on Kingston Road, he and I were the only ones home when he thought he'd heard a prowler in the basement. He yelled down the stairs, "Come out now or I'll shoot." I begged him not to, thinking a frightened teenager might be hiding, but he said anyone who broke into his house deserved to die.

Charging into the basement, he unloaded a full clip from his German Luger. The bullets ricocheted off the cinder-block walls. I stood at the top of the stairs, expecting to hear screams. As Dad climbed toward me, he said, "The bastard must have gotten away. I'm sorry I didn't get him."

I couldn't take any chances—I had to set a trap.

Staying low, I crawled around the backyard until I found a piece of flagstone—about the size of home plate—one of the many rocks Dad had dragged with us from the reservation. I got to my knees and slowly wobbled the heavy slab toward the door, keeping my eyes on the narrow panel of glass alongside it.

In seconds, Dad could turn on the lights and shoot me at point-blank range. Execution style, right through the forehead.

I inched closer, watching, afraid to blink.

A shadow darted across the window. Was that him? I dove to the ground, holding my breath, bracing myself, my face in the dirt.

No lights. No sounds.

I exhaled. I was just seeing things.

On my knees again, I reached the door and propped the rock against it like a lean-to, careful not to make any noise. Then I crept back into the woods.

I listened and watched. Nothing.

Now if Dad tried to burst through the back door, the flagstone would fall in on him, making a hell of a racket and most likely tripping him. That would buy me enough time to get away.

When I shifted my weight slightly, the light rippled across the front windows like a slow-motion wave. Was that Dad moving toward the door?

Or was I seeing things again?

Sweat poured out of me, soaking my T-shirt.

I couldn't lose my nerve, not when there was so much at stake. The Window Rock hayride scene flashed in my mind, followed by the assault on Query Man. No one could be better prepared for this. Under different circumstances, we would laugh at the poor fool who got the full Crow treatment.

Paper bag in hand, I crawled to the carport and under the Capri. I studied the wall of windows once more. My heart thumped so loud I felt certain Dad would hear it.

After seeing no change for several minutes, I got to work.

I shaved the potato to the approximate size of the tailpipe and shoved it deep inside and then wiped the residue with a rag and placed the peels in my jacket pocket. Another look at the windows, and I slid to the driver's side, away from the house, and pried off both hubcaps. I removed the lug nuts and valve caps, put them in my pocket, and twisted the valve cores slowly to keep them from whistling. Back on with the valve caps and hubcaps—everything in place so it wouldn't look like the wheels had been disturbed.

Next, the license plates. Under the car again, I pulled myself to the front bumper, unscrewed the plate, and wriggled to the rear and took off the other one. Returning to the woods, I shoved both tags under the neighbor's woodpile. It would be years before anyone found them.

I grabbed the five-pound bag of sugar and packet of letters and sat checking the house. Nothing except the rippling light.

When I crawled to the car this time, I headed for the gas tank, located on the driver's side. I removed the cap, inserted the funnel, and poured in the entire bag of sugar. Then I screwed the cap back on so Dad wouldn't notice anything wrong.

Now for the last, most crucial part.

Hunched down, I took several deep breaths and moved to the front of the car. Slowly, I stood up and taped the letters in their envelopes side by side on the windshield under the wipers.

Dad could have easily gotten me.

But still nothing.

As the coup de grâce, I glued the final letter directly to the windshield, facing out for everyone to see. The red words of Dad's confession glowed eerily in the dim light.

Escaping into the woods, I imagined the outraged look on his face when he read the letter and saw that it was stuck to the glass. And when he read the other letters, he'd realize he would be caught. It was almost worth hanging around to watch him.

After snaking my way through the trees, I ran to my car and took a circuitous route back to my hotel in downtown DC.

I felt powerful and invisible again.

Following a few hours of fitful sleep, I called Sally. "You'll be hearing from Dad, and he'll be furious. He'll demand to know if you've heard from me. Tell him you haven't." I rubbed my eyes, trying to push away the fatigue.

"Will he think I snitched?"

"We're way beyond worrying about that. Dad had to be stopped. I promise that's been done. He'll be angry with you but overwhelmed with rage at me. That'll divert him. He won't be driving his car for a while." I thought of the letters, especially the one glued to the windshield, and let out a shaky chuckle. "And he won't be going to Hatteras anytime soon."

"What'll I do if he shows up and tries to hurt me?" She cried softly.

"He'll probably threaten you, but he won't hurt you." I swallowed past the lump in my throat. "And he won't go through with Mona's murder. He accomplished his mission, though. I'm resigning my job."

"Why? What'd you do?"

"I betrayed him—or at least that's what he thinks. I rose above him at work and refused to go along with his crimes. He wanted revenge." My voice choked at the thought of battling Dad to the death for simply living my own life. "He knew you'd call me, and he expected me to fall into his trap. It was how he raised us. He's already damaged my reputation beyond repair—or he will soon."

"That's crazy. You aren't making any sense, big brother."

"None of this makes sense unless you know what makes Dad tick, and I do. He won't kill Mona without your help. And you won't help him. If you did, and he got away with it, he would hold it over you for the rest of your life. He's a weak man who manipulates others to do his dirty work. Don't let him control you any longer. There's nothing more to it than that."

"How'd you stop him?" she asked.

"By remembering everything he taught me."

CHAPTER 54

I took a shower and called in sick again, this time telling the truth about having a migraine. After eating breakfast at the noisy hotel buffet, I drove aimlessly, staying far away from Bethesda. My mind raced with all the possible scenarios.

My bosses would likely accept my resignation. Why wouldn't they? Plenty of talented candidates were available who wouldn't embarrass the department. Resigning would deliver a fatal blow to my career in Washington—no one does that without having a serious problem. In my world, losing this job would mean a complete loss of face and reputation. Dad counted on it, along with me being stupid enough to confront him in Hatteras.

When would he strike back? Right away? Or would he wait until he could catch me off guard? Maybe he would cut my brake lines or ambush me at night or get an accomplice to kill me. Given his history, nothing was off the table.

Where could I go to hide from him? At first, driving to Arizona felt like the right thing to do, but the more I thought about it, the less sense it made. My education, contacts, and job skills were all aimed at government and politics. What could I do there?

Albuquerque probably had the best opportunities, but it also had Mom. She would want to see me regularly and might even believe I moved back because of her. Even if Gallup had the right prospects, she'd be only two hours away. Living almost three thousand miles away from her was a blessing. She and Wally wouldn't drop in on me in DC.

After burning through a tank of gas, I went back to the hotel, more worn out and confused than I thought possible. Only one thing was clear—leaving Washington because of Dad would be a cowardly act. I'd be running from my fears again.

I stayed at the Harrington all weekend, and on Monday morning, I made it to work at the usual hour. I needed to give my resignation to Randy Russell, Secretary Block's most trusted adviser and one of my few friends at the USDA. When I burst into his office, I found him deep in conversation on the phone, so I went back to my desk, my head pounding. A long thirty minutes went by before Ann said, "Randy called and said you could see him now."

My hand shook when I gave Randy my letter of resignation.

"What's got you so upset, my friend?" he asked.

"I don't know what . . . what to do," I stammered. "My life is such a mess and I can't fix it. I'm resigning to keep from embarrassing our department." My eyes filled with tears.

"You're a dear friend and a good guy," he said. "It can't be all that bad. Relax and let's try to sort this out. Surely you don't have to resign. You worked hard to get this job. You beat out a lot of people for it, and you're doing great."

"No, I'm not doing great. My father planned something horrible, and if word got out, it would be very embarrassing to our office. I can't stay in good conscience."

"Have you done anything wrong?"

"No, but my father wants to destroy me."

"I'm on your side, and so is the big boss. If you haven't done anything, we'll stand by you. But you have to believe in yourself too. I've heard about your father's antics from some of your colleagues. Ann told me she's worried about you. Didn't you tell me he retired on disability? He can't hurt you here anymore."

"If only that were true, Randy."

"You're exhausted and distraught. My advice is to calm down, think about your future without being scared, and make the best decision you can for the long term. I won't accept your resignation and neither will Secretary Block. You aren't thinking clearly. Work hard, keep your head down, and let's talk in a couple of weeks."

"But—"

"No buts. Get to work and follow my advice. I'll always have your back, don't forget that."

When I returned to the bull pen, Fran grabbed my arm. "Hey, are you okay, buddy? What's in that big envelope you dropped off?"

"I can't tell you. Can you please give it back to me? You're a good friend, but for now, I can't say anything. I'm sorry."

The day crept by, minute by minute, hour by hour. I expected the worst. Would Dad show up at work? Would he have a gun?

Later that afternoon, Ann strode across the bull pen, her face pale and her eyes a little too wide.

"Your father is on the phone."

I jumped up and hurried to the closest empty office. "I'll take it in here. Thank you, Ann, for everything."

"Are you going to be okay?"

"I don't know."

Closing the door behind me, I watched the yellow light blink for several minutes. Sweat dripped down my back once again. I sat at the desk and slowly picked up the phone.

"I'll get you," came Dad's deep, threatening voice. "You've accomplished nothing. Your little stunt can't stop me. You're a child playing with a man. This ain't over, boy. And you know it. You better watch your step because I'll be right behind you. You're a goddamn cow—"

I quietly set down the receiver, knowing he'd speak for a while before realizing I had hung up. A sense of calm settled over me. Instead of reacting with my usual false bravado, I had at last refused to listen to his threats.

The greatest insult of all was to ignore him. Leaning back in my chair, I let out a sigh. My left hand shook uncontrollably, showing how much fear remained inside me.

Sally called me a week later. "Dad met me in the parking lot at school this morning. He was waiting when I pulled up. I didn't recognize the car. It wasn't his Capri. I was so scared, David." She started crying. "He said that you were no longer his son and if you ever interfered with him again, you would pay with your life. And he said I betrayed him too, and if I ever did it again, he'd make me regret it."

"I'm so sorry, Sally."

"He asked if I knew anything about the letters you wrote, if you had mailed them. He asked me at least three times. I kept telling him I had no idea what he was talking about."

"Good, the threat worked," I said. "The letters are insurance against him doing anything to Mona or you. Maybe someday I'll tell you the whole story—for now, let's put this behind us, okay?"

"I'll try, but it doesn't feel like he'll ever let us go."

"He will if we stop giving in to his demands."

"Easier said than done. He comes to Hatteras a lot and can drop by my trailer or school anytime."

She hung up crying. He still had control over her. I grimaced while putting down the phone, feeling a deep pang of failure because nothing had been resolved by my actions. Dad wouldn't change his ways or leave us alone.

I continued my job, but Dad wasn't finished with me no matter what he said to Sally. Within days, Mona chastised Sally and me in separate phone calls for not being respectful or helpful to our loving father. "Your father asks very little of you in exchange for a lifetime of love and devotion," she said. "He raised you and got rid of your mentally ill mother, who would have destroyed you. The least you can do is help him when he asks."

The irony of it all.

• • •

For the first two weeks after the showdown, I stayed at a friend's apartment. Everywhere I went, I looked over my shoulder, waiting for Dad's next move.

When I returned to my house, I bought dead bolts and slept in a sleeping bag in the kitchen. I left for DC before dawn, ran my five miles there, and took a shower at work.

I didn't leave the office until late. When I went home, I parked several blocks away and walked slowly to my house. I left every light on.

I hid a handgun in a window well. I even placed rocks in front of the doors in an arrangement that would let me know if they'd been disturbed.

I befriended a retired neighbor across the street who almost never left his house and asked him to keep a watch.

At work, people constantly asked me why I seemed so jumpy and paranoid. I couldn't answer, of course.

Dad didn't get away with his plan, but he left me so rattled I could barely function. He made me feel permanently vulnerable to future attacks, not just physical ones, but ones that would finish off my career.

In that sense, we both scored.

Who would ultimately win?

• • •

The summer came and went without any contact from Dad. As Christmas approached, I slowly became less fearful of an attack. Another year passed and still nothing.

Then on a cold, gray day in late January 1983, Ann walked across the bull pen. "Your father is on the phone," she said softly. "Do you want to take it?"

"No, but I will anyway."

Sweat immediately formed on my brow, and my left hand started to tremble.

His voice was as gruff as ever. "Your older sister has been totally disrespectful, and Sally isn't a damn bit better. Your brother isn't any help to me either."

Somehow, I was the best of the four at the moment. I chuckled to myself at the absurdity.

"I don't get any thanks or appreciation for all that I sacrificed and especially for getting rid of that crazy bitch mother of yours. No one visits me."

He acted as if we had been talking regularly. Had he forgotten our last conversation, or was this his way of pretending it had never happened—like his plot to kill Mona and what I had done to stop him?

In true Crow fashion.

After fifteen minutes of complaining, he said, "You're the only one I can talk to. Stay in touch. Why do I have to be the one who calls you?"

• • •

The following week, it was Mom's birthday. She and I hadn't talked since my Albuquerque visit almost six years before, so I took the special occasion to reach out to her again.

"I don't have your phone number, your address, or the phone numbers of any of the other kids," she said in her usual whiny voice. "If you don't want a relationship, don't ever call again."

"Can we start with happy birthday and go from there? I'll give you my home number, but I'm not there much. And you can have my office number, but only if you promise not to call too often because we're really busy. I'll try to call you more if you don't always bring up the past wrongs of the Crow family."

"What else is there to talk about?"

"Anything. Your son, Wally, how things are going in Albuquerque—anything else at all."

Within minutes, she had launched into the same old bitter script, and I told her I needed to get back to work. I waited a month and tried again but got the same results. Every call was a painful reminder that her life had not moved forward.

Then she began calling the office. If I was out or busy, Ann would tell her I'd call back when I was available. But Mom would call repeatedly until I talked to her.

Ann didn't know what to do. "How can I make her understand?"

"You can't," I said. "Something's wrong with her. When I tell her to stop calling so much, she claims she doesn't do it. She's stuck in some kind of arrested development as an angry child."

Mona called too, though not often. Sometimes she left messages on my answering machine. They were nearly identical—angry reprimands for not caring about my poor father who'd given every measure of devotion to his children. Each of us went through periods of being disowned, only to be back in his good graces when another one of us did something he couldn't tolerate.

That was mostly what the four of us talked about when we got together. No one ever brought up our childhood. We had each moved forward in our own way, not staying in touch much.

But I did learn a few years later that Dad pestered Sally to help him kidnap a rich Jewish woman for millions in ransom money. Sally simply didn't show up at the rendezvous point, which presumably stopped him. She wasn't sure.

As time passed, Sally saw Dad on many occasions in Hatteras with younger women. "They all look like they're on their last dime," she said. "How the hell does he find them?"

He just wouldn't quit.

EPILOGUE

I worked. I read. I ran. My understanding of politics and history deepened, but my inner world remained stunted. Friends told me I was guarded. I turned every serious conversation about myself or the Crow family into an inappropriate joke. Marriages failed.

By my early fifties, I still hadn't found any measure of peace—guilt and anxiety followed me everywhere. The self-help books lining my shelves hadn't helped, nor had the many therapists I'd seen. They were willing to listen forever to the story of my childhood but couldn't help me move past it.

I took several trips to Gallup and Fort Defiance, convinced I could somehow defang my childhood by reliving it. I remembered everything vividly, even the tiniest details—names of my classmates, street addresses, phone numbers, sounds, and smells. But the memories from 306 South Cliff Drive remained a scary blur.

One afternoon I sat in my car across from our

old house for several hours. Finally, the owner came over to me and asked me why I continued to show up. "Are you watching me?"

He was a thin, short Mexican man, like Ray Pino, but without the devilish smile. Nearly bald, he wore horn-rimmed glasses and had the softest voice for a man I'd ever heard.

I told him the Crow family had lived there many years before. He didn't believe me until I described the interior, including the chipped green-and-black tile in the basement, the crack in the shower, and the creaking, brown varnished steps that led to the kitchen.

He invited me inside.

A widower, the man had bought the house shortly after we left and raised four children there. "I've probably seen you a dozen times sitting in a car staring at the house or circling the block on foot. What happened here that constantly brings you back?"

A simple question, but he asked it with such kindness that the tears and memories came gushing out of me—Elephant Hill, cherry bombing the Navajos on Route 66, the Benny Paret fight, the knife-throwing incident, Lonnie swallowing the aspirin, ditching Mom.

He put his arms around me and pulled me to the couch. "Please sit."

I cried my way through more stories as he sat quietly and listened. When I finished, he fed me dinner in our old kitchen, which looked remarkably the same except for the table and chairs. When he asked me to come inside, it was still light. It was nearly two in the morning when I stood to leave.

At the door, I thanked him and extended my hand. He took it in both of his. "You can't change your childhood, but you can let it go," he said.

"I don't know. I've tried, but I could never unlock what I just told you. Maybe I needed to be inside the house, to talk to a compassionate stranger, to relive all that had gone wrong here—especially when Dad brought me back and I saw Mom sitting on the floor looking so hopeless. All the shame and guilt. Both my parents thought I was a coward on that terrible day, and I thought they were right, even if their reasons were different."

"That's a lot for a ten-year-old boy to carry around, don't you think? You just took a big step in telling me. None of that day or the rest of what happened was your fault." He smiled. "You're going to be okay, David Crow. Come by again anytime."

Back at my favorite hotel, the El Rancho, I jotted down notes about all the events in Gallup. I felt lighter but leery. Could I let go of the past? It stunned me how much blame I had assumed for everything.

The same tape had played in my head as far back as I could remember: "If only I had saved Mom. If only I had stopped Dad. If only I was a stronger person."

After a few hours of sleep and a fast run, I sat on the hotel bed and dialed my mom's number. "Do you think it was my fault that you were abandoned? Did you really think I could have saved you?"

"You deserve a lot of blame for not helping me, for not understanding my story, for not going with me when I had nowhere to go."

"But I was only ten years old. Do you really think I could have done anything to help you?"

"Yes, you were my oldest boy. You never came around to help and you still don't. You went with your daddy and ditched me." I quietly put down the phone.

Dad answered on the first ring.

"Do you regret being so cruel to Mom and abandoning her? Do you regret the brutal beatings you gave Sam and me? Do you regret what you did to Lonnie and Sally? How about the stealing, the buried body in West Virginia, the murder plots you tried dragging me into? Do you regret—?"

"Don't give me any of your revisionist crap! You never did what I wanted you to do. None of you kids are worth a damn. You complained constantly, and I never thought you'd be much of a man. And you're not. Don't ever call again with your whining bullshit.

You had it much better than I did. And much better than you deserved." He hung up.

Propping up the pillows behind me, I stretched out on the bed. At that moment, at age fifty-two, I wanted to be free of Mom, Dad, and Mona. They wouldn't—or couldn't—change and I couldn't change what had happened.

Then it came to me. The only way to be free was to forgive them—and forgive myself.

It was advice I'd heard plenty of times, but on that day in the hotel, I was ready to do it. In an instant, I stopped expecting anything from them. Their approval, friendship, understanding, empathy, love. And I stopped believing that Dad, Mom, and Mona were right about me—or any of us. I didn't want to carry around the burden of longing and guilt and shame anymore. I was done.

How else could I ever feel any joy or happiness?

It was as if a light went on inside my brain. It had been so simple, something I could have done long ago. But no tie is as strong as family, making it the hardest one to break.

It took time, but I became more relaxed and less anxious. I began to like myself and my confidence grew, as did my ability to share myself with others. The childhood memories I had buried came to the surface, but I saw them through a different lens, without anger or blame, as though they had happened to someone else. This allowed me to break the cycle that had defined my family for generations.

The benefits flowed. My lobbying firm flourished, and my two partners made it their firm also, becoming close friends and allies. My relationship with my children became stronger. Through lifelong friends, I met Patty, a wonderful woman who is now my wife. She was the first person I opened up to about my childhood. In the past, I'd always felt the need to omit and hide. Patty never judged me, for which I'll be eternally grateful.

When Dad was in his early eighties, he and Mona asked me to be their legal and medical guardian. He was weakened by heart disease and back problems, and Mona had dementia and could no longer care for him. The health services administration determined they were unfit to live alone. Intervening, I made sure they could stay in their own home in Hatteras with proper care. Patty and I often drove the six-hundred-mile round trip to see them.

Dad and I spoke almost every day, either over the phone or in person, about his time in prison and how he survived his childhood. Whenever he had the chance, he'd bring up the BIG LIE, going on about his Cherokee heritage and the vicious crimes perpetrated on him and his family by the white man. Dad had no remorse about anything, except for not killing more of the bastards who richly deserved it. When I asked him again if he felt bad about the way he'd treated Mom, he said, "Hell, no. Your mother should have died in Gallup."

At least once a month, Dad would call upset about something, whether it was figuring out a medical bill, getting his hearing aids to fit right, or programming his TV. Before offering to help, I'd say, "Dad, let me call Buddy for his advice." He roared with laughter every time. Our inside joke about his first San Quentin cellmate was still fresh after more than forty years.

By then, a decade had passed since I called him after my visit to 306 South Cliff Drive. He spoke as though the Crow children's lives had been idyllic. But there was no longer any reason to argue or question his version of events—I was free from all of it.

I'd done everything in my power to be his opposite, especially for my children and for Patty, the greatest blessings of my life. Dad knew I'd participated in the Big Brothers Big Sisters program, as well as mentoring hundreds of interns in my lobbying firm.

He laughed. "You always were a do-gooder. No one will give a shit what you do. Let me assure you of that."

I also mentored his accomplice's granddaughter. I felt such relief after tracking down George's family and apologizing to them. When I told Dad about it, his eyes filled with tears and he yelled at me to leave. The next time we discussed it, George was at fault. He was the reason they went to San Quentin. Dad told me to never bring him up again.

One night, after an open-heart operation he wasn't expected to survive, he grabbed my hand and motioned for a pad of paper and a pencil. He had tubes coming out of his mouth and IVs in both arms.

"Can you forgive me?" he wrote, his eyes filled with fear.

I gave him a big smile and squeezed his hand. "Of course. You're my dad."

But he did survive.

Two years later, Dad called me right after suffering a stroke and sounded like he had a mouthful of marbles. Until that day, his mind and temper had remained sharp, even as he approached the halfway mark in his eighty-fifth year.

The next morning, I made the three-hundred-mile drive with Patty to see how he was. His voice was clear, but his eyes were bloodshot, and he was confused about why I had come to see him. Within days he had a second stroke. When he was weakened to the point of barely being able to move, he was still irascible, scolding the doctors, telling them his brain was fine, but he had a bad back, and why the hell weren't they working on that? After a few days in the hospital, we moved him to a nearby nursing home.

A week later, on New Year's Day, I was summoned again. Dad was fighting with the staff about the "garbage crap" they were feeding him. By the time I got there, he'd fallen into a deep sleep. When he woke up, I knew it was the last time I'd see him alive. His eyes were swollen, no longer mean or angry—they were sad and lost. A nurse came in for a moment, giving me time to walk into the hall to collect my thoughts.

I told Patty that Dad would die soon, and I began to cry. She told me to go back to him, and that she would wait for me.

When I returned to Dad's bed, he stared at me. His piercing blue eyes regained momentary strength.

He asked me to lean down to his face.

Reaching up, he rubbed my head the way he did when I was a boy. "You were my favorite one. I love you, son. I always have. Please kiss me on both cheeks."

He had never uttered those words before.

I bent over and kissed him on both cheeks. "I've always loved you too, Dad . . . Goodbye."

Tears streamed down his face as he gripped my hand with the same powerful strength I remembered from childhood, his eyes now closed.

As I walked into the hallway sobbing, Patty put

her arms around me. "It's hard to say goodbye to a father, even to him."

There was nothing left to say. She took my hand and we went out into the rain. Except for a few words spoken at a drive-through, we were silent the whole way home.

The next day I drove to Dad's old house on Burning Tree Road. It had been torn down, but the foundation was still in place. I stood there in the cold for a long time, remembering the night of the showdown—and the full Crow treatment.

"Goddamn it, boy, make me proud even if it kills you." Dad's voice rattled around inside my head, as it always had and always will. "David, you're scrawny, you can't see, can't hear, can't fix a damn thing, but you are one tough little bastard, and the most clever son of a bitch I know. You could have talked your way out of San Quentin before God got the news."

I laughed. "Maybe so, Dad." I took one last look, turned, and walked away.

With the help of Ancestry.com, Patty and I traced my dad's family to eighteenth-century Northern Ireland and England. They settled in North Carolina and Maryland before the American Revolution.

There isn't a Cherokee among them.

POSTSCRIPT

Taylor Crow, Dad's father, served as a corporal for two years in the US Army Corps of Engineers, clearing roads and building bridges to aid troop movements. His ship, along with many others, was fired upon by German submarine torpedoes, as Dad said. Taylor saw combat in France and was treated for several weeks in a military hospital for unspecified symptoms. Later VA records show that he suffered from severe headaches and lung issues the rest of his life. He died at the age of fifty-one while working as a hired hand on a farm in Arizona. Taylor lived hard, drinking, fighting, and smoking heavily. There is no evidence Ella Mae poisoned him. She outlived him by fifty-eight years.

Cleo Cole, the man Dad and George attempted to kill before I was born, died a few years after the assault, blind and bedridden, angry until the end that justice had not been served. Smiley, his wife, lived for two more decades. Presumably, she didn't see the thirty-day notice in the Los Angeles newspapers asking if anyone objected to Dad's pardon because it went through uncontested in 1959.

George died broken and penniless in 1997. He never received a pardon for his violent felony conviction due to meaningless parole violations, including moving without telling his parole officer. His son, Jeff, who became a friend of mine, said his dad didn't tell him about the crime except to say, "Don't try to protect a lady's honor in California."

Buddy, Dad's first cellmate in the Q, served an eight-year sentence, as Dad had predicted. While in prison, Buddy lost both his car upholstery business and his wife.

Mona declined dramatically after Dad passed. Her dementia worsened, and she fell into a coma the last year of her life. She died in 2018.

Mom is eighty-eight years old and lives near her adopted son and his loving family. She and Wally were married for over fifty years, and he stayed devoted to her until the day he died. Without fail, Mom and I talk on the phone a few times a week. She still hates the Crow family and feels the need to say so in every call.

Lonnie, my oldest sister, is a college professor and lives with her professor husband. They have two adult children and three grandchildren.

Sam, my younger brother, and his wife work in the

medical field. He is the proud stepfather of three children. He never had the skin on his hand or stomach smoothed, and his left big toe still has a severe bend.

Sally, my younger sister, is a schoolteacher with two adult children.

I continue to work at my lobbying firm in Washington, DC. Over time, my eyesight deteriorated further, and I ultimately had five LASIK surgeries in Canada, several years before the procedure was approved in the United States. I have 26 percent hearing in my right ear and less than 9 percent in my left and can hear only with the help of powerful hearing aids and my highly skilled audiologist, Dr. Melissa Yunes.

My wife, Patty, and I have three children, all married to wonderful spouses. She and I live in the suburbs of DC.

ACKNOWLEDGMENTS

This book would never have happened had it not been for my friend John Campbell, who encouraged me to write my story. His excellent advice and insights helped me tremendously, as did his readings of different drafts of the manuscript.

My heartfelt thanks to my many other friends who did early readings: Melinda Schilling, Randy Russell, Laurie Flanagan, David Beaudreau, Angela Jamison, Sam White, Tom Edmunds, Tom Van Arsdall, Stephanie Binns, Mike Mitchell, Allyson Donaghy, David Sandum, Bill Osburn, Lindsay Mitchell, Debi Cabral, and Alexa Adams. The book is better because of their candid feedback.

A special mention to my niece Meredith, who read the book with a careful eye and helped guide me with regard to several sensitive Crow family episodes. And I thank my children and their spouses for listening to these stories over the years.

I am indebted to my editor and publisher, Sandra

Jonas, who took a raw manuscript and helped craft it masterfully, painstakingly taking it apart to make sure every detail was perfect and accurate. Her creative skills are second to none. I also want to acknowledge Jill Tappert, who worked with Sandra, for her careful editing and thoughtful questions. My gratitude as well to Trish Wilkinson for her superb preliminary editing and for introducing me to Sandra Jonas.

I thank the Navajo people for allowing our family to live on their reservation. My Navajo friends, Henry McCabe and Richard Kontz, as well my Menominee friend, Jim Fredenberg, were my guiding lights during childhood, and are still good friends today.

My warm thanks to my friend Jeff Wolverton, whose father, George, was Dad's accomplice. Jeff opened my eyes to the power of forgiveness.

I can't imagine how I would have survived my childhood without my siblings, Lonnie, Sam, and Sally (not their real names). I am especially grateful to my older sister for her encouragement. Nor would I be where I am today without the angels who appeared in my life when I needed them most: Evelyn, Rex Kontz, Chauncey Ford, Herm Davis, Tom Coleman, Randy Russell, and my Sigma Chi fraternity brothers. I am profoundly thankful to all of them.

And my deep appreciation to my amazing wife, Patty—my anchor, my partner, my friend—for her patience and steadfast support.

ABOUT THE AUTHOR

David Crow spent his early years on the Navajo Indian Reservation in Arizona and New Mexico. Through grit, resilience, and a thirst for learning, he managed to escape his abusive childhood, graduate from college, and build a successful lobbying firm in Washington, DC.

Today, David is a sought-after speaker, giving talks to various businesses and trade organizations around the world. Throughout the years, he has mentored over two hundred college interns, performed pro bono service for the charitable organization Save the Children, and participated in the Big Brothers Big Sisters program. An advocate for women, he is donating a percentage of his book royalties to Barrett House, a homeless shelter for women in Albuquerque.

David lives with his wife, Patty, in the suburbs of DC. For more information, visit his website: DavidCrowAuthor.com.

Made in United States
Orlando, FL
23 December 2021

12415916R00338